HAUNTED SKIES

THE ENCYCLOPAEDIA OF BRITISH UFOS

VOLUME FIVE

1972-1974

JOHN HANSON
DAWN HOLLOWAY

Front Cover by David Sankey

Edited by Jonathan Downes
Typeset by Jonathan Downes
Cover and Internal Layout by Jon Downes for CFZ Communications
Using Microsoft Word 2000, Microsoft , Publisher 2000, Adobe Photoshop.

First edition published 2010 by CFZ Publications

FORTEAN WORDS
Myrtle Cottage
Woolfardisworthy
Bideford
North Devon
EX39 5QR

ISBN: 978-1-905723-50-8

This Volume is dedicated to Margaret Fry, who has assisted us over the years, and two colleagues, who are no longer with us - Margaret Westwood, and Retired USAF Colonel Wendelle Stevens. It was published in the year of the Diamond Jubilee of H.M. Queen Elizabeth II (Veteran Ufologist Bob Tibbitts took this photo with his Kodak Brownie in 1963 at the age of 12. This was the first year that the Royal Agricultural Show was held at Stoneleigh, Nr. Coventry)

MARGARET FRY

We met Margaret Ellen Fry many years ago, at her home in Wales, and were enthralled with her account of what occurred on the 17th of July 1955, when, as a local young housewife living in Bexleyheath, Kent, she and her local Doctor witnessed the unbelievable sight of a UFO, hovering some 18ft above them, which, within a short space of time, actually landed on the junction of a road in Bexleyheath, Kent It seems incredible that this sighting of *something, or someone* - which we are constantly told by authority does not exist - happened now, over half a century ago!

We made a journey to the location with Margaret, a few years ago, and were astonished when she called at local houses, delivering a circular, appealing for any of the 'local children' who witnessed the event, to come forward. Margaret has an insatiable thirst for the UFO subject and feels very strongly that accounts, such as hers and many others, should be recorded for posterity.

Margaret was brought up in the Himalayas, and educated by a teaching order of Irish nuns. In 1947, she and her family left India and arrived in England, aboard the ship *Georgic*.

The UFO sighting was to change Margaret's outlook on life. She joined BUFORA in 1964, and was herself a founder member of Contact International UK, in 1967, established by the Earl of Clancarty - a senior member of the House of Lords. In 1993, she co-founded the Wales Fellowship of Independent Ufologists, and is considered to be a leading authority on the Berwyn Mountain incident of 23rd January,

1974. She is a woman of great charisma, who has also self published two books, '*Who are they?* And '*Link to the Stars*'

Norman Oliver, former editor of the Journal of BUFORA - British UFO Research Association:

> "*Margaret has been - and still is - an excellent UFO investigator and friend. Despite many personal problems and bereavements, she has always found the time to carry out numerous investigations into a great variety of peoples experiences in the field of UFO research, particularly in the Welsh area. Her open-minded approach and meticulous attention to detail in respect of these - and indeed her own experiences also - makes the books she has written concerning our subject ones that should not be missed.*"

MARGARET WESTWOOD

We met Margaret Westwood - an ex Police Officer - some years ago, at her address in Harborne, Birmingham, and have very much to thank her for. If it hadn't been for her interviews, held with various people, over the years, such as Chief Petty Officer Penrose, (1954) and Jean Hingley, (1979) and many others, we would have been none the wiser and our history of British UFO activity would have been flawed.

While she is now one of those forgotten people within the past UFO Community that never sought the limelight, her valuable contribution to UFO History should be recognised. There are, of course, many others like Margaret, who have worked to record for posterity, something whose presence Governments still steadfastly refuse to acknowledge.

We would like to think that we celebrate their work and commitment through the pages of *Haunted Skies* - the honour is theirs not ours.

WENDELLE STEVENS

Was born and raised in Minnesota. He enlisted in the Army shortly after High School.

He graduated from the Lockheed Aircraft Maintenance & Repair School, Aviation Cadet Training and Fighter Pilot Advanced Training, as a very young 2nd Lieutenant in the US Army Air Corps. After that, he attended the first Air Corps Flight Test Pilot School at Kelly Field, where he learned to fly all the aircraft of the Air Corps at the time, as well as a few US Navy aircraft.

During his long career in the military, one of his assignments

was the supervision of a highly classified team of technical specialists, who were installing hi-tech data collecting equipment aboard the SAC B-29s of the Ptarmigon Project - a research project which was photographing and mapping every inch of the Arctic land and sea area.

This equipment was designed to capture record & analyze all EMF emissions in the Arctic, photograph all anomalous phenomena, and record all disturbances in the electrical and engine systems of the aircraft, looking for external influences caused by UFOs. The data was then couriered nightly to Washington.

Unable to possess any of this information Stevens, upon his return, began his own research and collection effort, eventually amassing the largest private collection of UFO photographs in the world.

He began to publish reports on the events, and wrote many illustrated articles for many UFO publications. Disenchanted with the dearth of detail on contact events reported in books

and journals of the time, he began preparing detailed reports of his own investigations.

He published more than 22 books, all at his own expense, still seeking the elusive answers to the many questions raised by this phenomenon.

He was more than ready to assist us with a specific case involving a mysterious man who claimed he had the capability to change shape.

The investigation into this matter and the man's visit to the USA and Great Britain during the 1980s, will be the subject of a later volume and makes fascinating reading, especially after we learned that he met The Lord Hill Norton.

Wendelle was a Director of the International UFO Congress since its inception, and passed away on 7th September, 2010.

**Wendelle C. Stevens and daughter Cece Stevens
Laughlin Nv 2006**

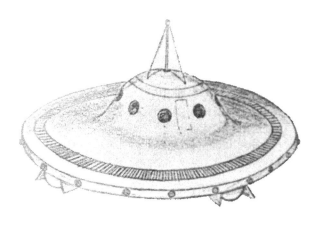

FOREWORD BY MATT LYONS

A t Volume 5 of this series, we find ourselves in the rapid development of research and investigation into the UFO Phenomena.

The late Allan J. Hynek had set a benchmark in the close encounters categories 1, 2 and 3 which through the subsequent formation of Centre of UFO Studies (CUFOS) in 1973. Jacques Vallee and John Keel had sent ripples of new thinking on the way of investigating UFOs and witness perception during events.

BUFORA continued towards its first extensive investigations manual and a young new investigator, Jenny Randles was to become increasingly well known for expanding research analysis. The UFO questions were moving away from the 'nuts and bolts' approach which could no longer hold an exclusive approach through the media, science fiction films and the public at large. In the U.K. the T.V. series UFO had certainly captured public attention, exploring defence, secrecy assertions and motives of a possible hostile alien presence.

I received a call from the authors, after Lionel Beer, BUFORA president, mentioned further cases and information related to our past cases and material. I was delighted to learn that someone had been planning just this major general project of covering UFO reports, even starting the first volume with cases which preceded the iconic Kenneth Arnold 1947 case. Having just finished two of our own archiving projects, the concept of a broader chronology of UFO reports was an exciting project and I have the highest respect for the time taken in producing the excellent volumes published so far.

This latest volume demonstrates the expanding cultural, scientific and analytical approach to the subject and forms an important link into the rapid and defining investigative procedures. It marks a time of the rise of conferences covering a vast spectrum of beliefs and approaches to the UFO phenomenon, with social, spiritual and astronomical and deep space approaches to the subject. The launch of satellites which were to travel beyond our solar system fired the imaginations for many and the growing serious approach to projects such as SETI (Search for Extra-terrestrial Intelligence).

A sound from a distant planet or the constant songs of pulsars, the UFO sightings that continue to amaze and capture the public's imagination, these continue to indeed be *Haunted Skies* to this day.

BUFORA highly recommends the whole series of *Haunted Skies* and it is one of our principal recommendations for the curious reader, serious investigator or researcher alike. John and Dawn are sincere and respectful researchers who have brought a wealth of material forward for you to enjoy and every book purchased will contribute further to the completion of the series, building a definitive and extensive collection that should be on anyone's bookshelf.

Matt Lyons,
Chairman of the British UFO Research Association, October 2011

Maude the Dog and Breeze the Cat - Our friends 'till the end

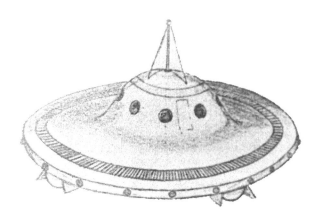

INTRODUCTION

T his volume of strange (and mostly airborne) events, describing things which continue to haunt the skies of the United Kingdom to the present day, covers the period between 1972 and 1974. In this Volume you will read of some even more fascinating cases, including reports of sightings of humanoids. These might seem far fetched and almost unbelievable, especially to the more sceptical. Indeed there was a time when we would have laughed at the very suggestion - but not now!

Contrary to the popular belief that sightings of UFO-related beings are extremely rare, researchers from MUFON's Humanoid Study Group (HSG) compiled a long list of such cases - over 1600 different entity incidents. HSG co-chairman, physicist David Webb said: *"Many of the reports are well documented, first-hand investigations, involving credible witnesses."*

Between 1966 & 1970 it is claimed that in the United States, hundreds of UFO researchers and witnesses were visited by the 'Men in Black'. The UK was also to receive its fair share of sightings of these anomalous visits which left UFO witnesses frightened and intimidated. There was a time during the early part of our research into this enigmatic subject when we felt that these people were members of a covert Government department, whose agenda was to intimidate people to keep quiet about what they had witnessed.

The evidence collected shows that this may well be probably *part* of the answer, but there are other instances when this is highly unlikely to be the case, taking into consideration, their apparent advance knowledge of detailed information on the person they contact, almost as if the individual had been under surveillance for a long period of time. They have been described as seeming confused by the nature of everyday items such as pens, eating utensils or food, as well as using outdated slang. Those who have encountered them say they produce identification, but when verification is later sought, the people described do not exist or have been dead for some time. Another defining characteristic of the 'Men in Black' is wide grins and disconcerting giggles. The phenomenon has been frequently reported since the 1950s and 1960s.

This is very puzzling, but one thing we do know is that their characteristics of reported behaviour remain unchanged. Invariably those threats can include threats of bodily injury, and harassment either through a personal visit by (normally) two or three 'men', often using motor vehicles with a number plate that has never been issued, or use of an unregistered untraceable telephone call. This might sound very far fetched but we have come across accounts involving many of these 'ingredients' right up to the present date. Some researchers, including John Keel, have suggested similarities between the 'Men in Black' reports and earlier historic accounts which were interpreted as demonic in nature. Would modern-day manifestations of the same UFO/Paranormal phenomena have been associated then as the work of the devil?

As we write, we are in the first quarter of 2012, an age dominated by Reality TV, the rise of the celebrity performer, and UFO documentaries which continue to attract the attention of the Public. Unfortunately many of these programmes do not in our view represent any serious attempt to show the true picture what has taken place based on proper scientific and rational investigation. You will all be familiar with these productions that rely heavily on clumsy sensationalism and offer nothing new. Fortunately, at long last many individual UFO researchers are being given the opportunity to air their views on the UFO subject. Interest in UFO's remains paramount, and in the news there is talk of space exploration to Mars and the setting up of a permanent base on the Moon by 2018.

Towards the end of the 20th Century, we contacted Gordon Creighton, the Editor of *Flying Saucer Review, ,* and asked if we could visit him at his home address in Rickmansworth, Hertfordshire. Gordon agreed to see us, but pointed out that, over the previous few years, he had been contacted by many people in the media, who had expressed a wish to interview him, but none of them had ever arrived!

Furthermore, he told us that since 1981, he had been prevented from airing his views on the radio and the TV, and that the authorities had effectively banned him form speaking about the UFO subject. We thought he was overreacting! After spending some hours with him he invited us both to be consultants for the magazine, which we considered a privilege, and we have never forgotten our visit We are sad that Gordon and the wife he adored, 'Eve' Joan Kathlyn Felice Creighton, are no longer with us. Both of them, right up to the end of their days, despite serious illnesses, endeavoured to ensure that the magazine was completed on time, even only hours before their deaths.

We should not forget them, or the magazine, which is still being produced by the current editor, Harry Challenger, and its majority shareholder Philip Creighton.

Within the pages of this volume there are one or two sightings that lie far from the shores of the UK, which may seem strange, bearing in mind our books are about cataloguing British UFO activity. However, we believe that while these matters normally lie outside the *Haunted Skies* geographical jurisdiction, it is possible there may be a connection with the English sightings, so we feel that it is of relevance to bring them to the readers' attention.

Sadly, although UFOs do not appear to have any boundaries, either in time or space, we are constrained by time and money.

We value the opinions of those researchers, of which some of whom have been involved in the UFO subject for over 40 years. One such man is Peter Hough, B.S.C. (Hons.), born in Nottinghamshire, and a prolific researcher of the UFO/Paranormal subject. He has written nearly twenty non-fiction books, and several hundred magazine and newspaper articles. He has also appeared in many documentaries and radio programmes, both in the UK and overseas. His new book - *Stench of Evil* - a supernatural detective thriller, is currently on sale on Amazon. Peter is working on a sequel - *The Devil Inside* - and we wish him every success. Here is what he had to say:

"The mid nineteen seventies was a watershed for UK ufology. It was the time when I became very active as an investigator for the Manchester UFO Research Association, after reading an interview with Chairman Peter Warrington, in the Manchester Evening News.

Then we were awash with reports of high strangeness cases, including close encounters with UFOs, entity sightings and Men in Black. Of course, there were many mundane cases too, and we solved these to the best of our abilities.

Of fundamental interest in this period is that the entities were mostly of the Nordic variety; tall, slim, with shoulder length blond hair. The so-called 'Greys' of North America was not in the British psyche yet. Whitley Strieber was yet to publish his communion with the goblin creatures, and Budd Hopkins was still busy exploring the 'missing time' of his UFO 'experiences' using hypnosis.

When the book tours of Strieber and Hopkins grabbed the UK media's attention, the reports we were getting from percipients evolved into descriptions of Greys, rather than our more local Nordic variety. I'm generalising of course, but there is no doubt that there was a shift in that direction.

Once again, it seemed the USA had exported an aspect of its own culture to Britain. Many sceptics said this proved that abductions and encounters were subjective hallucinations formed by current cultural paradigms.

Another view was that an objective phenomenon was using 'cultural tracking' to shape-shift and present itself to percipients according to what their expectations were. The jury's still out on that one".

EDITORIAL

Derek Samson

The recent wave of Ufo activity centered around the Banbury and Warwickshire areas has produced a "more than casual interest". Never before in all the history of Flying Saucers - has there been such concern - and so much enthusiasm displayed through the media of the radio press and television.

A subject of enormous dimension, far too easily ridiculed is fast becoming one of great importance cloaked with respectability. We live in trying times - in bewildered confusion - sometimes turning away from possibilities - from facts - from the truth.

Arthur Shuttlewood, once said, "Great truth's are forming in the void" . He questioned the possibilities, faced facts, saw the light and became another contact, or 'sensitive'. Arthur like so many of us had to make a decision, he chose that minute glimmer of possibility through which he entered into the full light of understanding.

My friends ! this is indeed the time of 'Decision' great truth's are forming they are in the 'signs in the skies' have you the courage of your own convictions ? can you faithfully decide ?, I already have. As a 'sensitive' much of the material in this and forthcoming issues will be through the guidance of my personal impressions received from the 'Unity of the Brotherhood of the Seven Rays' quote : " You, Derek have been waiting, with consideral patience, for this moment of decision. This moment of decision comes to all our workers on your plane - whether incarnate from a previous incarnation upon Earth or incarnate from other Planets within the Solar System, incarnated on Earth at this moment.

"Your work, from now onwards, is to teach - through the NICAP Journal by representation, in a palatable form, of some of the New Concepts. We do appreciate that the nature of the Journal links it very tightly with the subject of Space travel, space-craft, sightings etc; so that it is not possible to introduce the metaphysical, and this is why we suggested telepathy - as such, for inroads must be made from the scientific angle. As it has been recorded elsewhere, through many channels, that - THE FIRST CONTACT, telepathically made, has always been with Space-crews of Space-craft".

To my fellow colleague's and friends, all I can say for 1972 is "Seek and ye shall find".

Derek Samson

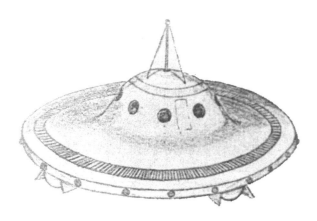

ACKNOWLEDGEMENTS

- Bob Boyd, of the Plymouth UFO Group for his assistance
- Bob Tibbitts, of the Coventry UFO Research Group, for the supply of a large amount of material collected by him over the years, and access to the Group's records and his own synopsis, *The Flying Saucer revelation.*
- Dan Goring, London-based UFO researcher for his assistance and access too many reports
- David Bryant for his assistance, illustrations, and general advice
- David Sankey, for providing illustrations to be used in the various Volumes of *Haunted Skies* and research into many UFO sightings, brought to our attention over the years. We would also like to thank Erica Williams, his partner, for her assistance and encouragement over the years.
- Derek Sampson, of NICAP
- Dick Thompson, Lincoln UFO researcher
- Frank Marshall, BUFORA
- Harold Bunting, DIGAP UFO researcher, of Stockport, Cheshire, for his advice
- Ian Mryzglod, of *The Probe* - thanks for your permission
- Ivan W. Bunn of the *Lantern Series*
- Jenny Randles, for permission to refer to her work
- John 'Dennis' and Ruby Llewellyn
- Kevin Goodman, for his support
- Lionel Beer, *Space-link Books,* for his assistance and photographs
- Lionel Cramp, Author and formerly involved with the Isle of Wight UFO Society
- Margaret Ellen Fry, head of the Welsh Fellowship of Independent Ufologists, for her valuable assistance in the preparation of a number of cases brought to her attention over the years, both in Wales and the Kent areas.
- Nick Maloret (WATSUP) for his encouragement and assistance with UFO reports.
- Norman Oliver, BUFORA
- Omar Fowler, head of the Derbyshire-based UFO investigations group, PRA (Phenomenon Research Association) formally with SIGAP, always willing to impart his own personal knowledge of many investigations carried out by him, covering decades.

- Paul Tricker for his assistance and submission of scrapbooks
- Peter Tate, from Bristol, who supplied a large amount of personal UFO memorabilia and information pertaining to investigations carried out by him, and his association with groups such as Probe, run by Ian Mryzglod.
- Philip Creighton Director of *Flying Saucer Review* for his assistance
- Philip Mantle, for his photographs, encouragement and foreword
- Peter Leek and his wife Pauline (Technical support) good friends
- Roy Dutton for his assistance and advice
- Steven Franklin, of 'Tom Cat Media', for his advice and illustrations
- Steven Pound, 'Art and Design Solutions', and partner Lyndsey Kelly
- Terry Hooper, for permission to use photographs and assistance
- Tony Pace, BUFORA
- Wayne Mason, from Stoke-on-Trent, for his preparation of a number of illustrations

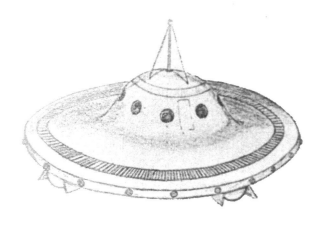

Volume 5
CONTENTS

Chapter One January - June 1972

Chapter Two July - December 1972

Chapter Three January - June 1973

RAF Pilot sights UFO, Soldiers sight UFO, UFO over Northumberland, UFO over Wales, UFO over Birmingham, Mystery Lights over Warminster.

Chapter Four, July - December 1973
UFO at Cradle Hill, Warminster, UFO's over North Cornwall, Close Encounter, Scotland, Close Encounter, Northampton, UFO over Cheshire, Encounter with ghost, Portsmouth, Close Encounters, at RAF Alconbury, Warminster - a personal view, Encounter on Cradle Hill, UFO over Wales, UFO over Kent, UFO over Orpington Kent, Close Encounter, Northamptonshire, UFO over Derbyshire, Sighting from Sky Lab 3, Close Encounter, Somerset, Visit from the' Men in Black', UFOs over Luton, Was there an Alien Incursion at Marconi Defence Centre? Halloween Mystery, UFO over Kent, Close Encounter, Nuneaton, UFO over Kidsgrove, Staffordshire.

Chapter Five January - June 1974
UFO over Lowestoft, UFO over Hampshire, Cross-shaped UFO over Kent, UFO over Bedfordshire, UFO over Derbyshire, UFO over Sunderland, UFO over Surrey, UFO sighted on the Berwyn Mountain, Horrifying encounter at Brecon, Is your neighbour a Martian? Strange 'stars' over Lincoln, UFO over Maidenhead, Ghostly 'figure' seen at Farnborough, UFO over Portsmouth, Close Encounter, at Barn Hill, Close Encounters Hartlepool, UFO over Worcester, UFO over Combe Martin, Early radio talk and UFO meeting, UFO Display over Birmingham, *Northern UFO News* (NUFON) Scientist Nick Reiter and his work, Examination of metallic debris found in Ohio, USA, Metallic debris found after UFO sighting, UFO Display, Bournemouth, A meeting that never was to be.

Chapter Six, July-December 1974
Rex Dutta and 'D' Notices, Vanished into thin air, Close Encounter, Dagenham, UFO over Cheltenham, UFOs over Stoke-on- Trent, UFOs over Surrey, UFO over Hertfordshire, Close Encounter, Bournemouth, UFO over Hampshire, UFO Display over Bedfordshire, UFO over Dorset, UFO over Portsmouth, UFO photographed over Bournemouth, Close Encounter, Aveley, UFO over Hornchurch Essex, UFOs over Rossendale Valley, Lancashire, 'Sky Watch' at Somerset, UFO sighting, Ben Nevis, UFO over Colchester, UFO over Kent.

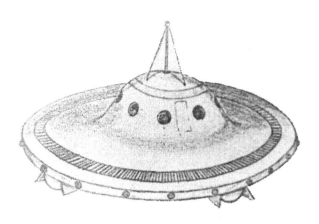

1972

This was a period of great unrest, beginning with a coal miners strike, which lasts for seven weeks, followed by 'Bloody Sunday', in Northern Ireland, when troops opened fire on demonstrators in Derry, killing fourteen people, as a result of which the IRA carried out attacks on the Mainland. Britain officially joined the European Economic Community, and unemployment exceeds one million for the first time; almost double that of when Edward Heath's Government came to power, less than two years previously. On a lighter note, *Jesus Christ Superstar* makes its West End debut and children were captivated by the publication of Richard Adams' novel, *Watership Down*

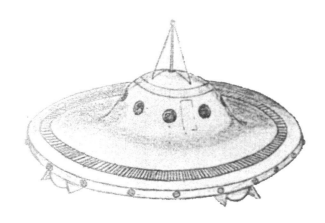

CHAPTER ONE
JANUARY-JUNE 1972

UFO over Shropshire

Mr. Mervyn Davies from Four Crosses, Llanymynech, Powys, was driving towards Knockin, along the A5, one evening, at 8.00pm., during the early 1970s.

"As I approached Knockin, I saw a bright, shining, silver object in the sky, and thought it was an aircraft.

While driving through the village, I was astonished to see what looked like a green ivy leaf, or diamond shape, in the sky - very low down. In fact, it was so low, I actually drove under it. I then stopped further up the road, got out, and looked back. There was nothing to be seen.

Some years later, I read about the Berwyn Mountain case and wondered if there had been a connection." **(Source: personal interview)**

At 1.00am on 3rd January 1972, Mr. Philip Edwards of Upper Park Road, Brightlingsea Essex, was awoken by an extraordinary 'rushing' noise. Thinking it was an aircraft about to crash, he ran to the window. When he looked out with his wife, they saw:

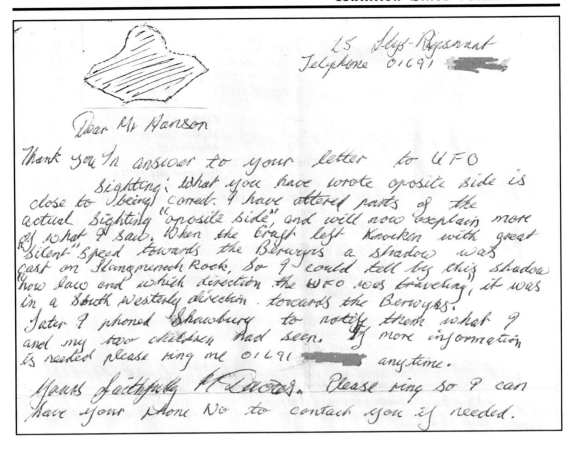

15 Sky-Rysnant
Telephone 01691 [redacted]

Dear Mr Hanson

Thank you In answer to your letter to UFO sighting. What you have wrote oposite side is close to being correct. I have altered parts of the actual sighting "oposite side", and will now explain more of what I saw. When the craft left Knocken with great "silent" speed towards the Berwyns a shadow was cast on Slangmenech Rock, so I could tell by this shadow how low and which direction the UFO was traveling, it was in a South westerly direction, towards the Berwyns. Later I phoned Shawsbury to notify them what I and my two children had seen. If more information is needed please ring me 01691 [redacted] anytime.

Yours faithfully [signature]. Please ring so I can have your Phone No to contact you if needed.

> "...a great light between us and the river, accompanied by a series of orange flashes from lights in the sky. The next morning I spoke to my sons, Richard and Charles, who told me they had also been awoken and had seen the lights."

Enquiries with the Police and the Army revealed no knowledge of anything that might have explained the incident away. (**Source:** *Colchester Evening Gazette*/BUFORA *Journal*, **Volume 3, No. 7 Summer 1972**)

UFO Display over Rickmansworth

At 10.15am on 12th January 1972, four workmen on Woodcock Hill, Rickmansworth, four miles from Watford, sighted a 'silver disc', motionless in the perfect clear sky, at an angle of 60°. A short time later, five more of these objects were seen moving at height in different directions. These objects were observed for a total of two and a half hours.

Enquires were made with London Meteorological Office, who pointed out that it was nothing to do with them, as they don't release balloons in batches.

One of the witnesses contacted the MOD and spoke to an official there, who seemed very interested in what he had seen, and asked him if:

"...he had told any others about the sighting, and were there any installations, or bodies of water in the vicinity?"

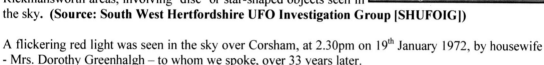

Enquires made revealed that a power line passed over the vicinity, and that the adjacent valley from Rickmansworth to Denham and beyond, contained a number of deep lakes, formed from gravel workings. This valley was the scene of at least a dozen UFO reports over the last ten years.

On the same day, a woman resident of Chalfont St. Peter sighted a number of tubular objects.

The following day, another sighting took place over the Watford/ Rickmansworth areas, involving 'disc' or star-shaped objects seen in the sky. **(Source: South West Hertfordshire UFO Investigation Group [SHUFOIG])**

A flickering red light was seen in the sky over Corsham, at 2.30pm on 19th January 1972, by housewife – Mrs. Dorothy Greenhalgh – to whom we spoke, over 33 years later.

"I was reading to my daughter, aged 4, at the time, when I became aware of a red flickering light just outside the range of my peripheral vision, but decided to finish the story before looking upwards into the sky, through the window, when I saw a huge bright red light, about six times the size of an aircraft, just hanging there, at a height I took to be several thousand feet.

I directed my daughter's attention towards the object and we watched, for a short while, before it flew away.

The next day, my daughter complained of some red marks on her stomach. I looked and saw three, in a triangular shape. I was shocked when I saw it because I had noticed similar marks on my stomach, which hadn't been there prior to the appearance of the UFO. What did defy explanation was the fact that Cyril also discovered an identical triangular inflammation on his stomach.

How could this be, as he was working some miles away? Within days the marks faded."

Exactly why people became afflicted with these medical conditions seems beyond comprehension, but if you consider those occasions when, as a result of UFO interaction, domestic electrical appliances in the house are rendered inoperative and cars are brought to a halt. Is it no wonder people find themselves unable to explain - never mind come to terms with the nature of puzzling medical conditions following an encounter with a UFO? **(Source: Ken Rogers)**

'Flying Saucer' over West Midlands

At 4.30pm on 20th January 1972, a saucer-shaped object was seen wobbling, a few hundred feet off the ground, over a block of flats close to Carters Lane Baptist Church, Halesowen, West Midlands, by three schoolboys on their way home. (see images opposite) We traced two of the boys who asked that their personal details be kept confidential fearing ridicule **(Source: *UFOSIS*)**

At about 10.30pm on 20th January 1972, Jim Todd - an electrician from John Readhead's shipyard, South Shields - was at work, with three other workmen, when crane driver - Jack Short - alerted them to something strange in the sky, the men looked up to see:

> *"...five roundish objects, high up, flying in a cross formation, heading eastwards over the sea; two were red, the others orange, yellow and blue. They were visible for two to three minutes."* **(Source: Isle of Wight UFO Society)**

UFO over Andover

At 1.43am on 21st January 1972, George Harris from Andover, Hampshire, sighted a circular object in the sky.

> *"It had a green glow around its outer edges. Through binoculars an inner ring of evenly spaced white lights could be seen. It was stationary, at first, but after about four minutes, it dropped vertically to take up a new position nearer the horizon, when it changed into an ellipse. The object changed position, once more - this time ascending until it reached an elevation of about 40°, slightly higher than when first seen. At 1.52am it became smaller, before finally disappearing from sight."* **(Source: *BUFORA Journal,* Volume 3, No. 10, Spring 1973)**

Close Encounter, South Yorkshire

In January 1972, Mr. Anthony Cureton was out walking the family dog with his two children – Jacqueline, and son, Tony - some 150yds away from their house at Kendray, Barnsley, in South Yorkshire, at 7.00pm - when they saw a strange torpedo-shaped craft, with what appeared to have two or three levels to it, full of dark lights, with a halo around, which descended vertically through the sky. The object, then about seven hundred feet above them, landed on the other side of a 6ft high concrete wall (forming the boundary line to a large complex of football fields).

According to the two children:

> *"...a 'pointed' face then popped up above the wall, showing pointed ears and large red eyes."*

Frightened, the children ran away and told their father, who was trailing a short distance behind them.

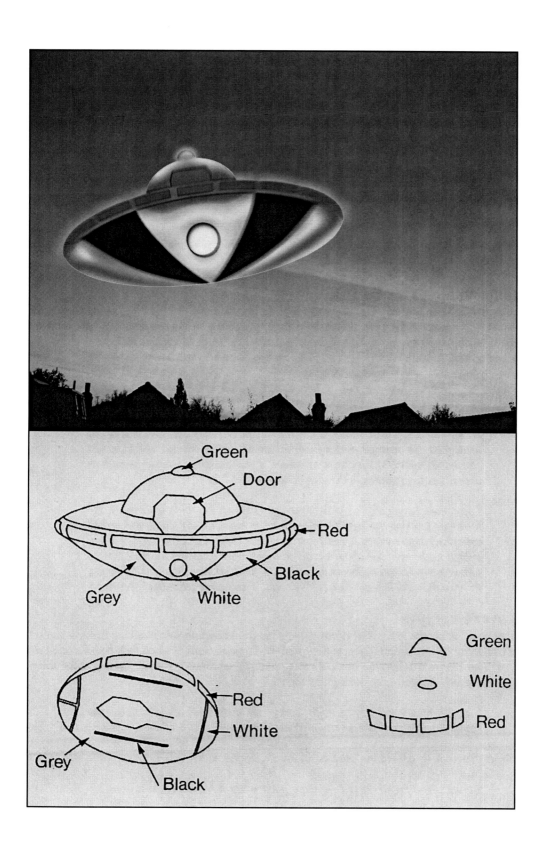

On looking back, there was no sign of the 'craft' and its 'occupant'

Mrs. Cureton confirmed that the children had arrived home in a very frightened state, and refused to go out in the dark for some time afterwards. Jacqueline, who was apparently the worst affected by the experience, could remember little about what had taken place, whereas Tony (who was older) had no problem remembering, with clarity, what he had witnessed. Mr. Cureton:

> *"I remember Tony mentioning this event, from time to time, and didn't attach much importance to it; besides, one UFO had been actually reported to have landed in the school playing fields, some years previously - around 1958, or 1959."*

Attempts to obtain further details of the incident, which allegedly took place in 1958, were unsuccessful. **(Source: Dan Goring - Editor of *Earth-Link*)**

Invisible Walker, Cradle Hill

In February 1972, Mike Murray was 'sky watching' on his own, one late evening, as his friend, Arthur Shuttlewood, was unwell at the time. As he stood there, pondering on the conversations held with Arthur about the 'invisible walker', wondering if there was any real truth to such stories, he decided (as the weather was so bad) to walk back to his car, parked a few hundred yards away.

> *"As I approached the car, I heard heavy footsteps from behind me. I stopped, wondering whether the noises could have been the result of the movement of a wild animal nearby. After hearing nothing more I continued on my journey, wishing I had a torch in my possession. Just as I was about to dismiss the strange noises from my mind, to my horror, the footsteps started up again, much closer to where I was standing - close enough to actually cause puddles in the tarmac to vibrate!*
>
> *Once more I stopped, so did the footsteps. I slowly began to walk away, the footsteps starting up again - almost as if blocking my path, the gravel crunching underneath. I could feel my heart thumping with fright. I stood rooted to the spot for about twenty minutes, until plucking up the courage to run to my Triumph Herald car, where I fumbled desperately with the key to open the vehicle's door and drive away."* **(Source: personal interview)**

UFO over Surrey

At 1.25pm on 4th February 1972, Neil Hards (9) and his friend Jacinth were walking towards the school room at Great Ormond St Hospital annex, Kingston-on-Thames, Surrey, when they heard a noise above them. They looked upwards into the sky, but seeing nothing, continued on their journey. After the noise was heard again they stopped, and looking upwards saw what Neil described as:

> *"...a silver coloured object, with 'scree' all over it. It made a noise like rough sandpaper, and kept stopping and starting."*

The object then took up a hovering position in the air, during which time it rocked from side to side.

> *"I could see a fin on the side of the object; when it rocked I saw one on*

UFO   MIRROR

International U.F.O Magazine

HEAD BRANCH: 37, The Close, Dunmow, Essex.

YOUR Ref. RTF2   Date 2/2/72   Reply to - HB

Dear Bob,

It is always nice to hear from you and now I am getting a little more
time free to answer mail things at this end are easing up. I start
a 5 day week again very soon I hope in two weeks time. I have saved
enough to be able to buy a Heidleberg Printing machine if I wished
but you see typesetting does take an alful long time and so I am
looking round for a quick method to obtain the same results. What is
needed would be a special typwriter to look like print. Thats quicker.

Would you like to help with the new magazine after you are settled
in on your new home, which incidently, youare lucky to get with the
price of houses going up I was told at a rate of about £1,000 a yerr.

If you like to help out, I want experts in all subjects of ufology
and its many manisfestations. If you want to help, you would have to
pick a subject you are very well with or just generalise etc, and
compile a dossier on it. You could publish this in SYNOONIC as well
and send the rest to me. I think I explained all this last time.
Anyway let me know what you think. We have just found out by the way
what SYNTONIC means: It means a harmony of radio waves or the only
wavelength for that frequency. Whatever made you choose that title?

My new mga is to be called COSMOLOGY NEWSLINK and may just about
wrap up ALL of space subjects and all there is in the cosmos.
Cosmology means: All there is in the universe etc.(See dictionary)

When I asked if you could help, I did not mean for you to give up
syntonic but to offer you your own section in Cosmology Newslink-
how does this strike you? You could of course advertise entirely
free of charge up to a full page advert in my new mag if you are
willing to help out. This way you will get orders for Syntonic and
your articles will help CN too. You could write a section in it and
then add that the full story etc on further details to be found in
syntonic. This I hope would be the only payment I could possibly
give you at present except for the 25 free copies for you to sell
for your own funds. All is very exciting this new venture. I look
forward to hearing your final reply.
I'll carry out a review for Syntonic if you would do the same for
Cosmology Newslink-you have my permission to mention the forthcoming
new magazine in Syntonic also when you receive a copy for assesment.
One vote was received for SYNTONIC in the International poll means
it is, sharing joint reading popularity as the 5th ufo magazine in
the world, with Perception and Space-Drive. All good wishes.
        Edward
        Edward Harr

the other side. It had an underneath, which was concave, and a red coloured 'bump' on the top, showing a thin gold coloured line running across it from front to back."

The object, which was seen for 2-3minutes, eventually disappeared behind trees, leaving the children very frightened by what had taken place. **(Source: Ken Philips, *BUFORA Journal*, Volume 3, No. 10, Spring 1973)**

Kensington Library, London

People were invited to a lecture held at Kensington Central Library, on 5th February 1972, at 7.00pm, by John Cleary-Baker, PhD., Editor of *BUFORA Journal,* to hear him talk on *'WARMINSTER - 7 years of Phenomena'.*

On 9th February 1972, a brilliant golden light,

> *"...with a central core of light running up and down - like flames of pure golden colour"*

...was seen by Mr. and Mrs. G. Farleigh of Poole, Dorset, at 3.35am, high in the southern sky. Ten minutes later, it disappeared from view towards the Purbecks.

Whilst we learnt of the possibility that a satellite was sighted in the western part of the sky, at 6.20pm on 8th February 1972, and may have led to other reports of UFO's, it is unlikely, in our opinion, that this is what the couple saw.

Fireball over Nottinghamshire

At 1.30am on 11th February 1972, Mr. William Dowman - a labourer by occupation - then 59 years of age, from Harby, Nottinghamshire, was in the process of going back to bed, after having visited the bathroom, when the bedroom lit up with intense light. Thinking it was a car he went to the window and saw with amazement:

> *"...a large spherical 'ball', as big as the full moon crossing the skyline. It had a pale green outer rim, with a yellow centre, like the sun. As it passed by, it swept the countryside with light. In 2-3seconds, it had gone from view, heading in a north-west to south-east direction."*

Is it possible, from the description given, that Mr. Dolman saw a fireball meteor, rather than a UFO? If this was the case, how many of us are given the rare opportunity to see such a brilliant example at first-hand? **(Source: Richard Thompson)**

Later that same day (11th February 1972) as darkness fell, two Loughborough schoolboys, Halit Akkan (11) and Warren Green(13)- residents of Mathews estate, Leicester - noticed an apparently square object in the sky, showing a central flashing red light and a light in each of its four corners. It was seen to hover before sinking in the light of powerful beams towards a field.
(Source: *Leicester Mercury*)

During the middle of February 1972, scores of people telephoned the Police, reporting they had sighted a brightly lit object moving through the sky over the Liverpool, Cheshire, and Wales area. Some accounts

MR. W. DOWMAN.

LOCATION AS SEEN FROM BEDROOM
WINDOW & FLIGHT PATH OF OBJECT AS
DRAWN BY OBSERVER.

included a white light, with a tail, that changed to a dazzling green flare. Residents in Rhyl, Prestatyn, Wrexham, Mostyn, Broughton and Birkenhead, also contacted the Police, some of whom had been patrolling the M6 between Birmingham and Preston, when mysterious lights were seen crossing the sky.

On the 17th February 1972, Mrs. Michelle Ryan and her husband were driving along Birkenhead Road, towards Moreton, at 8.00pm.

> *"It was dark. There were no street lights, due to a power cut, when my husband told me there was a lorry right on top of our back window. I looked round and saw two dull off-white discs of light in each corner of the rear window; it was as if someone was peering into the car. My husband slowed down, and then accelerated; the next thing they had gone."* **(Source: *Liverpool Echo*, 18/21.2.72)**

Kensington Library, London

People were invited to a lecture held at Kensington Central Library on 4th March 1972, at 7.00pm, by Charles H. Gibbs-Smith, M.A, F.M.A, F.R.S.A, member of Executive Committee of the history group of the Royal Aeronautical Society, and author of many Science Museum books and articles of Aviation History - *UFOs and Documentation.*

'Flying Saucer' over Sussex

On 5th March 1972, Mr. Francis Chard from Crawley, in Sussex, was walking home from East Crawley Railway Station, a few minutes before 9.00pm.

> *"As I walked along Haslett Avenue, forming part of the A.264 trunk road, I noticed an unidentified object hovering directly over an electrical transformer, carrying high voltage power into the town. It was 'mushroom' looking in shape, sharply etched against a background of yellow glowing light, about four feet in width. From the left and right-hand corner of the domed top were two red and blue in colour spotlights, shining downwards. It then started to move, completing an arc in the sky of about 180 degrees, passing behind my position, before shooting off towards the south-west."*

Francis rushed home and told the rest of his family, who watched the unidentified flying object - now looking like a bright yellow star hovering over a field, some two miles away - before fading from view, at 9.30pm.

In conversation with his mother, he learnt from her that the picture on the television screen had been replaced by what she described as *"interference, resembling tweed cloth"*, which she had never seen before, caused, one presumes, by

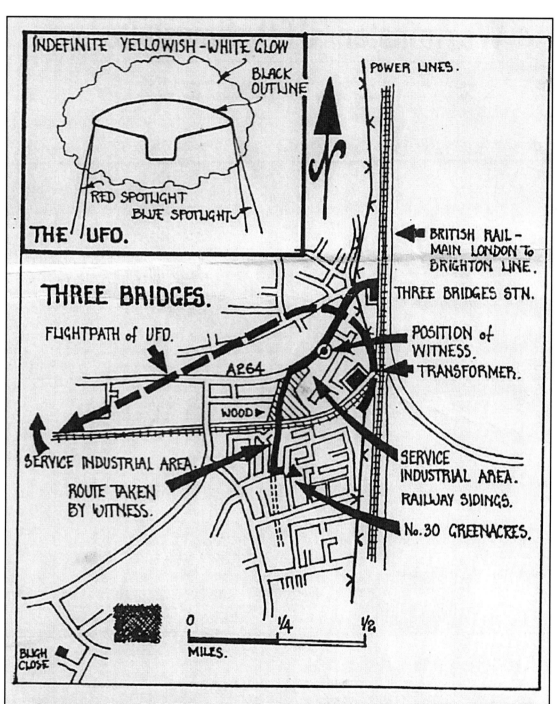

Flightpath of UFO over Three Bridges and Crawley. Inset: How the object appeared to witness. Cover drawing: UFO and transformer towers as seen over the fence from Haslett Avenue

Warminster UFO Newsletter

Presented as an Information Service for Persons Interested In Keeping
In Contact with Unusual Happenings in the Warminster District.

No. 4
MARCH 1972
PRICE 10p

SENSATIONAL PHOTOGRAPHS -
IF GENUINE

Professional photographers
Ian Scott and Derek Cooke
were taking pictures of Bishop-
strow Church last Autumn. Upon
developing - both were amazed
that they had captured on film,
a UFO, not visually apparent
to them at the time.

FULL STORY - PAGE 2.

Warminster UFO Newsletter

nº 8

10p

Presented as an Information Service for Persons Interested In Keeping
In Contact with Unusual Happenings in the Warminster District.

SUMMER NEWS SPECIAL.

LOCAL TALES AND LEGENDS

JULY 15th...

ufo..

..Prediction materialises.......

Another humanoid seen ?

Glider LANDS On Cradle Hill...

IMPORTANT NOTICE
for visitors to cradle hill !......

Following a security alert by the Army in Warminster (the Irish Rangers are at present stationed there) several parties of sky-watchers have been turned away from Cradle Hill (which is on the perimeter of the School of Infantry) by police.

A representative from this Newsletter enquired at Warminster Police Station as to whether any more skywatches would be permitted.

Warminster Police have been extremely sympathetic in this case and have agreed that skywatchers may watch from Cradle Hill ON THE CONDITION NO ONE PASSES BEYOND THE WHITE GATES onto Army territory. Failure to observe this rule could render trespassers to security checks by the Army.

The Newsletter has already provided a litter bin on Cradle. Skywatchers are asked by the farmer Mr. Geoff Gale to kindly follow the Country Code.

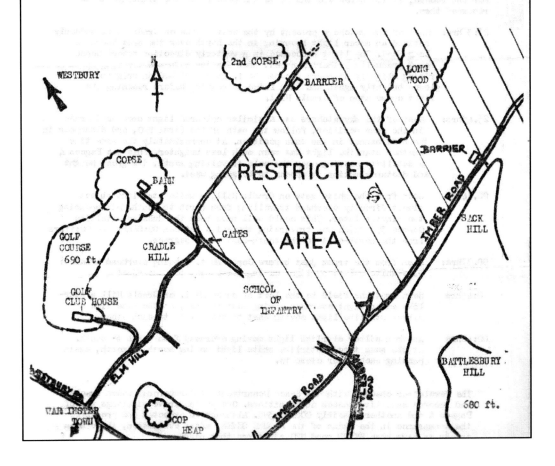

cosmology NEWSlink

SPACE - DRIVE

International Space Magazine

HEAD BRANCH: 37, The Close, Dunmow, Essex.

Ref. TF2   Date 15/2/72

Dear Bob,

Many thanks for your letter received today 15 Feb-hey thats a long time
isnt it?   Should be a day after you posted it-never mind..
Anyway you cheered me up, because I have just come back from hospital
I had an appendectomy operation-I often wonder if it was the right thing
they cut out? Anyway I was in and out in three days flat.Hi-speed Operations now-I think PERCEPTION should be aware of this rushing people out
of hospital nowadays. I am typing somewhat in agony-that means a delay
while I recuuperate until I can get the next magazine out.
I am also off work, but it will give me time to sort out for the next
and new cosmology Newslink.

Well, I could do with a lot of Contact report articles. I think Bob,
if you wanted to deal with this section in CN, you'd have to start from
the beginning-the history so to speak. Can you rustle up a dossier on
contact claims say before August? Perhaps earlier? I am not sure myself
of a publication date now. Yes, I do have a lot of your material I could
use, but does that mean you accept the position? Let me know. Also what
I would like to do is have on page two of CN the contributors and put
their photos alongside them : Therefore-

CONTENTS & SECTIONS ETC

CONTACT SECTION
by Robert Fibbitts

GHOST REPORTS
by ————

cm. ETC

m/station

2

Can you please send me a snap of yourself so that I can do the xxxxxxixxxx
your layout seen here.
photo I will put your column under
either Miscellaneous or whatever you
wish it to be placed under. Or perhaps
just General Topics. Titles for the sections
I am still trying to sort out.Nothing is
definite yet except Fred O Gardner has joined
me. So we have one expert. Now to get about
99 more. What a hell of a job I have set
myself. I'll be writing air-letters all over
the world-Then maybe I won't get the replies.
I will NOT bring out a specialist magazine
unless the specialist will do it.Or it will
be sheer hypocracy wont it? PTO

Lancashire Reps., Carol Rimmer, 1, Charles Ave., Birkdale, Southport, Lancs.
Sonia Hetmanczyk 15, Larkfield Lane, Churchtown ,Southport ,Lancs,. England
BRANCH. Janet Busell 75, Parkside, Estate, Rutland Road, Hackney, London
Voluntary Staff: Beryl Wallace, Malcolm Jay.

p.s you would go onto the staff notepaper too

As tyou said I may have some thoughts on what xxx I think you could do and if your speciality may look like becoming·UFO Contact cases with photos if possible-PHOTOS ARE VITAL or drawings and descriptions of aliens. I am still trying to get that UFO french magazine translated- I could of course put it under your name as you are in charge of this column-- see what I mean? Its working out alright. You could become the Editor of that Section in CN and contributors would send you these special reports. I will honour my promise and give SYNTONIC my full support once you can get it out again.. I'll be giving you full page cover with electronic stencil headings. YOU may possibly get more orders than me that way. You don't have to return the favour in Syntonic since this is owed to you..unless you want to so that CN gets read and your articles in SN get read and SYNTONIC gets read both together. I am sure this is the best move I have come up with for years for all local magaines like ours.

SYNTONIC means to tune in to a special waveband..reminds me of the time I had a crystle set when I was quite young and was without knowledge of course trying to tunexixxxix it in to outer space-yet I didn't believe for one moment there were anyone up there-but I was at least optimistic. If I was to get the radio amateurs licence and become a ham, the good idea would be for all the hams to form a link somehow and turn there apparatus skywards-still radio astronomy is very complex and all my wild ideas about contacting aliens are thrown out of the window. So it makes me think twice about so called contact radio claims from people with mere tape recorders out of the window and receive messages etc when Jodrell Bank with that massive dish hasn't such luck-they must be round the twist.. still with Cosmology Newslink Nothing can be overlooked even whacky way out things like this. Trouble is HOw to investigate things like this.I am not qualified to do so. I am a mere editor like yourself wishing only to get out a good publication. Its up to those who are not interested in the actual ink and type stuff of the matter, but are content to get out and be a reporter-like I tried to do once for a local paper.(That's bashing my head on the wall) Thinking of this, maybe I never sent you a copy of Sunrise-this was an all out attempt by a partner and I to produce a magazine in oposition to WEEKEND. NO.1 hit the market and every shop from central London to Takely Essex (a short way from here).But it crashed in the first issue although a vast bigger and better version was ready for number two which never appeared because of financial trouble-I have included one for you. The address is of course different today inside. There is NO sunrise anymore-just had the wrong partner also.

The unknown frightens and challenges you-well the unknown frightens every- one-what the mind does not know it senses great fear like an unknown road in the dark on a bike ride, with mini lights on it not being able to penetrate the darkness. I have had this experience and was petrified until I arrived at a town brilliantly lit. I wonder what sort of Evil those people feared from the Mothman in Gray Barkers Book Silver Bridge? Perhaps Bob the light will shine for some lot of people once our Cosmology Newlink gets out..but friend without you I can't do it,so I am counting on you a lot, and hope the length of this letter was worth it.I enjoyed pouring out all my news to you. Please let me know now about if you ARE accepting the position of CONTACT EDITOR and will send me your photo or negative. Edward.

the presence of the UFO. This abnormal picture as seen on the screen of a TV was to be brought to our notice on other occasions during reports of UFO activity.

Two weeks later, on the 19th March, the television set began to show heavy interference, at 8.40pm., similar to before. Francis ran outside and was astonished to see what looked like an identical UFO in the sky, but at a much higher altitude. He telephoned the Police, who sent an officer to the house, who agreed he could see the object - which was later explained away in the local newspapers as being the planet Venus! **(Source: personal interview/H. Watkins, *FSR*)**

At 7.50pm on 14th March 1972, Mrs. Lyons of Bridge End, Walthamstow London, was putting her baby down for the night when she saw, through the window, an *"orange, oval, or cigar-shaped object, surrounded by a hazy glow, standing vertically in the sky"* – About a minute later it vanished from view. **(Source: Ken Philips, BUFORA Report no. 1226)**

Sometime before mid-March 1972, Mr. Leslie Morris of Beechfield Road, Swinton Lancashire was walking home with his daughter, Marlene, when they noticed a strange red light in the sky. Les told us: *"It looked to be the size of a tennis ball, and appeared to be about 500ft up in the sky. It then hovered for several minutes, then turned and vanished."* Upon his arrival home, Les telephoned Manchester Airport about the incident but was told there had been no air traffic for at least quarter of an hour before the sighting. **(Source: *Eccles Journal*)**

They didn't appear to be the only witnesses. Whilst we cannot say it was the same object, The *Manchester News,* in their edition published around the same time period, told of a sighting by schoolgirls - Ellen Chapman and Fiona Cannon, who reported having seen four red lights in the sky, one of which was continually flashing and apparently leading the others across the sky. **(Source: *Manchester Evening News*)**

Humanoid figure seen, Wiltshire

Peter Mantell was cycling to Upton Scudamore, Wiltshire, accompanied by his friend, Ian, at 9.20am on 18th March 1972. Due to the extremely foggy conditions, Peter lost sight of Ian, who was, by now, well out in front. Peter said:

> *"I suddenly felt very dizzy, for no apparent reason, and decided to get off the cycle and walk. As I was doing so I glanced into a field, on my right, and noticed nothing, to begin with, but was then stunned to see a humanoid stood about eight yards away, in a field of grass. It was about 9ft. tall and stood perfectly still, allowing me to see it had three fingers, instead of five, the middle finger starting below what we would call the waist, an absence of any nose, with markings on the face, suggesting mouth and eyes. The 'figure' glistened, as though wet, and was wearing what looked like a tunic, with a sash and sock like shoes. The legs were short and stout, the arms reaching below the knees where the ankles would have been on a human. I shouted for Ian, being very frightened and unable to move. I watched in horror as the figure, whose left arm kept swaying to and fro, then touched its middle finger on the left-hand, on a black spot, or lump, and completely vanished."*

In an interview conducted by Ken Rogers, the Warminster-based UFO Investigator, Peter told him:

> *"Throughout the whole experience, I had been unable to stop my own left arm from rising slowly upwards before returning to its normal position - almost as if, in some way, emulating the movements made by the 'figure'."* **(Source: Ken Rogers/The Dewey Museum, Warminster)**

This was neither the first or last time we were to hear of sightings of similarly described entities, wearing what appeared to be a *"sash, worn diagonally across its chest"*, and similar symptoms endured by the witness, following the appearance of something that is clearly out of the parameters of everyday normality.

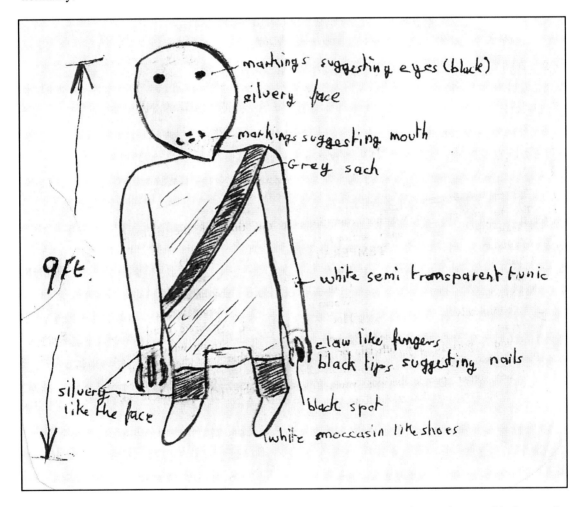

We cannot say there is any connection, but remain puzzled as to what it was that an elderly couple photographed some years back, while taking snaps of their cats in the lounge of their house. They didn't see anything at the time. However, they were sufficiently curious to contact us, wondering if we could offer any explanation as to what the figure was apparently standing outside their rear window. Was it a trick of the light or prank? The simple truth was we don't know and were unable to offer any explanation.

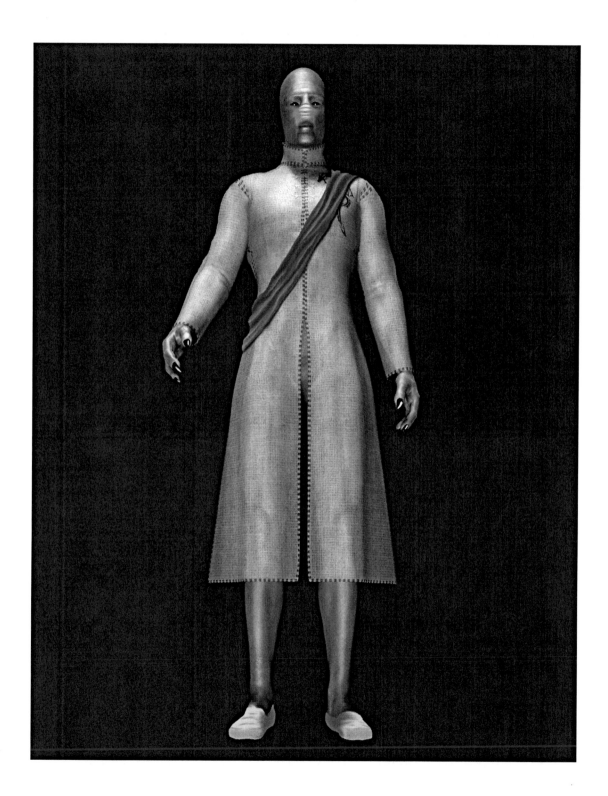

Over the years we were to come across many similar examples of strange humanoid shapes, seen walking across the ground. Their purpose, if they have any, defies our present understandings.

'Giant' seen near Warminster

In the same month, Mrs. Diana Granville Mathews, from Bath, was driving home near Norridge Common at 2.30am, along the Warminster to Bath road. It was a clear night, the surface of the road wet and shining after a recent rainfall.

> *"I saw an orange disc - perfectly circular, to begin with - crossing the road in front of my car; it came from the hedgerow, on my left, and sailed down to road level about 30ft away, before lifting and careering over another hedgerow. As it did so, it changed to oval in shape. I was startled and temporarily bemused, and a little frightened, so I decided not to stop on that isolated stretch of road.*
>
> *I was to receive another shock when, some few hundred yards into my journey, I saw, walking towards me on the other side of the road, a tall figure, dressed in all white clothing. He walked in a loping manner and was a giant of a man. You can imagine I was stunned by this strange sight so close to having just seen the UFO."*

Mrs. Mathews arrived home and went to bed. At 00.5am she was awoken, as though from a dream, by a sharp rapping sound on the front door of her house, followed by a voice calling gently and insistently *"I got up and went to the door; there was nothing there."* **(Source: Ken Rogers)**

This secondary development following on from the initial encounter appears 'part and parcel' of many Close Encounter cases. Did whatever it was latch on to her and follow her home? - Quite likely, in our opinion, bearing in mind other reports brought to our attention over the years involving such manifestations which occur fairly quickly after the initial UFO incident.

On the 24th March 1972, schoolboy Gavin Hudson from Overchurch Middle School, Moreton Road, Upton, Wirral, reported having sighted a large, silvery, *"...unpainted cigar-shaped object, heading from the south-west, towards the north-west"*.

By the time he had alerted the teachers and other pupils, it had gone from sight. **(Source: Martin Jones/*Merseyside Bulletin*, Spring 1972)**

Kensington Library, London

People were invited to a lecture held at Kensington Central Library, on 8th April 1972, at 7.00pm - **'UFOs COMMUNICATIONS and SEMANTICS'** - by Mr. C Maxwell Cade, M.I.E.E, M.I.E.R.E, A.F.R Ae S, F.R.A.S, Consultant to FSR, Psychical Researcher, Inventor, and author of many important scientific papers and books. Mr. Cade will discuss *"Who is trying to communicate with whom and to what extent is the message garbled"?*

UFOs over Cradle Hill, Warminster

At 9.20pm on 8th April 1972, a large golden ball-shaped object, with what appeared to be streamers trailing behind it, with a small red light following closely, was sighted low in the sky, heading towards Cradle Hill, by dozens of 'sky watchers', including Arthur Shuttlewood. Five minutes later, a silver coloured object was seen at high altitude, estimated to be moving at a speed of 5-8,000mph. At 9.50pm. an aircraft passed over Cradle Hill, heading in a north to south direction. Behind it (apparently following)

UFOs ACTIVE OVER WARMINSTER AGAIN

The heading is not a cliché but a mere statement of fact. Scores of sky-watchers witnessed no less than seven unidentifiable objects from watch points Cradle and Starr Hill on the weekend 8th/9th April 1972. Sky conditions were clear, no moon was visible and fixed planets were easily identified. The sightings are listed below in chronological order.

Location: Cradle Hill, Warminster
Date: Saturday 8th April, 1972.
Witnesses: Neil and Sally Pike, Arthur Shuttlewood, Diana Matthews, Cleeve Stevens, Peter Lawless and party, and the Cambridge UFO society. Local skywatchers Barrie Canner, Andrew Pritchard and Jim Wellings.

Account of sightings:

(I) 9.20pm. Large golden ball with faint streamers visible trailing out behind it, crossed the sky at fairly low altitude from North to South; visible for about three minutes. A faint red light was seen in the wake of the object. The speed was estimated to be fairly slow.

(2) 9.25pm. A siver coloured object passed directly overhead from South-West to North East. It was moving at a very high speed, estimated by one of the watchers as between 5000 and 8000 miles per hour, having completed the arc of the sky within two minutes. Both satellites and aircraft were discounted by all present due to great height and speed of the object.

(3) 9.45pm. Object first observed above copse near V.P.5. proceeding South-wards at a low altitude. It was silver in colour, like an exceptionally bright star and seemed to glide comparatively slowly across the sky. It faded out of sight within a couple of minutes.

(4) 9.50pm. Immediately prior to this sighting, an aircraft flying over V.P.5. in a Southerly direction had been observed, its identification lights being easily distinguishable. The object was golden coloured and first observed over V.P.5. travelling in a Southerly direction at seemingly much the same speed as the aircraft. Although the object was closer, when observed by two witnesses, it was seen to be definitely not a conventional aircraft. It was visible for approx 3 minutes.

(5) 9.55pm. Silver-coloured object observed at great height, flying South-wards above V.P.5. Visible for about two minutes. At the end it seemed to hover, then disappeared.

Location: Starr Hill, Warminster.
Date: Sat/Sunday 8th/9th April 1972.

Account of sightings:

(6) I0.45pm. Object appeared directly overhead of observation point. Silver in colour, it detached itself from a group of stars and seemed to hover for a few minutes before slowly fading from sight.

(7) 0I.I5 am. Golden object, circular seen first in Constellation of Cassiopeia by member of Cambridge UFO society. Travelling North West to South East Low altitude, slow moving. Dismissed as army flare or aircraft. Dimmed and 'blacked-out' suddenly whilst in horizontel flight. Duration of sighting I-I½ minutes. All present agreed on peculiarity of object. Witnesses included : Arthur Shuttlewood, Diana Matthews, Jennifer and William Yeadow from Bath, Roy Fisher, Tony Reynolds and Steven Evans from London, Francis Pullen, John Clark from Cambridge and Cleeve Stevens from Hertfordshire. Photographs were taken of the object by the London group.

was seen an object, resembling a golden 'ball of light' - definitely not an aircraft, according to the observers. At 1.15am on 9th April 1972, a golden object in the sky was seen from Starr Hill, observed in the direction of Cassiopeia, heading slowly north-west, at low altitude, by many people, including Arthur Shuttlewood. **(Source: Ken Rogers)**

A dull yellow tinted object was seen falling like a leaf through the sky, over Cradle Hill, Warminster, at 10.00pm on 15th April 1972, by Bristol residents - Mr. J Beecham, Mr. Davies and Mr. Porter. Believing something had landed, they hurried over to the copse but nothing further was seen. **(Source: Ken Rogers)**

At 2.00am on 24th April 1972, a Manchester woman - Mrs. Taylor - who was suffering from insomnia, happened to look out of the window, opposite a tall factory chimney, when she saw a glowing, yellow-white ball shaped object, out of which emerged a 'figure', wearing boots, described as: *"...similar in appearance to an astronaut, landing on the moon"* After two hours, the object eventually disappeared from view. **(Source: Roy Dutton, Joan Nelstrop & Peter Rogerson)**

'Flying Saucer' landing - Great Barr, Staffordshire

In approximately 1972, Karen Hills was then living in Castle Drive, Great Barr. She told of being awoken in the early hours of the morning by a whirring noise outside. On going to the curtains to have a look outside, she saw:

> *"...a huge machine, its base surrounded by light. Inside the clear dome on top, I could see bright lit machinery. I rubbed my eyes several times to make sure I wasn't dreaming, but it was still there. I was very frightened and awoke my sister by shaking her, but she wouldn't listen and told me to shut up. I went to have a another look and it was still there, although it had moved slightly. I went back to bed and lay awake, feeling very scared."*

In 2011, we traced Karen (50) and spoke to her at some length about her sighting. She had this to say:

> *"I can remember being in my bedroom. I used to share a bedroom with my sister and heard a strange noise outside. I looked out of the window and saw this real bright light, this circular thing - a bit like a cup and saucer whirring away.*
>
> *It was absolutely huge. I tried to wake-up my sister and couldn't. I wondered if I'd had a dream, but it seemed so real. I remember seeing it later in the distance between the houses. I did have a very odd dream, involving a massive UFO which was calling the people. I remember going up this ramp thing into the UFO. Inside the UFO there was this seating all the way round.*

SECTION B.

In the boxes below, please sketch what you saw

1. Object/s seen

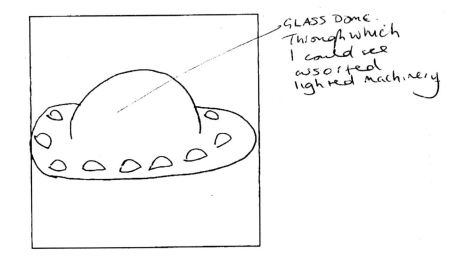

GLASS DOME.
Through which
I could see
assorted
lighted machinery

2. Panoramic view, including any buildings or points of interest, also indicating position of object and manoeuvres if any indicated by a dotted line.

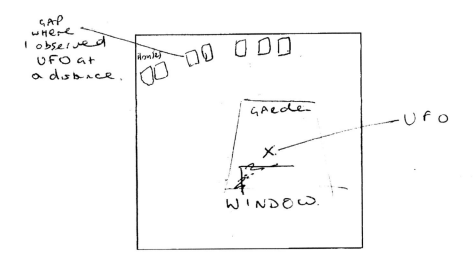

GAP
where
I observed
UFO at
a distance.

Houses

GARDEN

UFO

X.

WINDOW.

I looked around and saw people I knew. We were waiting to leave. There was an arch with a corridor and there was somebody - a weird looking character - just standing there. It wasn't frightening but bewildering. I think that this was a dream. The amazing thing is that when I spoke to my sister, she told me she had also dreamed exactly the same dream."

Having talked to Karen, it was obvious that she was a very genuine, intelligent woman, who remained curious about the sighting and the strange dream that both she and her sister experienced. We are well aware of the implications of what this strange version of events might mean, to some people, but Karen was aged seven or eight at the time, hence her limited recollection of what took place. One thing is assured, she is not the only one to sight something like this. What they are and where they come from is the ultimate question, but whether they exist is not in contention as far as we are concerned. **(Source: Irene Bott, Staffordshire UFO Group)**

UFO fleet over Reading

During the early 1970s, Kate Saunders was a front seat passenger in a car being driven by her boyfriend home from a nightclub in Bracknell, at midnight, when the car spluttered and came to a halt.

"I sat in the car and looked across the road, and saw a dark disc shape object ascend from behind some trees. After a little while the car started and we drove home. I was pretty scared, by this time, and although my boyfriend hadn't seen it, he seemed pretty concerned. We pulled up outside his house and as we got out we saw a large craft moving silently overhead that had a searchlight underneath it, panning left and right as it moved forward.

We ran into his house and his Dad came out with a camera, hoping to get a few shots. At a later date, his Dad had the film developed and was told that the film had been overexposed.

After a while I decided to go home and asked him to take me, but because he was shaken up he asked his sister to come with us. It was a clear, cold night, and as we drove to my house, we were watching the sky and could see more of these craft overhead - no sound, complete silence. I ran in and went up to my room. I didn't try to wake my parents, as they were strict about what time I should be home. I sat looking out of my window until dawn and saw dozens of craft in the sky, travelling towards the Newbury area.

We never told anyone, but some years ago I was talking to my brother and he said he was watching the same thing on the same night.

It was reported in the local newspaper, but was explained away as being the Armed Forces on a joint operation. I really thought that it was an invasion of some sort and was unable to sleep properly for many weeks after the sighting." **(Source: WWW.2012)**

UFO Display over Worcestershire

In spring of 1972 (it may have been a little later) local farmer Trevor Edmunds, from Gorcott Hill - just outside Redditch, Worcestershire (dwarfed now by a giant telecommunications tower) - was out walking, late one evening, contemplating the loss of four acres of his land, due to construction of the new dual carriageway, when he noticed a 'circle of lights' hovering silently in the sky.

"I gazed at them with great curiosity. They were far too big to have been any aircraft. They then started to curl in and out of each other before moving left, towards the direction of Studley."

Despite the incident having happened over 30yrs ago, Trevor's memory of the event remained vivid and was, according to him, the oddest thing he had ever seen in his life. No doubt if this was reported today one may feel that this was an example of laser lights. **(Source: personal interview)**

Kensington Library, London

People were invited to a lecture held at Kensington Central Library on 6th May 1972, at 7.00pm., by Roger Stanway - a solicitor and amateur astronomer of some repute, being a director of the Newchapel Observatory and co-author of the *Flying Saucer Report*, internationally acclaimed as a blueprint for efficient investigation – *Investigations of Landing Cases.* On a personal note we have had the pleasure of talking to Roger Stanway, who withdrew completely from any research and investigation of the UFO subject many years ago. In 2011, Roger reiterated his belief that UFOs are examples of something demonic in origin rather than extraterrestrial, which appears to be more likely from the nature of evidence accrued over the years, although one cannot rule out that if we can send probes to other part of the universe, is it possible that we have also intercepted theirs?

We wished him well and thanked him for allowing us permission to refer to some of the sightings that he and Tony Pace were involved in during the 1970's

At 9.55pm on 15th May 1972 retired Nurse Florence Freeston from Cherry Avenue, Kirby Muxlowe, Leicestershire, contacted the Police after sighting an object, resembling:

"...a car's headlight, in the shape of an umbrella, with something attached to it. It looked like a burning parachute, and remained stationary until covered by clouds, it was positioned neat to the Moon in the sky" **(Source: *Leicester Mercury*, 16.5.72)**

A group of five yellowish-white lights were seen flying over Nairnshire, heading on a north-west to south-east course, at 9.30pm., by Dr. & Mrs. Finlay, then living at Brackla, in May 1972. The couple told of seeing them,

"...apparently descending from the direction of Ben Nevis, quickly followed by a group of six similar objects and then a single light. Ten minutes later, the display was over". **(Source: *The Nairnshire Telegraph*, May 1972)**

UFO over Lincoln

The following evening, Michael and his father, from Ermine Street, Lincoln - both keen amateur astronomers - were outside in the garden at 8.15pm. Michael noticed something strange, low in the sky, moving over nearby rooftops. His first reaction was to think it might have been Venus, but then he realised the colour and position was all wrong. On looking at the object through the telescope, he was surprised to see:

"...a diamond shape, with a red ball of light in the centre, showing a variety of colours in a sequence I had never seen before, with a red glow surrounding the outer 'diamond', with a fainter red inside. The best way to describe what we saw is for you to imagine three circles, one inside of each other - the outer yellow, the inner green, with a golden red centre. As it moved slowly through the sky, it pulsated before being lost from view, as it disappeared behind some houses." **(Source: Richard Thompson)**

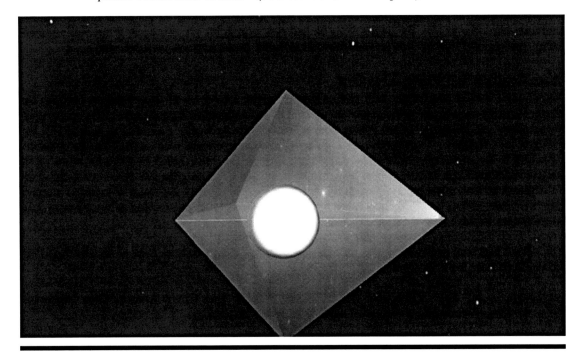

UFO over Wiltshire

On 18th May 1972, John and Joan Lewis were driving along the Shaftsbury to Warminster Road, when they sighted three lights, forming a triangle, motionless in the sky, over treetops, near Cowdown Hill.

> *"We watched, with amazement, as two of the lights blinked out, leaving one shiny orb in the sky. Suddenly, in a blink of an eye, appeared nine glowing objects. They stayed in the air for about three minutes and then drifted slowly to our left, forming a figure 2. We later reported what we had seen to Police Sergeant Jack Bosley."* **(Source: Jack Bosley/The Dewey Museum)**

On the 21st May 1972, Mrs. Dorothy .Fear of Boreham Fields, Warminster, was on her way to the shops when she noticed *'a silver disc-shaped object'* between two large black clouds, towards the direction of Starr Hill, which slowly moved up to each other, taking 15mins to do so. Five days later a European UFO conference was held involving the attendance of important dignitaries as shown in the accompanying photo.

EUROPEAN UFO CONFERENCE, MAY 26th & 27th, 1972

Left to right :

CHARLES BOWEN, *Editor, " Flying Saucer Review."*
HON. BRINSLEY, LE POER FRENCH, *International Chairman of CONTACT.*
CTESSE R. D'OULTREMONT, *Belgium.*
CAPTAIN E. I. A. MACKAY, *BUFORA.*
DR. J. CLEARY-BAKER, *BUFORA.*
French Delegate.

On the 30th of May 1972 Wiltshire resident Mrs. Dorothy Fear found herself witnessing further examples of UFO activity, while looking through the windows of a telephone box, when she saw:

> "...*a red ball-shaped object in the sky, somewhere over the Dene, in the direction of Heytesbury. It was still there after I made my call.*" (**Source: Ken Rogers**)

Incredibly, Mrs. D. Fear found herself sighting something unusual in the sky for the third time on the 1st June 1972 after having left her daughter's flat at Woodcock House, at 10.15pm.

> "*I looked across Kingsdown School and saw a peculiar shaped white coloured cloud, in a clear sky. It was visible for some ten minutes, before disappearing from sight. Later the following morning, at 3.00am, my son, Clive, and I, heard this humming noise over the house. I looked out of the window, but couldn't see anything.*" (**Source: Arthur Shuttlewood**)

UFO over Hartlepool

At 10.30pm on 8th June 1972, a mysterious object, described as resembling "*a flying electric light bulb*", was seen by residents of Wingate, Hartlepool. They included James Anderson, who was driving through Wingate with his wife, Rita, when the car in front of him skidded to a halt.

> "*The people jumped out and looked up into the sky. I saw a brilliant light in the sky, like an electric light bulb. It was making a terrific noise. It seemed to fly along for a few seconds before stopping, and then it shot straight upwards at speed.*"

Another witness included Mr. Richard Roberts, who was driving home with his two sons from the *Fir Tree* Inn, when he saw:

> "*....something came from the west, towards the east coast. I thought it was a rocket, at first. It seemed to hover for a few seconds and then climbed vertically, making one hell of a rumbling noise as it did so. It was like a brilliant spinning light, with a centre and a sort of flare around it.*" (**Source: *Northern Daily Mail*, 9.6.72/personal interview**)

On the 12th June 1972, David Harris - a Police Officer with the South Wales Constabulary - was off duty, at 11.45pm., when he saw what he believed to be an aircraft in trouble, flying low over Llangeinor Mountain.

> "*The object was about the size of a bus in length. I waited for the explosion. There was nothing - just silence. I drove to the Police Station and telephoned Air Traffic Control, at Rhoose Airport. They confirmed no aircraft were in the vicinity. I then reported the matter to the Police control room, at Bridgend.*"

As a result of submitting a report, David received considerable ridicule from his colleagues and some very offensive remarks made by Senior Officers, who suggested he was lying. (**Source: personal interview**)

UFO landing, London

On 13th June 1972, Miss Shirley Devereux and her parents, of Danebury Avenue, Roehampton, London, sighted a cluster of light landing in Richmond Park, at 10.00pm. Miss Devereux later said:

> *"It hovered above the park, 30ft. above the ground, and then moved across the park but stopped near the Priory. Between then and 12.15am, we saw a number of other lights converging on the same spot where the previous one had come down; they were so bright you could see them clearly with the naked eye. The lights were a brilliant orange and seemed to go dull. Just before they landed, I saw a distinct saucer-shaped object behind them."*

According to Gordon Creighton, Editor of *Flying Saucer Review*, this was not the only occasion when things had been seen to land in the park. Apparently, another resident in the area - Mrs. Joan Kinneir - had observed a flaming object descending into the park, some years previously. **(Source: *Barnes and Mortlake Herald*/Gordon Creighton)**

On the afternoon of the 28th June 1972, a UFO was seen flying over the Penhill area of Swindon, Wiltshire, and was reported to RAF Lyneham, who confirmed they had received a number of reports. One of the witnesses was local woman - Wendy Eales.

> *"It was about 12.30pm when my sister, Lesley, came in and grabbed binoculars. It was white, with a ring around it, and spinning very fast. It didn't frighten me. I was fascinated."*

A shining silver globe was seen in the sky over Scarborough during the same afternoon by residents of Princess St, before it moved away towards the north east. One of the witnesses was Mr. R. Sewell,

> *"I don't know what the hell it was; it was around silvery thing with a point on top. It's hard to say how high it was, but certainly higher than the low cloud"*

Other reports of a similar object seen on the same day came in from Coventry and Norfolk, but the sightings were later explained away as a weather balloon by RAF Lyneham - which appears highly unlikely, bearing in mind the nature of the sightings concerned. **(Source: *Evening Advertiser*, believed to be 29th June 1972/*Scarborough Evening News* 29.6.1972)**

In summer of the same year, David Jones and a friend from Balham, London, were looking out of the first floor window of their flat, at midnight, when they spotted a single light, low, above the terrace house roofs, some distance away.

The light was seen to divide into two, then rapidly into three, as it approached their position, at a fast speed. They were clearly able to see:

> *"...a wedge-shaped craft, flying so low we could plainly see a man in a high collared, black or navy blue uniform, looking back at us, from inside some type of cabin. The craft passed over the roof, emitting a sound similar to air displacement, and then turned around and came*

back over the roof, emitting another whooshing sound. It appeared to be emitting a dull red flame from its centre. The craft then disappeared in the direction it was first seen coming from." **(Source: UFO Reports/ Albert Rosales)**

UFO over Coventry

At 11.30pm on 29th June 1972, a red, green and silver, object was sighted over Coventry by Leamington woman - Katherine Laws - who called the Police. They attended and confirmed they had the object under observation, which appeared to have *"a fan-shaped tail"*. This was yet another sighting later brought to the attention of local UFO Investigator Bob Tibbitts, who was to discover that on occasion rational answers could be found!

Bob received a telephone call from a young man, who had read Katherine Law's account in the *Coventry Evening Telegraph*. He told him that he had also witnessed a total of 29 UFOs over the Leamington area, during the same evening, but that, more importantly, he was *now* watching two of them in the sky! Bob Tibbits later wrote:

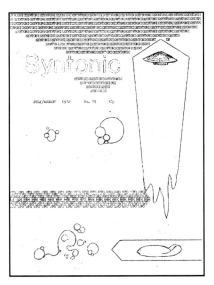

"About 15mins later, he turned up at the house and offered to take me to see the objects, and clutching binoculars and coats in our hands, we rushed from the house.

Excitedly, my wife and I leapt into the car, accompanied by the young man, and made our way to a high point along the road near Lillington. He pointed out the UFOs in the sky.

I peered at them for several minutes and then, feeling almost totally deflated, said to him, 'They are stars, nothing more I'm afraid!'" **(Source: as above/ SYNTONIC, July/August 1972 Coventry Evening Telegraph, 3.6.72)**

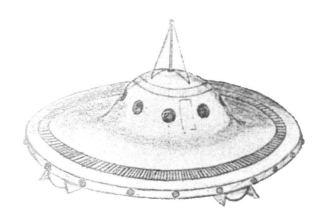

CHAPTER TWO
JULY-DECEMBER 1972

UFO over Brighton

In July 1972, as the sun began to set, a silvery object was seen flying across the sky over the coast of Brighton, by a woman and her daughter, out exercising the family dog.

A few days later, the same couple were astonished to see a 'repeat performance', when a large red 'light' appeared moving from the east, at 10.00pm., which they thought was a satellite, but dismissed this as a likely explanation when it stopped in mid-air, for a few minutes, before rising upwards into cloud cover.

They watched, hoping for a another glimpse of the 'visitor', and were rewarded, a short time later, when it appeared, once again, close to its original location - now projecting bright rays of light, before disappearing ,once more, into cloud.

To their amazement it reappeared, slowly descending in a peculiar *"rocking motion - 'like a leaf falling through the sky' – then it stopped and shot upwards, never to be seen again"*. **(Source: Leslie Harris, Bournemouth UFO Group)**

In the summer of this same year, two young girls, aged 9, were walking across a field in Malden, Essex, at 9.00pm when they sighted what they initially believed to be some sort of new electricity pylon, until they realised this was not the case.

In an interview, later conducted with UFO Investigator Andrew Collins, the two girls described seeing:

> *"...a silver orange dome like object, showing a number of portholes along the edge, which showed clear light; its bottom portion was covered by trees and it appeared transparent. There was a ghostly glow around the edges. We became frightened and ran away."* **(Source: as above/*FSR*, Volume 22, No. 4, 1976 - 'British reports Old and New', Jenny Randles)**

UFO over Warminster

At 1.45am on 13th July, two civilian drivers who were on night exercise with the Army, on Salisbury Plain, sighted a blue light moving about erratically in the sky, for several minutes. They estimated the light to be south of their position, towards the direction of Heytesbury.

At 1.55am on the same date, Mrs. Booker from Corton - a small village situated some 6 miles from Warminster - got up to go to the bathroom. On her return to the bedroom, she noticed a large bright light through the window, high in the sky, towards the south-west direction. After watching it for some time, she rang her neighbour - Mrs. H. Ley - at 2.00am, and alerted her as to what was going on. She said:

> *"I thought, at first, it was Jupiter and went outside to have a look; it then diminished in size and disappeared, but reappeared immediately. I picked up a naval telescope and looked through to see a circular shining spot in the sky. By this time the 'light' had moved to our far right, westwards, and was now much lower in the sky.*
>
> *I went outside, once again, and noticed that the light was definitely moving and seemed to be sending off rays to the bottom right. I also thought I saw a smaller light crossing in front of it and around it on several occasions. The diminishing and reappearing action happened several times during the hour we watched it. Finally the light grew smaller and moved westwards, until disappearing from sight, at 2.55am."*

They were not the only ones to report something strange that night. A married couple from Sutton Veny, told of being awoken at 3.00am by a kind of whistling noise - like a boomerang being skimmed through the air. Later that evening, Alan Smith from Torquay, Devon, was with four other 'sky watchers' on Cradle Hill, when they saw a bright, slowly moving, amber coloured light above the copse on top of the hill, which became a common sighting over this locality, and were labelled 'amber gamblers' by many of the sky watchers. **(Source: Peter Paget)**

Police Officers sight UFOs

Police Constable Brian Nichols, of North Walsham, was on duty, at 9.15pm on the 25th July 1972, when he noticed a strange 'light' hovering in the sky above the village of Happisburgh. Thinking it was a flare fired at sea he radioed the Police force control room and asked them to contact the coastguard, who confirmed they had no knowledge of any ship in distress near Eccles-on-Sea. The Officer got out of the Police car.

> *"As it approached closer, I could see the outline of an object behind the flickering light, transparent in nature, reminding me of a polythene bag, with a candle burning in one corner, totally silent. It then disappeared from view over the direction of Stalham, at a speed I estimated to be a hundred miles per hour, which ruled out any chance of it being a plastic bag, as there was no wind."* **(Source: Ivan W. Bunn/personal interview)**

In the summer of the same year, Police Constable Keith George was on patrol with another colleague, travelling along the A26, near Mereworth, Maidstone, heading towards Tonbridge, Kent, at 2.20pm, when they sighted:

> *"...two objects, at what appeared to be high altitude, flying in a diagonal formation. They were tube-shaped, but flying 'sideways'. They were moving slowly, but then stopped and reversed, at enormous speed, for a short while (10 seconds) - then continued forward as before, and accelerated fast forward out of sight.*
>
> *This was reported over Force radio and we were instructed to go to Tonbridge Police Station and then took a phone call from an RAF officer, after which we were sent forms to fill in. We never heard another word about it and took a great deal of 'stick' from other officers. I can give the name of my colleague, but as I no longer know his whereabouts, feel it is unfair to name him without his permission.*
>
> *We never sought publicity over this - the opposite, in fact. I did think it would be mentioned in the latest list of MOD sightings and cannot understand why it has not been."* **(Source: www.uk-ufo.co.uk)**

Strange 'figure' seen - Cradle Hill, Warminster

On 26th July 1972, Robert Mason, accompanied by his friend Stephen Barnett were conducting a 'sky watch' on Cradle Hill, Warminster, when, as the light began to fade, they caught sight of what looked like a small man, or boy, standing in the clearing in front of a nearby barn. Excitedly they ran over, hoping to confront the figure, but despite a search of the locality, found nobody there.

Although the sighting was outlined on page 96 of *'The Warminster Triangle'*, by Ken Rogers, an examination of personal papers stored at The Dewey Museum, in Warminster, by Ken after his death revealed the story did not end there.

After completing the 'sky watch', the two men returned to their lodgings. While ascending the stairs leading to the communal bathroom, before retiring for the night they heard the sound of running water and presumed another guest was using the bathroom and stood waiting on the landing. The door opened and a woman came out, entered the bedroom opposite, and promptly vanished in front of their eyes!

Thursday, July 20th, 1972

A few days ago Mr. Tony Justice informed me, quietly and matter-of-fact, that not just one but several "flying saucers" had been observed by him. The first, one evening two years ago near Warminster in Wiltshire, was "a big orange ball travelling fairly slowly, about 50 m.p.h., and about 500 ft. in circumference, which came towards us over a hill. When about half a mile away and at a height of about 2,000 ft. it changed course abruptly and went across Salisbury Plain. It had a red pulsating light at rear."

Likewise at Warminster, with 15 or more others, he saw a streak of light travelling at "something around the speed of light," and then an orange glow at the end of the streak, this orange going elliptical and disappearing as a streak. UFOs (unidentified flying objects) Mr. Justice claims to have noted additionally include pinpoints of light resembling stars.

He agreed that if these objects were not natural phenomena, they could have been mass-produced on this planet and not necessarily the inventions of beings from outer-space. But he is convinced they were the latter.

Tony Justice - genuine and sincere.

Whether this incident was connected to the earlier sighting is something we cannot answer. For all we know, there may well be an innocent explanation for the appearance of the small figure; maybe it was a hoaxer at work. However, even if one chooses to completely disregard the earlier matter, how can we explain, rationally, the 'ghostly' events which occurred in front of the men's eyes as anything but inexplicable? We would have liked to have found out far more about where they were staying, and the history of the house itself. **(Source: The Dewey Museum, Warminster)**

UFO over Norfolk

In summer of the same year, Lilian Nettleship of Bradwell, Norfolk, was walking through Gorleston, near Gt. Yarmouth, with her small son, at around noon, when she saw:

> *"...a large dark grey 'U'-shaped object crossing the sky, east to west, before it partially disappeared through some light cloud. It looked like three metal cans, stuck together with a matt metallic finish. I ran over to the other side of the road to follow it, but it went too fast for me. I drew other people's attention to it before it went out of view".*
> **(Source: Ivan W. Bunn)**

UFO over Hampshire

On 3rd August 1972, a mysterious red, glowing, light was seen hovering over the New Forest, Farmington, Hampshire, at 11.35pm., by Sir John and Lady Chichester, at Battramsley Lodge, Boldre before suddenly dropping downwards, at terrific speed, behind a line of trees. A short time later, a similar object appeared in the sky to the north and circled the area, once, before it, too, disappeared.

E EDITOR :	
M MANAGING EDITOR :	...rt ...ondon, W.1. ...l: 01-723 0305
S SUBSCRIPTION DEPARTMENT :	...ing ...London S.E.3.

LIONEL BEER
(SPECIALIST BOOKSELLER)
15 FRESHWATER COURT
CRAWFORD STREET
LONDON W1H IHS

SPACELINK

An independent magazine specialising in

UFO NEWS — FLYING SAUCER TOPICS — SPACE NEWS

PLEASE REPLY TO M.

17 September 1972.

R W Tibbitts Esq
43 Tanners Lane
Tile Hill Village
Coventry, CV4 9HX.

Dear Bob

You may recall that we exchanged correspondence last year when you expressed interest in helping with SPACELINK. Recently after sorting through old correspondence I found your letters, and it appears nothing further happened. This may well be my fault, as I have had numerous problems during the past year, which have made major inroads into my precious sparetime, not least of which was having my flat broken into at one stage.

Anyway I don't wish to bore you with my problems, and let me say that recently I have been able to bring a lot of paperwork and letters up to date.

I am writing now, as a matter of courtesy, to ask if you are still interested in helping with SK, after this long interval? Should you be interested, may I remind you that I think you offered to produce a list of U.K. UFO and related magazines. I would still like this. I had it in mind to grade it into three sections: 1st - the four leading magazines, 2nd, the major local UFO club magazines, and 3rd, the remaining newsletters and very small circulation magazines, possibly including those newsletters which contain a small proportion of UFO material eg. Interplanetary News, NICAP JOURNAL etc.in relation to their total contents. If you would like to do this please go ahead, I could still use it as a basis for the U.K. list.

You also mentioned in one of your letters that you were a compositor. I wonder if you could type-set a special article for me for SK? The article is technical and too long to be typed up using an ordinary typewriter, as it would occupy too much space this way. If it were type-set in a suitable point size it would probably fit in nicely. Can you help? I would be willing to pay something towards having this article (on propulsion) set, and otherwise I will look round for a jobbing printer. Incidentally, do you still work for the Coventry Telegraph?

Yours sincerely

Lionel

L E Beer

According to Sir John, the 'light was described as scarlet in colour and pulsating regularly as it *"wandered about the sky"*. Lady Chichester added that: *"Through a pair of binoculars it looked like a circular object, with red flames projecting from a mass of holes on its outer surface. We then reported it to the* Southern Evening Echo *Newspaper. I've no idea what it was, although I did wonder if it could have been an experiment carried out at Porton Down.*[*]*"*

Sir John tried to ring Hurn Airport but received no reply; he then contacted the Police at Lyndhurst who sent out two officers but by the time they arrived there was nothing to be seen. **(Source: personal interview/*New Milton Advertiser*, 19.8.72)**

At 8.45pm on 6th August 1972, Liverpool resident – Victor Stevens, and his wife - were sat watching the sunset when they noticed a bright object stationary in the sky at extreme height. Vic,

> *"We watched it through binoculars. After about three minutes, it veered rapidly towards the westerly direction, and then it halted in flight for a couple of minutes. During its movement we saw what looked like a condensation trail, like that made by a jet aircraft. There appeared to be red flames issuing from its rear. At 8.57pm it sped rapidly out of sight, towards the west. We also saw a jet aircraft in the sky at the same time, but this was an easily recognisable object."* **(Source: *Merseyside UFO Bulletin*)**

UFO over Bath

Mrs. Barbara 'Babs' Honey was then living at Upper Milford Farm, Bath, with her husband.

> *"During the early hours of the 7th August 1972, we were awoken by a bright light shining into the bedroom. We looked out of the window and saw what looked like a gold 'eyeball', with 'lashes' of light, slowly flying through the sky, making this weird 'beating noise' - like a heart beating. My husband, who was very sceptical of such matters, was astonished. Thirty minutes later, it was lost from view as it entered a bank of cloud."* **(Source: personal interviews/*Bath Weekly Chronicle*, 10.8.72 – 'Eyeball in the sky')**

UFO display over Warminster

From the *'Sky Watchers'* log kept by Cleve Stevens, to whom we contacted - then a regular visitor to the Warminster area, during the 1970s period - we learnt of a sighting, which took place at 11.10am. on 9th August 1972, involving John Lewis, a hairdresser by profession.

> *"I was watching a jet fighter 'loop the loop' high in the sky, and was about to fetch a pair of binoculars to obtain a closer look, when, all of a*

---

* Defence, Science and Technology Laboratory, Porton Down (United Kingdom facility for Military research, located at Salisbury, in Wiltshire) Porton Down is one of the United Kingdom's most sensitive and secretive government facilities for military research, including CBRN defence. The Defence Science and Technology site occupies 7,000 acres (28 km). It is also home to the Health Protection Agency's Centre for Emergency Preparedness and Response, as well as a small science park, which includes companies such as Tetricus Bioscience and Ploughshare Innovations. Porton Down was originally opened in 1916, as the Royal Engineers Experimental Station, as a site for testing chemical weapons. The laboratory's remit was to conduct research and development regarding chemical weapons agents, such as chlorine, phosgene and mustard gas, by the British armed forces in the First World War.

sudden, this object, looking like a gigantic frozen snowball, dwarfing the size of the aircraft, appeared from the direction of Norridge Wood, near Cley Hill.

It shot past, and then stopped in mid-air over the Downs to the North. From out of this enormous object emerged two smaller 'white things' that spun out to either side of the 'balls', resembling solid white clouds. They dropped downwards in a perfect white triangle. I rushed inside and grabbed the binoculars but, when I dashed outside, the two white fleecy, cloud-like, 'things' had gone. The larger object then faded away and out of sight."

On the 10th August 1972, Mr. William Jelly - an employee of London Airport - was shooting pigeons, south of the Airport, at 12.30pm, when he was astonished to see what looked like a whirlwind pass over in a west to east direction. It appears that this whirlwind had sucked up a large quantity of loose straw from outside the airport perimeter as, on the same day, it was reported there was a fall of straw from the sky over Heathrow, which we presume was the same material taken from London Airport. Interestingly, it was reported that pilots had encountered layers of straw, suspended in the air at high altitude. On the 14th August 1972, straw was reported falling over Heston, in Cambridgeshire. **(Source: Arnold West)**

At 3.00pm on 13th August 1972, a dirigible, or Zeppelin-shaped object was seen in the sky close to Gatwick Airport, by an off-duty officer watching aircraft. According to the witness, it was seen heading north-east to south-west, with its rear end enveloped in blue smoke. About a minute later the smoke cleared, leaving no sign of the mysterious object.

Humanoid figures seen Warminster

We also learnt of an alleged sighting, bordering more on what one may ascribe to ghostly phenomena, rather than the visitation of any alien intelligence, involving *"three gigantic humanoid figures"*, seen standing in a triangular formation at the edge of a field, close to Starr Hill, at 9.00pm on 13th August 1972, by a group of six 'sky watchers'. The 'beings' were described as:

> *"...at least eight-foot tall, with large domed heads, no apparent necks, wide shoulders, slim waists, and long dangling arms"*

This was followed by a beautiful fragrance, accompanied by warm air, which flooded over them, accompanied by loud thumping noises heard from some nearby bushes. The 'figures' then approached the group of 'sky watchers', *"one of whom apparently walked right through one of the 'figures'"*, at which point the 'beings' vanished from sight.

Admittedly, such incidents seem almost unbelievable, until you either experience them for yourselves (or speak, as we have done, over the years) to others who appear to have witnessed the presence of similarly described 'alien' figures on the slopes of the same hill, and some very strange objects in the sky. They included Neil Pike, to whom we spoke, on many occasions, with regard to regular visits made to Cradle Hill and other locations, with his ex-wife, Sally, (which included the sighting of a giant figure) but we should take into consideration the actions of hoaxer - Molly Carey - who was on the hill that night, although it stretches the bounds of feasibility to accept the hoaxers could have orchestrated anything like this.

LOOK OUT, LOVERS!

By HARRY WARSCHAUER

The men from outer space could be 'beaming in' on your intimate moments

SAY, FELLAS, have you heard the one about the Englishman, the Irishman and the brawny young farmer from Brazil?

Between them these three gentlemen have started a flap in flying saucer circles . . . and, just as intriguingly, revealed a possible *new dimension to sex.*

It could be that when certain people make love they send telepathic signals into outer space.

Flying saucers home in on them and, hey presto, the saucers land on Earth rather as jets approaching Heathrow sometimes follow radio signals from the airport to get on to the runway.

It may sound a fantastic theory and it's easy to imagine Romeos changing their patter to (girls be warned): "It's not sex I'm after . . . I just want to contact the flying saucer men."

But at least one expert on unidentified flying objects is seriously considering the sexy wavelengths possibility.

Too shy

He is Mr. Norman T. Oliver who has raised the subject in "Gemini," the leading U.F.O. journal which he edits.

"I feel sure lots of people have had such contacts but are too shy to come out into the open about them," he said. "I'd like to hear from them."

Several eminent men are consultants to "Gemini." They include Air Marshal Sir Victor Goddard and Dr Geoffrey G. Doel, the radiologist.

Last week Mr Oliver, 40, an accounts executive with the Metropolitan Water Board and a member of the British Astronomical Society, solemnly told me of these remarkable experiences claimed by three men.

The first, of a 27-year-old ENGLISHMAN, was on the Derbyshire - Staffordshire border

6 He said he had made love to his girl-friend at his home and then felt impelled to go out into the country.

He saw an unidentified

Air Marshal Goddard: "I suppose sex comes into everything nowadays."

Norman Oliver: Three fascinating tales of sex and flying saucer people.

flying object — a UFO — which landed about half a mile away.

After waiting about 10 minutes one of the UFO crew, who looked like an ordinary human being, came to meet him.

He told the contactee that his craft came from outside our solar system.

Rhythm

They had not come specifically to contact him. It was merely that his love-making had established a kind of telepathic line of communication between him and the saucer people.

In certain humans, sexual activity "charged" them to a rhythm compatible with the telepathic wavelength of any beings from outer space within range. The rhythm gave them a beam to home in on.

The contactee said the man from the saucer spoke English well, but had some difficulty about some of our more specific sexual terms.

He explained that their planet was very much like ours, and so were the people. But they were more highly developed and lived two to three times longer. Their way of reproduction was similar to the human way. **9**

According to some reports quoted by Mr. Oliver, a number of Earthlings have actually had sexual intercourse with the flying saucer visitors.

The young BRAZILIAN farmer, for instance. He was ploughing when his tractor went dead and a spacecraft landed near by.

He was carried aboard, undressed, disinfected and had blood samples taken.

Then he was joined by a nude saucer girl, a well-made, blue-eyed blonde with

thin lips, high cheekbones, freckled arms and no body hair.

She embraced him, and they made love. The farmer was then given his clothes back and escorted off the saucer, which took off.

Later the farmer found his tractor was working.

A very similar incident is reported to have happened near Belfast.

A young IRISHMAN is said to have been backed out one night by an intense light from a spacecraft.

He came to on the craft, his head and wrists secured. There were four men and a girl who was blue-eyed and blonde, with high cheekbones and freckles — just as the Brazilian experienced.

The Irishman, too, had sexual intercourse with the girl—who told him they came from another galaxy and wanted the seed of Earth men.

Said Mr. Oliver: "I was a little concerned about touching on sex in the magazine in case some of our readers objected.

"I don't want people to think that we want everybody to make love in the hope of contacting extraterrestial beings. So far nobody has objected to the article."

What do Mr Oliver's consultants on "Gemini" think of the article?

Dr. Doel, a member of the Royal College of Surgeons and a Licentiate of the Royal College of Physicians, told me:

Very good

"If you accept the possibility of contact by extraterrestials you must accept every aspect of such contacts as possible. And that must include the sexual.

"I think the article is very good. From our point of view, this is only a very minor aspect of U.F.O. research but you cannot leave it out."

SUNDAY PEOPLE
6/8/1972

THE SUN, Wednesday, February 2, 1972   15

Watching on Cradle Hill: Ken Rogers, Moreen Butler and Jim Wellings   Pictures: ROBERT BAMBER

Keith Palmer with some of his evidence

earthly manifestations as council meetings, annual dinners, and cat shows.

Sceptic

For the first nine months after Warminster put itself on the UFO trail, Shuttlewood was not only a sceptic, but he wasted no opportunity to put his scepticism into print.

In the sitting-room of his house in Portway, Warminster, he spoke of the moment when he saw the light.

"It was a Tuesday night in September, and I had taken some notes up to my study to write an article for the local paper.

"Suddenly I was aware of something glittering through the window.

"I looked up, and saw, coming from the direction of Cradle Hill, something that looked like a giant airship, except that its forward end was rather pointed. It was more like a huge white banana. I pointed my camera at it, and felt electricity flowing through my arm.

"This really frightened me.

"Then it suddenly began to revolve, and, as it came nearer, I reckoned it was about 200ft long, and about 75ft deep.

"It changed colour to a glossy yellow, and then red. And then it was gone.

"It moved terrifically fast, and yet there was no noise at all." For Shuttlewood, an ex-RAF bomber housewife, kept vigil on Cradle H

And now, just s Shuttlewood, assi he reckons he has 700 UFOs.

Ken Rogers, 22 assistant manager shopping comple something stran pening strongly send out the UFO Newsletter e

Visit

"I think there festation of energ minster which ga appearance of are in the sky," said h

But there is a core which is con visits from other

Then there is that if you dre through all the

Even the police have seen them

THEY say that if you were to ride a cock horse into Banbury these days, the chances are that no one would notice.

Why? Because everybody is looking straight upwards.

This historic Oxfordshire town, immortalised by nursery rhyme, is currently being given a new lease of life by UFOs. A thousand of them have been spotted since August 25, 1971.

Nowhere in the world

have reports of strange sightings in the sky been received by the police in such mind-boggling numbers.

Crowds

Not only by the police, but from them as well, because four witnesses to come forward have been a police inspector, a constable, a police cadet, and the wife of a police sergeant.

Every night crowds of

sightseers congregate on the Burton Dassett Hills, just north of the town, to skywatch.

Keith Palmer, 25-year-old Banbury warehouse manager, and the British director of the International UFO Society, has been kept busy investigating each new sighting.

"The first thing to explain is that we have discounted about 97 per cent," he said.

"But that still leaves 30 sightings in the last five

months which we believe to be totally unexplained."

The photographs of several UFOs were taken by Paul Beckham, of Rochester Way, Twyford, Banbury, and show a saucer-shaped object with bright lights on its underside.

One UFO eye-witness was Mrs Ina Wood, a 29-year-old housewife, of Woodhead, Banbury.

She looked out of her kitchen window last October, and saw a low, whitish vapour trail in the sky.

"It suddenly appeared, then stopped, and, as I watched, it began again in a different place," she said.

Planet

Palmer, who believes in visitations from other planets, added: "We have a number of American air bases around here, and I am absolutely convinced that they are doing secret tests with a circular craft.

"The Ministry of Defence has appealed through

our local paper for full details of the various sightings, and it has even sent an RAF squadron leader down to examine our findings."

Palmer receives from the Radio and Space Research Station at Slough, Bucks, regular information on the movements of American and Russian satellites, as well as up-to-date positions of other visible planets, and is careful to check with these records before "recognising" a UFO sighting.

DO YOU BELIEVE IN UFOs? HAVE YOU EVER SEEN ONE? Write to: UFOs, 30 Bouverie Street, London, EC4Y 8DE. £1 for every lett

Neil was to send us a UFO photo of what he (and many others) was to label the appearance of the 'Ambler gambler'

At 2.30am, the following morning, a married couple from Surrey, were sat in their parked car, near Longleat woods, when they saw two small red lights emerge from the wooded area, and leap into the sky; one headed over to Cley Hill, the other, east, toward Warminster. The couple made their way to where the UFOs had first been seen, and heard strange shooting sounds. The wife felt a presence and ran back to the car, followed by her husband, who claimed he saw: *"...an awesome goat-like creature, with scales on its belly - like a fish - fluorescent green in colour.* (**Source: Ken Rogers, *The Warminster Triangle* (Coates and Parker)/*Warminster News*, September 1972 – 'More humanoids seen around Warminster'**)

UFO Display over Winsford

During the same period, a number of people living in Pulford Road, Brindley, Winsford, sighted a number of mysterious lights in the sky, which began on the evening of the 15th August 1972, and went on being seen over the course of the next 4-5 days. It was believed they were occurring over the direction of Jodrell Bank and the Pennines area. According to Mrs. Lucy Howard of Pulford Road, they were seen as:

> *"...flickering red lights; sometimes four, other times singly."*

Other reports described them as brilliant fluorescent lights seen to rise vertically off the ground and grow in size as they did so. Explanations in the media included reflected light from low cloud, caused by electric trains moving along the rail, planes refuelling, or even reflected light from aircraft on Manchester Airport, bounced off cloud! (**Source: *Stoke-on-Trent Evening Sentinel*, 18.8.72 - 'Sky at night of UFOs!**)

In the early hours of the 16th August 1972, 'bright lights' were seen hovering in the sky over Hounslow, Middlesex, by a Police Officer, who described them as showing a number of strange black spots over their surface. The Officer reported the incident to his colleagues at Hounslow Police Station who confirmed the object was still in the sky and was hovering over the direction of Acton and Chiswick . They weren't the only ones office workers in Central London also contacted the Police after sighting the object. Enquiries made by the local Newspaper, the *Acton Gazette*, seeking further information about the incident, at Hounslow Police Station, met with a denial, although enquiries with the Police at New Scotland Yard confirmed a UFO sighting had been reported to them by an officer, whose identity they declined to reveal. (**Source: *Acton Gazette*, 17.8.72**)

On the evening of the 17th August, pensioner Harold Emson (70) sighted an object, which was white in colour, motionless in the sky, over Newcastle. The object was still there some hours later, but now orange in colour. He contacted the local newspaper, the *Stoke-on-Trent Evening Sentinel,* who published his sighting. A spokesman for the Manchester Weather Centre suggested he may have seen a weather balloon, released from Liverpool, the previous day. (**Source: *Stoke-on-Trent Sentinel*, 18.8.72 - 'Pensioner sees UFO - twice'**)

Phantom footsteps Cradle Hill

Neil and Sally Pike were to experience for themselves, at first hand, a phenomenon which was to be labelled, 'the phantom footsteps', or 'the invisible walker', at 10.00pm. on the 22nd August 1972. Neil said:

> *"We heard a sound, like a large animal was trapped, behind a hawthorn bush on the track way leading up to the ranges. I shone my torch around the area but couldn't see anything. Suddenly, we heard the*

sound of what we thought were heavy footsteps, crashing through the cornfield, and seemingly approaching our position; we left immediately, feeling quite frightened."

Neil and Sally (now divorced from each other) were to provide valuable assistance to the authors, over the years, with their assessment of the 'UFO scene' and of people involved. Here is a rare photo of Neil, taken at Starr Hill, during that period. (**Source: personal interview with Neil**)

Landed UFO Lancashire

At 2.00am on 24th August 1972, Heald Green residents - John Taylor and his wife, Sandra - were driving home along the Ripponden Road, between York and Thirsk, when Sandra asked her husband to pull up, after telling John she could see something in a field next to the road.

John, who was later interviewed by a reporter from the *Stockport Advertiser*, described what happened next:

> *"We saw this thing in a field beside the road. We couldn't see its base, because of a high hedge. It was about 20ft tall and a great deal more than that across, and glowing a weird luminous colour. At one time I would have laughed at anyone saying things like this, but it was a weird experience and when the door began to open, nothing would have made me stay around."*

Mrs. Taylor called at Cheadle Hulme Police Station, and reported the matter. She was surprised to hear from the officer that they had received other calls from people, who told of seeing a similar UFO, including one man that had stopped his car to take a closer look. (**Source:** *Stockport Advertiser,* **Cheshire, 24**[th] **August 1972)**

Between the 24th and 31st August 1972, Jane Sullivan (19) of Rose Hill Park West, Sutton, sighted something unusual from her bedroom window, at 3.30am. She later told a reporter from the *Sutton and Cheam Herald* what she had seen:

> *"At first I thought it was an aircraft, but it was very low in the sky and had no flashing light. After about five minutes, there were two bright flashes - like those you get from railways lines when it's raining."*

Her father, who was sceptical about the existence of UFOs, said that he had looked through binoculars and seen an object, pitted like a golf ball. The Air Ministry confirmed that they had received a report from one other person, and suggested that Venus was likely to have been the explanation. (**Source:** *Sutton and Cheam Herald,* **31.8.72 – 'UFO baffles the Air Ministry')**

Bryce Bond - New York Journalist

Another person who visited Warminster, during 1972, was New York Journalist - Bryce Bond, whose account of what he experienced on 26th August 1972, was later published in *The Fountain Journal,* No. 3, 1976.

> *"We drove over to Starr Hill, another ancient burial mound area, which the Romans built on, with a few of the remnants still in evidence, located in the valley wheat fields all around, with high hills and ridges in the background. The sky started to clear, now filling up with thousands of beautiful stars, but still no UFOs! It was getting late and I still hadn't interviewed Arthur Shuttlewood. I caught up with him and crawled into one of the nearby cars to keep warm, while I interviewed him for the American radio listeners.*
>
> *Arthur told me three large entities, about eight feet in height, had been seen in a little hollow, which he pointed out, and that in their presence, people had felt a great warmth, and were engulfed by a scent of roses and violets.*
>
> *Suddenly, he pointed to a peculiar light that had appeared in the field in front of us and said to me, 'I'm very glad that you are here tonight, Bryce. There, in front of us, is a UFO. Notice the triangle shape and the coloured lights going around it; that is a very good sign'. It then started to lift in a weird pattern - then just disappeared. I was flabbergasted.*
>
> *While describing it on tape to the American listeners, a brilliant white one popped up, about 25degrees off the horizon, and did a little dance. Arthur jumped from the car and flashed his torch at the object, using Morse code. The object flashed back the same, did a little dance in the sky, and disappeared from view."*

After interviewing other witnesses, Bryce made his way back slowly to the parked cars, when he heard a noise - like some crushing down the tall wheat at the side of the track - very odd, as there was no wind blowing.

"I looked out. The Moon had just come out, shining brightly. There, in front of my eyes, a large depression was being crushed down in an anticlockwise pattern, shaped like a triangle, measuring about twenty feet from point to point. I stood there, for a few moments, and experienced a tremendous tingling sensation, accompanied by a sweet smell and warm air. I made my way back to Arthur, who pointed out some landing impressions in the section fronting the bar, a 30ft. circle and a cigar-shaped one, both in an anticlockwise fashion. I was happy my mission had been a success."

While one could argue that the 'lights' may have been the work of hoaxers, it is clear the creation of the simplistic 'crop circles' could not fall into this category. Unfortunately, there are no easy answers but plenty of theories available to explain this type of phenomena. They include, alien/UFO interaction, shifts in the earth's magnetic field, creating a current that flattens the crops in its path, and whirlwinds (surely unlikely in this instance) - the plain simple truth is we just don't know.

According to a close friend of Bryce's, Cetin Bal, Bryce describes much more fully what may well have been the same incident that he says took place in 1974, at Cradle Hill, during an interview held in 1987, although rather curiously there is no mention of any contact with 'alien beings' was the following

version of events embellished or did Mr Bryce omit what appears to have been contact with an alien species – we shall never know as Mr Bryce has passed away. What seems highly probable is that incident took place in 1972 as opposed to 1974, but there are inconsistencies with the times given, Bryce makes a reference to 5pm and time for tea, which means an afternoon sighting rather than night time........

According to Bryce:

> *"Arthur was talking to the people, and encouraged them to go off to sky-watch a little, and commune with the energies and meditate. So, I took off down a little dirt tractor path that leads to another field, ducked through a fence and went into a field with long golden 18 inch tall grass, or possible hay.*
>
> *I walked about 20 to 30 ft in or so, and stopped and stood for a while just looking at the sky for UFOs. I sent out telepathic thoughts of peace and love to the universe. After a while, I noticed that I didn't hear the people talking anymore, and thought they had all just settled down to meditate a bit. It was a beautiful day with the sun shining and some clouds moving slowly in the sky. I stood in the field and closed my eyes to send out a prayer, when I noticed an unusual energy building up around my aura. I thought it was very peaceful and felt a loving vibration as if being caressed by Angels.*
>
> *Suddenly I smelled the intense and intoxicating beautiful scent of Lily of the Valley flowers with a mixture of honey! I felt very calm and almost euphoric with the smell and the energy surrounding me, and then began to feel a tingling pressure in his temples surrounding my head accompanied by a strange whirring sound above me. I tried to look up and turn around and couldn't feeling held still in place by a gentle pressure. I opened my eyes and saw forming around me a perfect circle in the grass, being pressed gently down in a clockwise direction. The energy then changed in front of his eyes - a bit blurry for a few seconds, enabling him to see superimposed around me, with the grass still moving, the interior of a spaceship, and some translucent people!"*
>
> *In a few more seconds I was standing inside the 'physical spaceship,' and surrounded by a beautiful space woman with large blue eyes, dark hair, and dressed in a form fitting medium blue space suit. In front of me stood a smiling benevolent alien, being about seven feet tall, with kind, large, amber green eyes, no hair, a short and somewhat flattened nose, very small ears, and long slender fingers.*
>
> *He was wearing a dark blue gray spacesuit, with a reflective belt, and a shimmering silver white cape. Both of the aliens spoke to me telepathically, and asked me some questions, like," How are you feeling? Are you thirsty? We have been watching you for some time."*

Bryce said he had telepathic information transferred into his thoughts and mind regarding energy and healing, and that he was taken aboard a craft from out of which he was able to see the Earth. Some 15munutes later he was told they were bringing him back and that someday, maybe, they would meet again. He thanked them all for the experience and said *"God bless you all".* The aliens smiled at him and said, *"Good-bye, and bless you too".* Suddenly, Bryce told me he began feeling the tingling energy throughout his body, with the smell of flowers surrounding him! Then in seconds he was standing back in the golden grass again, in the centre of a perfect crop circle the sky was now darker.

Soon he felt the energy shifting around him, and he began to hear the sound of a slight wind in his ears, and birds chirping in the distance. Suddenly, he heard Arthur yelling" *Bryce! Bryce! Where are you? Bryce!"* he replied, *"I'm here, Arthur, in the field!"* Bryce found now he could finally move his feet, and sprinted in seconds through the field, under the fence and up the dirt path, towards Arthur, who asked him: *"Where have you been? We've been searching for hours!"*

Bryce replied, *"I was on a spaceship! Come see the circle I was standing in, Arthur!"* Bryce and Arthur, and some of the group, walked towards the field. Arthur, upon seeing the crop circle, exclaimed: *"We searched around the area and you were not here! Bryce, you had disappeared!"* Bryce was amazed - they searched for him and he was missing. Bryce asked, *"Arthur? What time is it, because my watch has stopped?"*

Arthur said, *"Bryce, it is close to 5:00pm, you have been missing for a few hours."* Bryce exclaimed, *"Wow! That's incredible, because it felt like 10 to 15 minutes to me."* Arthur said: *"They took you man, they took you for a ride! Let's go talk it over some tea now mate."*

Bryce and Arthur then walked with the rest of the group out to the dirt road, and drove back to the town of Warminster to share tea. Later, they discussed the amazing encounter Bryce had, as well as the UFO sightings all the people had that day. Bryce mentioned how having that experience changed him forever, as well as the small group of people who were witnesses. (End of interview)

The reader will have to form their own judgement about a version of events that, on the surface, seems almost too strange to believe. We did email Cetin Bal, in 2012 many times, asking if he had any further information about this interview and his relationship with Bryce, but never received an answer - which seems strange. Was there some embellishment here; following what was no doubt an apparent genuine sighting? We shall probably never know. **(Source: Cetin Bal 2011, WWW Peter Paget, *Fountain Journal*)**

In the same month, Alan Shepherd from Hartland Road, Reading (who was to sight more than one UFO) was saying goodbye to his parents, at 9.00pm. Just as Alan and his wife were about to re-enter their house, they noticed an object descending through the sky.

"At first we thought it was an aircraft, on fire; it was shooting out all different colours of light from its rear. As it approached closer we saw that this was no aircraft, as it had no wings. It was like a long rocket, only more streamlined. We thought it was going to crash but it levelled out, allowing us to see that it was all black in colour.

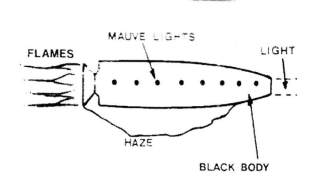

It was longer than a Jumbo Jet, but about the same width. My wife's stomach turned over and my hair felt as if it was connected to electricity. After a couple of minutes, the object made a sharp turn, sharper than any aircraft, and went off in the direction of Basingstoke." **(Source: Leslie Harris/John Ledner/*Scan Magazine,* Issue No. 11, January 1976)**

UFO over Suffolk

We spoke to Paul Tricker, living in the Ipswich area of Suffolk, after discovering a UFO had been sighted over the town in the summer of 1972, by a number of people, including Paul - then aged 18, at the time.

"Until that night I was a non-believer, a legacy of my father's influence, who firmly believed people who saw such things were as the result of an over-imaginative mind. It was a crystal clear evening, no clouds, the time 10 pm., when I noticed a bright light, not arching and unlike a shooting star, heading towards me. It then stopped in mid-air, hovering over the nearby Whitehouse estate, close to Bamford village. I tried to fathom out what it was. It then began to pulse large coloured lights - unlike any aircraft, which often flew from and to RAF Woodbridge and Bentwaters. I was unable to discern any structure because of its brightness.

Suddenly, it performed a series of instant accelerations and stops, doing virtually 180 degree turns in the air, zigzagging across the sky. I took

careful note of the way in which the lights seemed to be connected to its speed. When it was hovering, I saw a white light; when moving, the coloured lights came on. When stopped, the white light came on and the coloured lights ceased. It then rushed upwards into the sky, at a colossal speed, and disappeared."

Paul pondered whether the speed of the object could reach light speed and beyond, which would be impossible to calculate, but if these UFOs were capable of such speed, were they from the future, past, or a different dimension? **(Source: personal interview)**

UFO over Trowbridge

At 11.45am on 8th September 1972, Mrs. Sally Pike was sat outside in a deckchair at her Trowbridge home, when she saw:

"...a transporter aircraft flying low over our estate, heading towards me, followed by another plane. I think the second plane had its side door open; it was so low I could almost see inside it. Following the second plane and chasing it around its body and tail was a silver object flashing in the sun.

I picked up my husband's binoculars, which were close by, and saw that it was bell-shaped and like no other aircraft I had seen before. It was 6-8ft across and silent, although the noise of the transporters would have drowned it out anyway. The objects seemed to be playing 'tag' with the plane, although the pilot gave no visible indication that he could see the object. The plane was low enough for me to see the pilot quite well through binoculars.

After a minute or so later, the plane moved across the estate and I gradually lost sight of it and the bell-shaped object. I then rushed indoor and telephoned Arthur Shuttlewood and also told my husband about the sighting. When I went out again, 15minutes later, I glanced up and caught sight of a glint high in the sky, I didn't have time to get the binoculars again, but watched as this flashing object, which may have been the UFO, moved rapidly off and disappeared." **(Source: Ken Rogers/personal interview 2012)**

USAF scrambles fighter Jets

What would those people have said if they had known that at 6.00am on the 14th September 1972, a UFO was detected by USAF radar in Southern Florida, which led to two military Jets being scrambled into the pre-dawn skies by the North American Air Defense Command, after a glowing circular object appeared on the radar scopes?

The fighters were dispatched from Homestead Air Force base, south of Miami, and ordered to use their onboard radar systems to search for the UFO. According to an Air Force spokesman, who was later interviewed, he said: *"If it had proved hostile, we would have destroyed it."*

Although no trace was found, one of the Pilots - Major Gerald Smith - confirmed there was definitely something in the sky over the City: *"We were getting height cuts from two different military installations."*

Enquiries revealed the object had first shown up at 4.20am and was attributed as being a *'hard target'* by F.A.A Air Traffic Controller - Mr. A.W. Brown, while his associate - Mr. C.J Fox said: *"It was a good clear target."*

Visual reports came in from witnesses on the ground, who described the object as: *"...being a silver/ white in colour, and cigar-shaped."*

Other reports told of strange lights - some blinking, others unusually bright over the County. Amazingly, the Air Force explained the incidents away as being weather phenomena, or Venus, which was exceptionally bright at that time of the year. **(Source: *UFO Investigator,* October 1972 - 'Jets scrambled to intercept UFO')**

DECEMBER 1972

UFO INVESTIGATOR

NICAP

NATIONAL INVESTIGATIONS COMMITTEE ON AERIAL PHENOMENA

NICAP ■ SUITE 23, 3535 UNIVERSITY BLVD. WEST ■ KENSINGTON, MARYLAND 20795 ■ A NONPROFIT CORPORATION FOUNDED 1956

Radar Returns Still Unexplained
Florida Sighting Stirs Debate

Was it a solid object violating U.S. air space or was it simply a distant planet? This is only one of several unanswered questions remaining in the wake of one of the most interesting UFO cases on record for 1972.

The dramatic case *(UFO Investigator,* Oct. 1972) occurred during the pre-dawn hours of Sept. 14 when tower operators at West Palm Beach International Airport reported sighting a "glowing circular object" northeast of the airport.

During the next two hours, an unknown object was spotted on three radar screens, sought by Air Force jets, observed by an in-bound airlines pilot and hunted by a county sheriff in a police department helicopter.

Interpretations of the Palm Beach episode appear to be as numerous as there were witnesses. The Air Force, which scrambled its jets two hours after receiving the initial sighting report, found nothing in its search and concluded that the object observed by many was Venus, which is exceptionally bright at this time of year in the northeastern sky.

Others, however, have argued with this conclusion, noting that it fails to

(See Florida, page 4)

Flight Controller Bill Brown *(above),* a principal witness who claims to have seen the object visually and recorded it on his radar screen, stands beneath the West Palm Beach control tower. The tower *(left)* offered, according to many, an ideal platform from which to observe the reported UFO. Weather conditions Sept. 14 were almost "perfect," according to Weather Bureau officials, thus seeming to eliminate the "weather phenomenon" solution frequently offered for concurrent radar and visual sightings. *(Photos courtesy National Enquirer)*

Saturn-shaped UFO over Brecon Beacons

On 14th September 1972, villagers living on an housing estate at Croespenmaen, Crumlin, Monmouthshire, contacted the Police, after they sighted a bright orange object in the sky in the north-west direction of the Brecon Beacons.

The UFO, which was in the sky for approximately two hours, was seen to change rapidly in colour and size, before disappearing from view when an aircraft flew overhead. The object was first sighted at 8.30pm by Robert Philips, who was on his way home from Oakdale. He watched it for about 30mins and then telephoned the Police. Robert later said:

> *"The object looked like an inverted soup bowl, with dark rings underneath it, which appeared to be spinning. Three times it disappeared at the approach of an aircraft. On the third occasion it didn't reappear."*

One of the Officers who arrived at the scene was Police Sergeant Clive Williams from Blackwood,

> *"I saw an orange/red circle in the sky, which seemed to turn over to a cone shape. Its colour changed from red to white, to green. It then moved away rapidly. The next morning I visited the scene in daylight. It must have been something in the sky, as there were no mountains obstructing the view."*

ENGLAND Western Mail 16th September 1972

'Soupbowl' in the sky villagers in a spin

THREE POLICEMEN called in after villagers claimed they had seen an object in the sky like a flying saucer said last night there was no doubt the sightings were genuine.

Police were called after the object was reported by at least 20 people on a housing estate at Croespenmaen, Crumlin, in Monmouthshire.

The bright orange object appeared in the sky on Thursday night in the North-West in the direction of the Brecon Beacons, and changed rapidly in colour and size, said the witnesses.

Disappeared

It was in the sky for about two hours, finally disappearing when an aircraft flew overhead.

A spokesman at Glamorgan (Rhoose) Airport said last night that two Cambrian Airways Viscounts had landed at the airport at about the same time and could have passed over the area where the object was sighted.

Western Mail Reporter

But as far as he was aware nothing unusual was spotted on the airport's radar.

The Crumlin area lies directly beneath Green One—the corridor for aircraft flying between Britain and America—but a Civil Aviation Authority spokesman said pilots in the area at the time had not reported anything strange.

The object was first spotted at 8.30 by Mr. Robert Phillips, aged 24, a plumber, of Meadow Walk, Croespenmaen, who was on his way home from Oakdale.

He watched it for about 30 minutes through a telescope borrowed from a neighbour, and then phoned the police.

He said the object looked like an "inverted soupbowl with dark rings underneath it which appeared to be spinning." Three times it disappeared at the approach of an aircraft, but on the third occasion it did not return.

One of the policemen called to the scene, Sergeant Clive Williams, of Blackwood, said he saw an orange red circle in the sky which

seemed to turn over to a cone-shape "Its colour changed from red to white and green and it moved away rapidly," he said. "I revisited the site in the morning and it must have been something in the sky for there are no mountains obstructing the view."

Satellites

All officially reported Unidentified Flying Object sightings are investigated by the Ministry of Defence in case there are any defence implications, such as foreign aircraft.

Of the sightings reported in 1971, 160 were aircraft, 28 were satellites or space debris, and 11 were balloons.

Another 62 were meteorological and natural phenomena, and 27 turned out to be either flares, fireworks, lights on tall buildings, or flocks of birds.

FOOTNOTE: In Taree, New South Wales, Australia, a UFO which had baffled scientists and panicked animals was identified yesterday . . . the planet Venus.

The Police confirmed details of the incident had been forwarded to Air Traffic Control, at West Drayton. A spokesman at Glamorgan Rhoose Airport commented that two Cambrian Viscounts had landed at the Airport at about the same time, and could have passed over the area concerned! According to the MOD, of the sightings reported to them in 1971, 160 were aircraft, 28 were satellite or space debris, 11 were balloons, another 62 were meteorological and natural phenomena, 27 were flares, fireworks, lights on tall buildings, or flock of birds. **(Source: *The Western Mail*, 16.9.72, 'Soup bowl in the sky - villagers in a spin')**

During the same evening (14.9.1972) a mysterious light was seen zig zagging through the sky over Clackmannan by Gordon Gillies of Gean Road Aloa. **(Source: *Glasgow Evening Citizen*, 15.9.1972)**

UFOs over Essex

On the evening of 16th September 1972, Danny Harle (15) and Colin Hastings (18) from Hainault, Essex, were on their way to Kingswood Youth Club, at about 8.00pm through pouring rain along Harbourer Road when they noticed three peculiar 'clouds', motionless in the sky above them, glowing with brilliant light, accompanied by a deep electric hum. As the sound grew louder, one of the 'clouds' changed into a small triangular shape and rushed away across the sky, leaving an incandescent trail.

The second 'cloud' then vibrated from side to side, at an estimated height of approximately 400ft., while the third suddenly shrunk into a tiny pinpoint of light before increasing in size - now cigar-shaped. This tilted and appeared to move closer towards the youths, who now frightened ran to the safety of the youth club. When they looked back, there was just the vibrating 'cloud', which began to dart about in the sky 'as if lost'. It then turned triangular and vanished in the same direction as the other. The boys telephoned the Police at Barkingside, and were surprised to learn that one of their officers had reported seeing similar objects over Hainault the previous evening at the same time which was reported to Air Traffic Control at West Drayton. **(Sources: Essex UFO Group/*Ilford Pictorial and Guardian*, 20.9.72 - 'UFO terrifies Hainault youths'/*Redbridge Guardian*, 22.9.72/*Independent Weekly/ Western Mail*, 16.9.1972 - 'Soup bowl in the sky put villagers in a spin'/*Redbridge Guardian and Independent*, 22.9.1972 - 'Something in the sky', *FSR*, Volume 18, No. 6, November/December 1972)**

On the 24th September 1972, a bright light was seen in the sky over Horsham Park, West Susssex, by Mr. Michael Fiest and his girlfriend, at 8.00pm. According to the couple, the object executed a number of repeated movements in the sky, which included moving backwards and forwards in the air in a wide arc, for approximately two minutes, before vanishing behind a clump of trees. **(Source: BUFORA)**

Landed UFO, Buckinghamshire

Ernest Scott from High Wycombe, holder of a pilot's licence, was to find himself witnessing another example of UFO activity - this time just after midnight. He was travelling towards Marlow, on the A4155, between Henley-on-Thames, in winter 1972 - a journey that normally takes between 35-45mins.

As he approached a bend at the end of a long, straight, part of the road, he noticed some lights by the verge of the dual carriageway ahead of him. When he drew nearer, he was astonished to see a strange object in the bushes by the side of the road.

> *"It was the size of a telephone kiosk, with a conical top, with four fluores-*
> *cent strip lights, pulsing with light, that moved slowly from top to bot-*

tom, attached to the outside of the object, which I thought would have been hexagonal if you could have looked down from the top."

Mr. Scott decided to stop, but his mind went blank as he approached it.

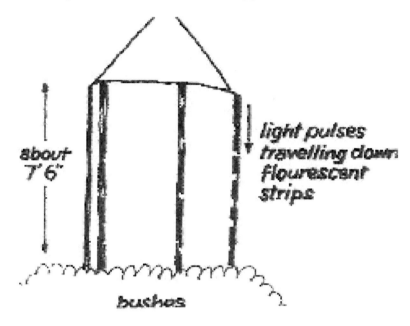

The next thing he remembers was driving through Marlow, some miles further, and looking at his wristwatch, when he realised it was about one and a half hours later than when he last looked. An examination of a map of the area shows us the site of a Roman villa on the outskirts of Medmenham and a nearby Hill Fort. **(Source: John Makin -serving Police Officer/Nicholas Maloret, WATSUP)**

UFO over Lincolnshire

Boston, Lincolnshire, newsagent - Thomas Trinder - and his son, Alan, were opening up the shop at 4.30am on 3rd October 1972, when they saw:

"...a glowing orange and green cigar-shaped object, with what looked like tiny flames projecting from each side, floating slowly across the sky, close to the crescent moon".

When they looked out again, at 6.30am, it had gone. Enquiries were made by Reg Greaves of Skegness, who interviewed Tommy and his son with the RAF and the MOD. A spokesman for the RAF told him: *"We have nothing that could move that slowly."* **(Source: Reg Greaves/Richard P. Colborne, BUFORA Investigator, Issue 1)**

The following day, at 10.25pm, it was the turn of Mr. Bryan Bishop from Winsford, Cheshire, to sight something unusual, while working on night duty outside in the works yard.

> *"I saw a series of five lights approaching across the sky. When they were overhead I was able to see that there were, in fact, eight lights forming a 'diamond'. The centre one appeared hazy; I was unable to discern whether this was eight objects or one object carrying eight lights. They were visible for four minutes and were travelling at a moderate speed across the sky in an east to south-east direction."*

Mr. Bishop is an amateur astronomer and familiar with the night sky. He does not believe what he saw was any natural phenomena. **(Source: Gordon Clegg)**

At 9.30pm on the 8th October 1972, Mr. & Mrs. Brown were driving from Northampton to Bedford, when Mrs. Brown sighted a strange object through the windscreen in the sky south of the A 824 road, at an angle of 45° off the horizon, Mr. Brown stopped the car to allow a better view of the UFO, which they described as:

> *"...triangular in shape, with flashing lights outlining the triangle, three on each side, flashing clockwise. From its base were three more lights appearing to project vertically downwards from beneath."* **(Source: Kath Smith, Isle of Wight UFO Society/*UFOLOG*)**

UFO over Lancashire

Four days later, on the 8th October 1972, ex-Legionnaire, John Byrne - then working as a Security Guard for Ferranti's Cairo Mill, Oldham - had just 'clocked in' to the security point, at 11.55pm., next to the cycle shed, near the car park, when he heard what sounded like a swarm of bees moving through the air.

In a tape-recorded interview held with UFO Investigators - Gordon Clegg & Ron Drabble - Mr. Byrne had this to say:

> *"I looked upwards over my right shoulder, and was amazed to see a large, slightly oval–shaped, object descending vertically towards the car park, directly overhead. It was black at the back and lit-up at the front, with a blue/white fluorescent light shining through a bulge, or 'window', covering approximately one third of the base of the object. I thought the object was going to descend on top of me. I tried to move but couldn't. My fear then changed to terror. My right arm was devoid of any feeling. The hairs on the back of my neck felt as though they were standing on end."*

The object then moved downwards until its base was almost level with the top of the mill tower, (90 ft.), and halted in mid-air, blocking out Mr. Byrne's view of the sky.

Although John didn't see anybody in the 'craft', he felt as though he was being watched. Suddenly, the object flipped over onto its edge, with its underside facing the mill wall, showing a dome, about one third as high as the object itself, illuminated by blue/white light and an upper surface of blue metallic sheen.

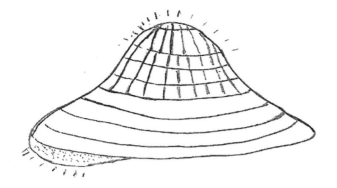

However, this could have been caused by a refection of the white light from the dome. Less than half a minute later, without warning, the UFO then shot straight up, nose first, into the sky, at terrific speed.

Almost immediately, Mr. Byrne found he was able to move and ran back towards the checkpoint at the main gate, where he found the factory cat cowering in a corner - a position it remained in for two days, refusing food and drink. **(Source: Richard P. Colborne, National Investigations co-coordinator, BUFORA/Issue 1, *The Investigator*, February 1973/Jenny Randles/ *Yorkshire Post* 21.10.1972)**

At 6.45pm on 20th October 1972, Mr. John Hedger of Oxford Road, Wallington, Surrey, sighted:

> *"...six bright lights in the sky. They made up a formation that was roughly rectangular and were individually recognizable as discs. They were white in colour and stayed in the same position for about three minutes, until cloud obscured them from sight."*

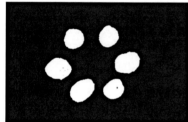

During the same year, Mr. Clive West - then the owner of Ceres Hotel, Bude, in Cornwall - was driving home with his family, along the A303, across Salisbury Plain, when they saw what they took to be a star in the sky.

They soon realised this was not the case when further observation revealed the presence of two red lights, which were circling it.

> *"It was about 500yds from the road and at an altitude of about 400ft. As it dropped lower, it lit up the whole area with its brilliance. The two red lights remained on opposite sides of the UFO. When the object 'touched down', they left and departed skywards."*

Mr. West, previously employed as a reporter and photographer for the news media, made an appeal in the newspaper. Subsequently, he was contacted by another family from Salisbury, who had also seen the same UFO. **(Source: *BUFORA*/Issue 1, John Hedger - Investigator)**

UFO over Lincoln

At 6 45pm on 22nd October 1972, Harold Rollins - a retired railway worker, living in Queen Elizabeth Road, Lincoln, with his wife - happened to look out of the window, when he saw a strange luminous object slowly descending in the sky. Harry shouted for his wife to come and have a look. The couple then stood watching as the object slowly settled in the air, between two houses opposite, 30-40ft. away, allowing them to describe fully what they saw, later, to Richard Thompson, the Lincoln-based UFO Investigator who came to see them.

"It was a round 'ball', about 30ft. in diameter, bright red in colour, with a mauve tint. Projecting outwards were streaks of golden coloured light - a bit like the rays of the sun against a backcloth of pale mauve. We watched in amazement as it slowly began to move away, eastwards, before losing sight of it." **(Source: Dick Thompson)**

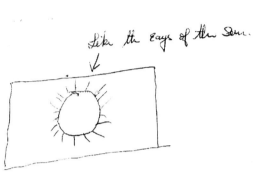

UFO over Nottinghamshire

Mrs. M. Sadler of Ashbourne, Nottinghamshire - a local magistrate by occupation - was driving to Clifton Smith Hall, at 6.55pm on the 24th October 1972, accompanied by a friend - Mrs. A Hughes - when they noticed an object, which they first thought was Venus, moving at a fairly fast speed 45° off the ground.

As they drove through Clifton, they were surprised to see that the luminous object was now hovering above a clump of trees.

In a later interview with a reporter from the *Asbourne News Telegraph*, she told him:

> *"Although it was possible to imagine spikes sticking out of the sides of the object and a fluctuating emission of light, I was certain it had been moving, and then stopped, borne out by the object's relative position to a telegraph pole. It was this changing of motion that had aroused my interest, and others, from the Hall."*

At 7.40pm the object sank slowly from view behind trees and disappeared from view.

During a search on the internet in (2012) we learned that Clifton Hall is a Georgian style Grade I listed building, and ancestral home of the Clifton family. The building recently attracted a reputation in the national media of being haunted, after Anwar Rashid, the millionaire owner of Clifton Hall, and his family, fled the premises - apparently driven out by its ghosts. On 21 September 2008, *Sky News* covered the story in an article entitled *Millionaire Flees Haunted House.*

> *"A millionaire businessman has become so spooked by the 'haunted' £3.6m mansion he bought last year that he has handed the property back to the*

Paul Nunn is the young man being filmed on the stairs; the person with the camera is Lee Roberts.

The T.A.P.I.T. team have gone from strength to strength, since 2006. In 2008, the organisation enjoyed national and global recognition for their investigations into paranormal activity reported at Clifton Hall, Nottingham, world - not just in the UK, but also in Australia, Hungary, and German newspapers and TV. Paul Nunn (insert) told us:

> *"The team are already looking to build on past successes and moving forward to continuing their work. They are constantly researching new locations of investigation. In addition to this, they plan to return to many of our old haunts to update our continued research.*
>
> *Currently the team consists of eight regular members, who will tell you of the great energy, trust and respect they have for each other. This has helped many of them to develop as individuals as well as a team. This development has enabled many members to pursue their own interests and studies in many of the areas they investigate, which include: Psychic Mediumship, Photography, Spiritualism, Psychology and Parapsychology".*

bank. Anwar Rashid, 32, described how he, his wife, and their four young children, lived in fear after they began hearing screams in the corridors, shortly after moving into Clifton Hall. They also claim to have seen apparitions and heard knocking on the wall of the 17-bedroom mansion in Nottinghamshire. But it was the sight of blood spots on their 18-month-old son's bed clothes that finally forced the family to abandon their luxury home."

Mr. Rashid said, comparing his experience to Nicole Kidman's film, *The Others:*

"We were like the family in The Others. *The ghosts didn't want us to be there and we could not fight them because we couldn't see them. The day we moved in we had our first experience. We sat down in the evening to relax and there was a knock on the wall. We heard: 'Hello. Is anyone there?'*

We ignored it the first time, but two minutes later we heard the man's voice again. I got up to have a look, but the doors were locked and the windows were closed. On another occasion my wife went downstairs to make milk for the baby, at 5.00am, and she saw our eldest daughter watching television.

She said her name, but she wouldn't respond. My wife realised something was up, so she went back upstairs to check on her, and found her fast asleep in her bed.

When we found red blood spots on the baby's quilt that was the day my wife said she'd had enough. We didn't even stay that night. It was the last straw; we felt that they had come to attack us. It was really emotional."

We contacted Paul Nunn and asked him about his knowledge of the Manor.

"Clifton Hall certainly did not disappoint and gave us some interesting results. I can honestly say that this was the first and only investigation in which we had to stop what we were doing and regroup, just to get everyone's focus back - an eerie location, which really did give some of us a scare."

Darren Brookes, whose security firm previously guarded the hall for five years, said some of his staff 'refused point-blank' to work there. He said they reported sightings, such as a monk walking through the grounds, a woman in the graveyard, falling over, and chairs moving in one of the rooms.

Mr. Brookes, of Sovereign Security UK, said:

"I've often put officers, who know absolutely nothing about the house, in there - and after a night on duty they have quit."

UFO over Heywood

At 8.40pm on 25th October 1972, Alan Brown was out walking his dog near the boundary with Castleton, when he heard a roaring sound in the direction of the north-west part of the night sky. Puzzled, he looked through a pair of binoculars and saw:

> *"...a lentoid-shaped craft, moving from north-east to south-east. It was gun metal grey, or dull pewter in colour, and was flying at a height I estimated to be 800-1,000ft, at a speed of about 15mph, as I watched it for three minutes. I saw that it was displaying four lights - one white, two red, and one white. Whilst the object gave the impression of having a propulsion system, no exhaust emissions were visible.*

> *The best comparable analogy to the sound produced would be steam under very high pressure being discharged. The object headed towards the south-west, still making the roaring noise. All of sudden it just vanished from view, like a TV set being switched off."* **(Source: UFO INFO Exchange 30A Library/BUFORA/**some accounts give this as 1977**)**

UFO over Cheshire

On 3rd November 1972, schoolboys - Damon Munday (10) brothers Dale (10) Wayne (13) and Anthony (16) from Verdin Comprehensive School, Winsford, in Cheshire - were walking home to their home in Pulford Road, at 5.00pm. as dusk fell, when they saw a glowing, bright cigar-shaped object, hovering in the sky above the School, which was then seen to move towards the right and slowly disappear, as if going behind something in the sky.

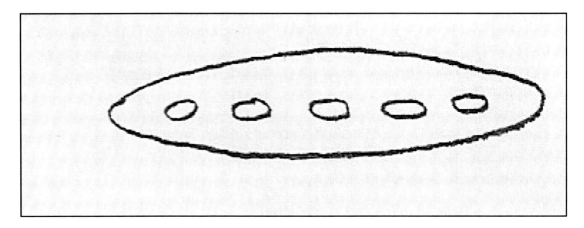

Upon their arrival home, the boys told neighbour - Mrs. Mary Roberts - what they had seen. Suddenly, to their amazement the object reappeared in the sky, once more, over the school.

Mrs. Roberts fetched Mrs. Barbara Munday to show her, from which the following description was taken:

> *"It was a bright cigar-shaped light, with tapering ends, at an elevation of about 20 degrees in the sky, giving off a yellowish-white light, as brilliant as a full moon. Along its length were six dark portions, or specks - like portholes. It then began to increase in size until twice its original length, before decreasing in size, like a 'ball of light', before vanishing inexplicably from view, a few minutes later. It was really weird watching it. When it did go out, I was really thrilled with what I saw."* **(Source: BUFORA/*The Investigator*, Issue 1, Bob Skinner)**

Dr. J. Allen Hynek

In 1972, Dr. J. Allen Hynek published his classic book, *The UFO Experience* - A scientific study presenting his categories for grouping UFO sightings, from which was coined the phrase, 'Close Encounters'. In 1973, he started the *Centre for UFO Studies* and served as its Scientific Director, until his death in 1986. *Close Encounters of the Third Kind* describes confrontations between humans and alleged 'Aliens' from landed, unidentified vehicles. Statistics drawn from over 800 UFO entity sightings received during this period, left him pondering why these 'creatures' should resemble humans so closely, and he theorized whether they could be mechanical robots, whose environment is very similar to ours on Earth. A rare photo shows him during a visit to the UK. **(Source: Stephen Shipp, 1982, *Probe*)**

Michael Williams with Dr Hynek.

Ian Mryzglod (right) with Dr Hynek

Close Encounter, Gloucestershire

Incidents involving UFOs and their 'Alien' occupants will always be treated with suspicion, despite determined efforts made by the witness to convince their fellow peers that what she or he experienced occurred as a result of an incursion into our physical plain of existence, rather than anything subjective in nature.

Over the years, we were to come across a number of accounts involving the appearance of humanoid figures, seen close to their 'vessel', often apparently observed to be carrying out some form of examination of the ground. Their resemblance to people of Scandinavian descent has led to them being labelled 'Nordics' - a description which forms a familiar background to other cases we were to come across over the years.

On 5th November 1972, John Hickman from Tewkesbury, in Gloucestershire - an employee of Severn Trent water board, then living at 12 Station Lane, Tewkesbury - described to us what he witnessed:

> *"I was putting the children to bed, after having taken them to bonfire celebrations, held on waste ground* (formerly the old railway yard at the rear of his garden, in Rope Walk, Tewkesbury), *at 5.30pm., when I glanced through the bedroom window and noticed a patch of green coloured mist in the air to my right, approximately 30ft off the ground, some 60ft from where I was stood, in Cotteswold Gardens, and first presumed it was smoke, or the residue of a firework, as the bonfire was still burning, with people gathered around it.*

A patch of green mist then appeared between the two houses, situated at the end of the garden, and slowly changed into what looked like a large bubble, about 20ft. in diameter, surrounded by a blue/green luminous glow. Inside the bubble was what I can only describe as a painted white light.

As this light cleared, I was confronted by the amazing sight of two 'figures', which became clearer as the mist subsided. They appeared to be sat down in front of a type of hooped headrest. I watched, daring to breathe, fearing what might happen if they realised they were being observed.

They appeared to resemble males in build, rather than females, and were identically dressed, wearing a black garment - looking like leather, or plastic, covered in little whorls of patterns over it. Behind their heads were what I took to be pointed collars. I can't be sure whether these collars were part of the seat's headrest, or their apparel.

The one nearest me seemed much older than his companion. He had thick, long, bulky, wavy hair above his shoulder line, with a pronounced wrinkled skin, like elephant hide. His partner looked very similar but his hair was

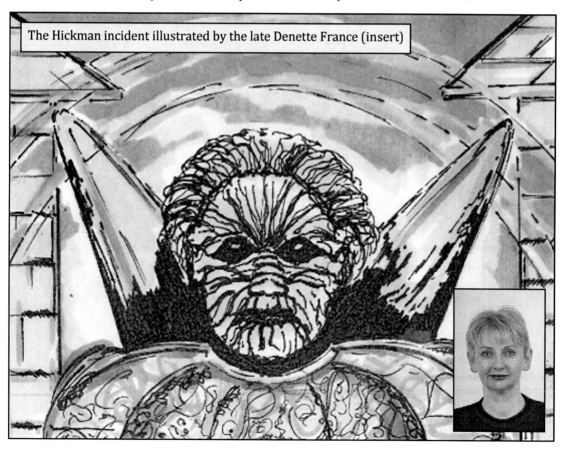

The Hickman incident illustrated by the late Denette France (insert)

receding, creating an impression he was younger. I struggled to get a grip on myself, knowing this was no dream. I quietly opened the window, which was beginning to steam up, wondering if the whole thing was some kind of reflection - it was still there.

I closed the windows and continued to watch them for about ten minutes - then shouted to my wife to come upstairs and have a look. While waiting for my wife to arrive, I saw the elder of the two 'figures' slowly turn his head, raise his arm, and point towards me, as if realising they were being watched. His companion also turned, both of them now looking straight at me. I felt my blood run cold when this happened. Within a split second, the 'bubble' changed colour to a green glow and accelerated away, gaining

QUEST INTERNATIONAL

SIGHTING REPORT FORM

QUEST INTERNATIONAL IS AN ORGANISATION WHICH SEEKS THE ANSWER TO ONE OF THE MOST ELUSIVE MYSTERIES OF OUR TIME... THE INVESTIGATIVE BUREAU HAS RESEARCHED THOUSANDS OF REPORTS PERTAINING TO THE UFO PHENOMENON OVER THE YEARS, AND OUR INVESTIGATORS WHO ARE EXPERIENCED IN THIS FIELD WILL VISIT AND TALK WITH YOU SHOULD THE NEED ARISE.

ANY INFORMATION GIVEN TO THE ORGANISATION WILL BE STRICTLY CONFIDENTIAL. WE WELCOME YOUR COOPERATION AND SHOULD YOU REQUIRE FURTHER INFORMATION REGARDING QUEST INTERNATIONAL OR UFO MAGAZINE, PLEASE WRITE TO:

THE SECRETARY P.O. BOX 2, GRASSINGTON, SKIPTON, NORTH YORKSHIRE, BD23 5AU

FULL NAME: (MR MRS MISS MS) ... JOHN HICKMAN

ADDRESS: HUNTERS LODGE,

OLD ROAD NORTH, KEMPSEY, WORCS WR5 3SZ

AGE: 49   OCCUPATION: S/E WATER CONSULTANT

TEL (HOME): 01965-824729 TEL (WORK): ———

QUALIFICATIONS (IF ANY): C&G CRAFT AND C&G ADV PLUMBING / NEBBS
+ WATER RELATED QUALIFICATIONS

APPROX YEAR.
SIGHTING DETAILS

DATE: 1972   DAY: SATURDAY   TIME: 19:30 TO 20:00 AM/PM
NOV 5TH ?   BONFIRE NIGHT

PLEASE GIVE EXACT LOCATION OF SIGHTING I.E., TOWN, COUNTY, AND A GENERAL DESCRIPTION OF AREA (OPEN LAND, BUILT-UP AREA, POPULATED, MAP REFERENCE (IF POSSIBLE), STREAM, VILLAGE, ETC):

THROUGH BEDROOM WINDOW OF 12 STATION LANE, TEWKESBURY
GLOS. THE OBJECT APPEARED BETWEEN MY HOUSE AND THE
PROPERTY AT THE REAR, (COTTESWOLD GARDENS.

DID ANYONE ELSE OBSERVE THE PHENOMENON? IF YES, PLEASE GIVE DETAILS. INFORMATION SUBMITTED SHALL BE DEALT WITH IN THE STRICTEST CONFIDENCE: I DO NOT KNOW.

1: ....   2: ....

3: ....   4: ....

A CONTROL PANEL. AFTER A FEW SECONDS THEY
(THE TWO IN THE BUBBLE). TURNED THEIR HEADS
TO THEIR RIGHT AND APPEARED TO BE LOOKING
AT THE FIRE WORK DISPLAY. I CAN ONLY DESCRIBE
THE TWO PEOPLE AS MALE. THE ONE LOOKED
VERY OLD SAY 150 to 200 YEARS, THE OTHER ONE
LOOKED BETWEEN 60 & 70 YEARS OLD. THE OLDER
LOOKING ONE HAD LONG GREY WAVY HAIR and
HAD GREY SKIN THAT LOOKED LIKE ELEPHANT
HIDE. THE YOUNGER ONE WAS SLIGHTLY
BALDING ALTHOUGH HE TO HAD GREY SKIN HE
LOOKED A LOT YOUNGER THAN THE OTHER. BOTH
OF THEM WORE IDENTICAL CLOTHES. THAT LOOKED
LIKE A TYPE OF BLACK PLASTIC WITH A PATTERN
THE COLLERS WERE RIGID AND POINTED.
BECAUSE OF THE POSITION THEY WERE SAT
LOOKING TO THEIR RIGHT I COULD SEE
CLEARLY THE BACK OF THE SEAT ON WHICH
THEY WERE SITTING IT WAS SHAPPED THUS.

← ? HEAD REST

← BACK OF SEAT.

I COULD NOT BELIEVE WHAT I WAS
SEEING, SO I queitly OPENED THE WINDOW
AND TOOK A GOOD LOOK OUTSIDE TO SEE
IF IT WAS SOME KIND OF REFLECTION,
BECAUSE OF THE POSITION OF THE BUBBLE.
THERE WAS NO WAY THIS WAS A REFLECTION
I QUIETLY CLOSED THE WINDOW AND CONTINUED
WATCHING FOR A FEW MORE MINUTES, THE
WINDOWS KEPT ON STEAMING UP AND I
KEPT CLEANING THEM DOWN WITH MY HAND

TO ENABLE A BETTER VIEW. I HAD BEEN WATCHING FOR ABOUT 15 MINUTES WHEN I SHOUTED TO THE WIFE TO COME UPSTAIRS AND LOOK. BECAUSE THE WIFE DID NOT COME UPSTAIRS AFTER A FEW MINUTES I RAN DOWN THE STAIRS AND TOLD HER WHAT I COULD SEE FROM THE BEDROOM WINDOW, AND THAT I WANTED HER TO CONFIRM WHAT I WAS SEEING. I RAN BACK UPSTAIRS TO THE WINDOW AND WAS LOOKING AT THE TWO PEOPLE IN THE BUBBLE, WHEN THE OLDER ONE OF THE TWO WHO WAS SITTING IN THE FAR SEAT, SLOWLY TURNED IS HEAD AT WHICH TIME I COULD SEE HIS FULL FACE HE RAISED HIS ARM AND POINTED HIS INDEX FINGER STRAIGHT AT ME. AT THE SAME TIME THE OTHER PERSON TURNED AROUND AND LOOKED AT ME. SEVERAL STRANGE FEELINGS CAME OVER ME. AND I CONTINUED TO WATCH THE BUBBLE. WITHIN A SPLIT SECOND THE BUBBLE CHANGED COLOUR TO a GREEN GLOW, IT THEN STARTED TO MOVE BETWEEN THE HOUSES. I RAN DOWN TO THE LANDING TO LOOK THROUGH THE WINDOW AND SAW THE GREEN LIGHT ACCELERATE AT AN ANGLE OF ABOUT 30° AND SUDDENLY CHANGE DIRECTION EASTWARDS TOWARDS THE COTTESWOLDS. IT VERY QUICKLY DISSAPEARED AND THE WIFE COULD NOT CONFIRM THAT SHE COULD SEE THE GREEN LIGHT FROM THE LANDING.

We met John on a number of occasions, initially with Redditch-based UFO researcher - Denette France - to discuss his extraordinary sighting, involving the arrival of what can only be classed as non-human beings. We have pondered why sightings like this (and there have been many similar ones worldwide) are humanoid in shape. If John Hickman's encounter was the only one, we could apply the laws of logic and rationality to it. Honesty dictates we wouldn't have believed him, but he is not the only one to have reported a 'close encounter' like this. At the end of the day, the only person who truly knows is John.

SUMMARY OF EVENTS

PLEASE DESCRIBE IN YOUR OWN WORDS THE CIRCUMSTANCES OF YOUR SIGHTING/EXPERIENCE. (USE ANOTHER SHEET OF PAPER IF NECESSARY):

WE HAD RETURNED FROM THE BONFIRE EARLY AND PUT THE CHILDREN TO BED. THE BONFIRE WAS HELD ON THE OLD RAILWAY YARD. I WAS LOOKING OUT OF THE BEDROOM WINDOW AT THE FIRE WORKS WHEN A GREEN COLOURED MIST APPEARED TO MY RIGHT. AT THE TIME IT LOOKED LIKE SMOKE. THE GREEN MIST DRIFTED ACROSS BETWEEN THE BUILDINGS AND SUDDENLY STOPPED. WITHIN A FRACTION OF A SECOND WHAT LOOKED LIKE A LARGE BUBBLE APPEARED. THE OUTER CASING OF THE BUBBLE GAVE OFF A BLUE/GREEN GLOW, WITHIN THE BUBBLE WAS A WHITE LIGHT. LOOKING INTO THE BUBBLE I COULD SEE TWO PEOPLE. THE TWO PEOPLE WERE SAT ON CHAIRS INFRONT OF WHICH APPEARED TO BE

WEATHER AND LIGHT CONDITIONS AT TIME OF SIGHTING (TICK APPROPRIATE BOX):

THIN CLOUD ☐	HEAVY CLOUD ☐	CLEAR ☐	MIST ☐	DRY ☐	HEAVY RAIN ☐
DRIZZLE ☐	SNOW/ICE ☐	WARM ☐	COLD ☐	CALM ☑	WINDY ☐
DARKNESS ☑	DAYLIGHT ☐	DAWN ☐	DUSK ☐	MOON ☐	STARS ☐

WAS THE OBJECT/PHENOMENA SEEN IN THE VICINITY OF ANY OF THE FOLLOWING?

CIVIL AIRFIELD ☐	MILITARY AIRFIELD ESTABLISHMENT ☐	AIR ROUTE ☐
POWER LINE ☐	RADIO OR TELEVISION MAST ☐	QUARRY/MINE ☐
STREET LIGHTS ☐	RESERVOIR/RIVER/CANAL/WATER ☐	WOODLAND ☐
MOOR/FARMLAND ☐	ANCIENT MONUMENT SITE ☐	URBAN AREA ☑ BACK GARDEN BETWEEN HOUSES

PLEASE TRY TO DRAW WHAT YOU OBSERVED TO THE BEST OF YOUR ABILITY:

BLUE / GREEN OUTER RING

WHITE LIGHT
OLD ONE BACKREST
YOUNG ONE BACK REST
CONTROL PANEL
? DARK BLUE/GREEN UNABLE TO SEE THROUGH

LONG WAVEY GREY HAIR.
HIGH COLLER AROUND NECK
SUIT LOOKED BULKY.
COLLER LIKE WINGS UPRIGHT REAR OF SHOULDERS
LARGE EYES.
GREY SKIN GRAINED LIKE LEATHER (ELEPHANT SKIN) VERY WRINKLED
THEY LOOKED VERY INQUISITIVE BUT SENSITIVE TO ME WATCHING THEM.
"(THEY LOOKED FREINDLY)"

Page two:

HOW LARGE DID THE OBJECT APPEAR IN/ON THE GROUND, COMPARED WITH THE FOLLOWING OBJECTS HELD AT ARMS LENGTH? (REMEMBER, A GARDEN PEA HELD AT ARMS LENGTH WOULD COVER THE FULL FACE OF THE MOON):

PIN HEAD (STAR) ☐   MATCH HEAD ☐ (PLANET)   PEA ☐ (MOON)

ONE PENCE ☐   FIVE PENCE ☐   TEN PENCE ☐

OTHER PLEASE STATE: _APPROX 8' DIA IN THE WHITE LIGHT AREA_
BUT APPROX 15' OVERALL ACROSS THE SURROUND. LIGHT.

IF YOU HAVE EVER SEEN A SIMILAR OBJECT BEFORE, OR EXPERIENCED THIS PHENOMENON IN THE PAST, PLEASE GIVE BRIEF DETAILS:
_NO_

DID THE OUTLINE OR ANY PART OF THE OBJECT APPEAR: SHARP ☑ FUZZY ☑ TRANSPARENT ☑

STRUCTURED ☐ DETACHED ☐   IF YES, PLEASE GIVE DETAILS: _Very difficult to explain_
how something solid can be seen inside a bubble of
light with a dark outer light covering the main structure in the Atmosr.

DID YOU OBSERVE ANY FIGURES OR MOVEMENT ON/IN PHENOMENA?: YES ☑ NO ☐   IF YES, PLEASE DESCRIBE YOUR EXPERIENCE:
I watched the movement of Two people inside the light bubble
They observed the Fire work Display and the one pointed his
finger at me and both turned and looked at me. THEY SEEMED TO
_   communicate with_
                                                  EACH
DID ANY ANIMAL DISTURBANCE OCCUR. IF YES, PLEASE STATE: _NO_   OTHER,
                                                                WITH
                                                                HAND
                                                                MOVEMENTS

HAVE YOU OR ANY OTHER WITNESS TO THE EVENT SUFFERED PHYSICAL, PSYCHOLOGICAL EFFECTS, PRIOR TO, DURING, OR AFTER YOUR EXPERIENCE/OBSERVATION?: IF YES, PLEASE STATE:
_NO_

HAVE YOU ANY OBJECTION TO YOUR NAME OR OCCUPATION BEING PUBLISHED IN CONNECTION WITH YOUR SIGHTING/ EXPERIENCE?:   YES ☐   NO ☑ _but not my Home address !_

SIGNED (WITNESS): _J Hutson_   DATE: _16 / 11 / 95_

INVESTIGATOR: _____   DATE: /   /

IF YOU WOULD LIKE FURTHER DETAILS OF HOW TO OBTAIN MORE INFORMATION ABOUT THE UFO PHENOMENON, PLEASE TICK THIS BOX: ☐

PLEASE RETURN THIS FORM TO:
JHANSON, 3, REDDICH Rd
ALVECHURCH
Page five   _B48 7RS_

THE DIRECTOR OF INVESTIGATIONS,
QUEST INTERNATIONAL,
P.O. BOX 2,
GRASSINGTON, NEAR SKIPTON,
NORTH YORKSHIRE, BD23 5AU.

☎ 24 HOUR UFO HOT LINE
[01756]
752216

PLEASE INDICATE THE DIRECTION THE OBJECT WAS FIRST SEEN (MARK 'A'), AND LAST SEEN (MARK 'B'):

NORTH

WEST

B EAST

A

SOUTH

PLEASE NOTE: TO HELP YOU ANSWER THIS QUESTION; THE SUN SETS IN THE WEST AND RISES IN THE EAST. AN O/S
MAP COULD HELP YOU ANSWER THIS QUESTION MORE ACCURATELY - DO NOT GUESS.

DID THE OBJECT MOVE IN FRONT OR BEHIND ANY OF THE FOLLOWING? PLEASE TICK APPROPRIATE BOX:

CLOUDS ☐   HILLS ☐   TREES ☐   BUILDINGS ☑   OTHER (PLEASE WRITE): ☑

IT TRAVELLED BETWEEN THE BUILDINGS AT AN ANGLE OF SAY
30° AND THEN CURVED OFF TO THE EAST

IF YOU OBSERVED THE OBJECT WHILST TRAVELLING IN A VEHICLE, PLEASE GIVE DETAILS OF MAKE, SPEED, ROAD
SURFACE, VISIBILITY, LIGHTING ETC:

N/A

DID ANY SPECIFIC MALFUNCTION OF THE VEHICLE OCCUR? (E.G.) POWER FAILURE, HEADLIGHT FAILURE, BATTERY
FAILURE, ENGINE FAILURE, INSTRUMENT MALFUNCTION, EXCESSIVE HEAT INCREASE WITHIN VEHICLE. DID ANY
PHYSICAL DAMAGE OR MARKINGS APPEAR ON OR IN VEHICLE. PLEASE GIVE DETAILS IF APPLICABLE:

N/A

APPROX
HOW LONG WAS THE PHENOMENA VISIBLE FOR: SECONDS: _____   MINUTES: 2φ /30 HOURS: _____

DID YOU HEAR ANY SOUND ASSOCIATED WITH YOUR SIGHTING?: YES ☐   NO ☑   IF YES, PLEASE
DESCRIBE WHAT YOU HEARD:

DID YOU OBSERVE THE OBJECT THROUGH ANY OF THE FOLLOWING? (PLEASE TICK APPROPRIATE BOX):

NORMAL EYESIGHT ☑   SPECTACLES ☐   BINOCULARS ☐   TELESCOPE ☐

NORMAL WINDOW GLASS ☑   DOUBLE GLAZING ☐   CAR WINDOW ☐

WAS MORE THAN ONE OBJECT OBSERVED? IF SO HOW MANY, AND WAS A PATTERN OR FORMATION OBSERVED?:

ONE

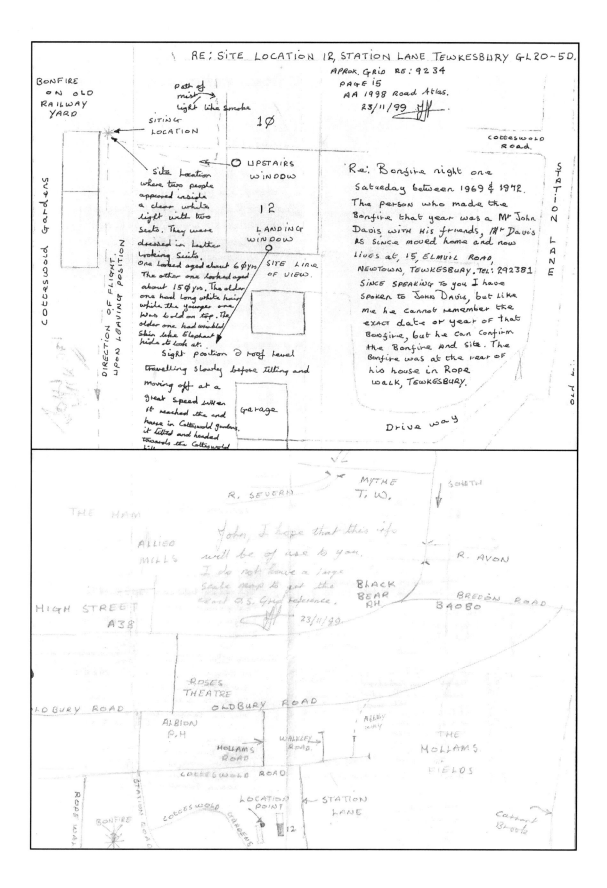

RE: SITE LOCATION 12, STATION LANE TEWKESBURY GL20-5D.

APROX. GRID RE: 9234
PAGE 15
AA 1998 Road Atlas.
23/11/99

BONFIRE ON OLD RAILWAY YARD

Path of mist
Light like smoke

SITING LOCATION

10

COTTESWOLD ROAD.

STATION LANE

○ UPSTAIRS WINDOW

12

LANDING WINDOW

Site Location where two people appeared inside a clear white light with two seats. They were dressed in leather looking suits.
One looked aged about 60 yrs. The other one looked aged about 150 yrs. The older one had long white hair while the younger one was bald on top. The older one had wrinkled skin like Elephant hide to look at.

COTTESWOLD Gardens

DIRECTION OF FLIGHT UPON LEAVING POSITION

SITE Line OF VIEW.

Re: Bonfire night one Saturday between 1969 & 1972. The person who made the Bonfire that year was a Mr John Davis with his friends, Mr Davis as since moved home and now lives at, 15, ELMUIL ROAD, NEWTOWN, TEWKESBURY. TEL: 292381. Since speaking to you I have spoken to John Davis, but like me he cannot remember the exact date or year of that Bonfire, but he can confirm the Bonfire and site. The Bonfire was at the rear of his house in ROPE WALK, TEWKESBURY.

Sight position @ roof level travelling slowly before tilting and moving off at a great speed when it reached the end house in Cotteswold gardens. it tilted and headed towards the Cottesworld hill.

Garage

Drive way

OLD

√2

R. SEVERN

MYTHE T. W.

SONTH

THE HAM

ALLIED MILLS

John, I hope that this info will be of use to you. I do not have a large scale map to get the exact O.S. Grid reference.

R. AVON

HIGH STREET A38

BLACK BEAR P.H.

BREDON ROAD B4080

23/11/99

ROSES THEATRE

OLDBURY ROAD

OLDBURY ROAD

ALBION P.H.

WALKLEY ROAD

ASHLEY WAY

THE HOLLAMS FIELDS

HOLLAMS ROAD

COTTESWOLD ROAD

ROPE WALK

STATION ROAD

COTTESWOLD GARDENS

LOCATION POINT

STATION LANE

Carrant Brook

BONFIRE

12

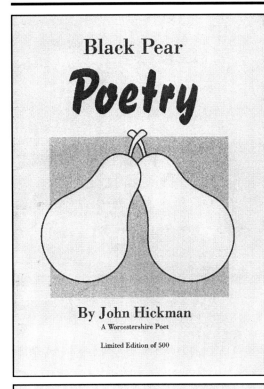

Black Pear

Poetry

By John Hickman
A Worcestershire Poet

Limited Edition of 500

John Hickman: Born 23rd April 1946 in Droitwich Spa, Worcestershire. Started writing poetry at an early age. Over the years he has had many poems published and gives out to friends copies of his booklet, "Black Pear Poetry".

John's interests are many and include such things as water dowsing, pipe location using dowsing rods, gardening and caravaning.

John's work as a senior operations engineer in the water related industry involves a great deal of travel. Through meeting different people across the country he is inspired to write on various subjects.
However upon reflection John feels that one subject that does not go away is his feeling for the future of mankind. Because of this he has written several futuristic poems under the heading; "The Millennium".

speed, heading towards the Cotswolds."

John has never budged from what he saw all those years ago, and was later inspired to write a number of poems, one of which refers to this particular incident.

'A flash of light across the sky,
the soft blue green mist attracts the eye.
Then in a flash, less than the blinking of an eye,
the light has disappeared in the distant sky.
Are these the visitors from other worlds,
sometimes seen but never heard?
Described in detail when they are seen,
but concrete proof there's never been.
So do you believe what people say,
or await the proof the scientific way?'

(Source: personal interviews)

Close Encounter, Sussex

Someone else who maintained he saw the occupants of an 'Alien' craft, during winter 1972, was Howard Johnson - now a Councillor (2005) from Spalding, in Lincolnshire. He was then living in Beacon Road, Crowborough, in Sussex.

"At 11.30am, I happened to look through the bathroom window - then fitted with clear glass, not frosted, as the style is now - when I noticed a saucer-shaped object heading towards my direction, low down in the sky, about 75yds away from the house, solid looking, rather than anything substantive. It then came to an abrupt halt, allowing me to see a transparent dome on top, with a bank of flickering multi-coloured lights underneath. I watched with disbelief, deliberately forcing myself to look away, expecting that when I returned my gaze it would have gone, but this didn't happen. Unbelievably, I could see three 'figures' standing inside the dome.

Two looked like the entities now referred to as 'Greys', although I was unaware of such terminology then. The third occupant looked more human in appearance and was taller than his two companions but completely bald, and wearing a silver coloured uniform, apparently manipulating something out of my view.

All of a sudden, they seemed to realise they were being watched. The 'craft' slowly moved away, until lost from view, over Tunbridge Wells. I shouted out to the rest of the family, who dashed outside, but unfortunately, by this time, there was nothing to be seen."

The incident still haunts Howard, despite the passing of years, who feels unprepared to accept what he witnessed was irrefutable evidence of any 'alien' life-force, but remains mystified as to the reason for the appearance of this 'craft', and it's never to be forgotten occupants. He was shown the illustration of the 'craft' seen at Bexleyheath, in 1955, by Margaret Fry, and confirmed it *identical t*o what he saw on that date. **(Source: personal interview)**

UFO photographed over Arizona, USA

Although our next sighting did not take place in England, we decided to include it. We felt that it was worth bringing to the attention of the readers, as it was investigated by a man whom we were proud to have known - retired USAF Colonel Wendelle C. Stevens. In addition to this, the object had been

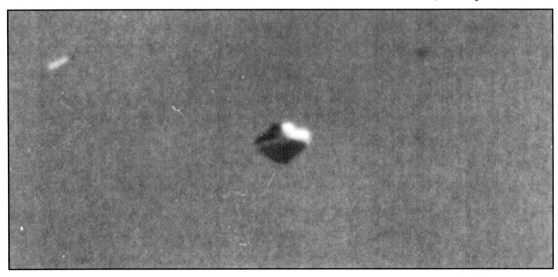

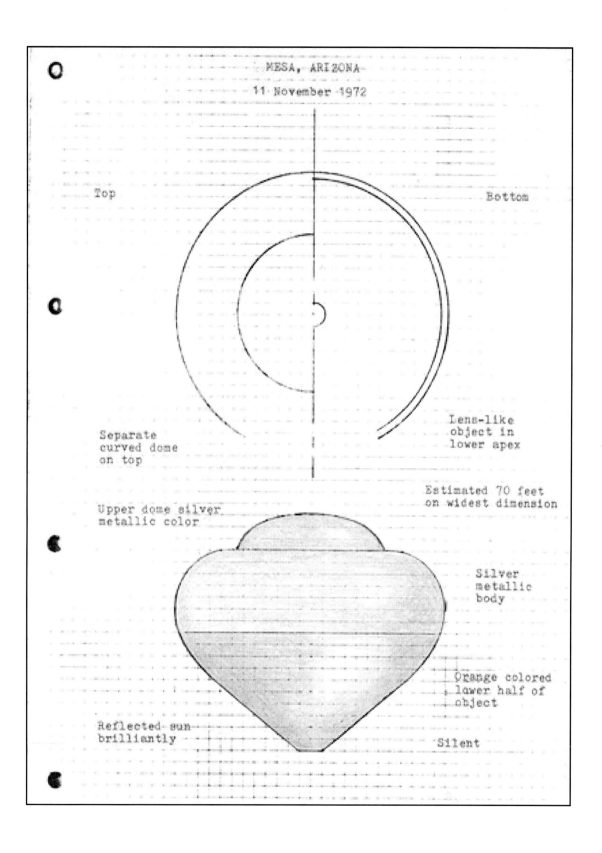

MESA, ARIZONA
11 November 1972

Top   Bottom

Separate
curved dome
on top

Lens-like
object in
lower apex

Upper dome silver
metallic color

Estimated 70 feet
on widest dimension

Silver
metallic
body

Orange colored
lower half of
object

Reflected sun
brilliantly

Silent

photographed. Shortly after noon on the 11th November 1972, Shawn Cheves, age 10, was with a group of boys, playing in the garden at his friend Scott's house, at Mesa, Arizona, USA, when he noticed a glint of light on the fence. Looking around, he noticed high in the sky and far away, a bright shining object and brought it to the attention of the others.

> *"It resembled a silvery meteorological balloon, but when observed through binoculars, which one of the boys had gone to fetch, it looked more like a fat silver ice-cream cone, or an upside-down bell, and it had a smaller dome on top of the rounded upper domed surface. It was completely silent, and there was no smoke trail."*

Not knowing what to do, Shawn called around at Mr. Lee Elders' house and asked him to come out and see it, suggesting it might be a UFO. Mr. Elders, who was watching the beginning of the Arizona State football game on his television, waited for a commercial break before going out to observe. When the break came on, he picked up his 35mm Asahi Pentax SLR camera, with a 200mm telephoto lens, and went out into the street. He looked towards the east-south-east direction they were pointing; at an angle of some 40° elevation, and saw the object.

> *"It was very bright and shiny - like a mirror ball in the sky. I did not see any flashes and felt that the light was all reflected. It looked like a small shiny BB high in the sky. The object, which was completely stationary in the sky, then very slowly began to move closer to us."*

At 13:55hrs. Mr. Elders took the first 3 photos. After standing around for some minutes, he became bored and went back into the house to watch his football game. It was the annual homecoming game and was the most popular of the season. Curiosity getting the better of him, he came out again on another commercial break, a little later, and took the last picture at 14:05hrs. By then the object was somewhat north of its original position. The children watched it until it went out of sight, 35 to 40 minutes later. **(Credit: Cece Stevens and Wendelle Stevens/UFO Photo Archives)**

UFO display, Warwickshire

Clusters of mysterious 'lights' were seen darting about in the sky by Rita Tallis - a resident of Ullenhall Lane (just off the A435 Birmingham to Redditch Road) at 6.00pm on 11th November 1972. She later said:

> *"I telephoned a friend of mine, Susan Harris, living a short distance away, and asked her son, Keith (aged 15) to cycle over to my house and take a look for himself. After Keith arrived, I stood in the garden, accompanied by my husband, Gordon, and other family members, watching these strange multi-coloured 'lights' darting about in the sky over the Danzey Green area of Warwickshire, at which stage we decided to call the Police."*

Two Police Officers arrived, a short time later, one of whom was P.C. William Hunt. Unfortunately, by this time, the 'lights' were no longer to be seen. P.C. Hunt advised the family to contact them again, should the 'lights' reappear.

Oddly, no sooner had the Officers departed when the 'lights' reappeared in the sky. Rita's husband telephoned the Police again, who told him they were already aware, as the Officers were now, themselves, actually witnessing a number of mysterious 'red lights' rotating in the sky, over Henley-in-Arden.
In a conversation which took place between him and Rita Tallis, following the Officer's return to their

house, he told her:

> *"It was like a lighthouse. One of the objects projected a beam, like a searchlight, shining downwards onto the ground. The 'lights' then moved towards Birmingham, leaving a solitary 'white light' behind. Within a short time this, too, rose upwards at a sharp angle and headed away, following the same direction as the previous objects."*

Enquiries made at Elmdon Airport, Birmingham, revealed nothing untoward had shown on Radar. We also spoke to Keith Harris, who recalled seeing the multi-coloured light forms 'cavorting' about in the sky - totally unlike anything he had ever seen before in his life. **(Source: personal interviews/*Sunday Mercury* 12.11.1972 'Observers including Police see objects over Beoley)**

Another similar display of strange 'lights' in the sky took place on the other side of the Warwickshire border, over Barnt Green, Worcestershire - a small village, just outside Birmingham (approximately 20mins away from the scene of the previous encounter) according to William Matthews - an elderly resident, living in the village, sometime during November 1972.

> *"I was in the back garden, pointing out the various constellations to my wife, when we noticed a cluster of stars moving across the sky. Suddenly, to our surprise, they broke-up into fragments, or particles of light, which split into separate directions, moving backwards and forwards in the sky - unlike any ' shooting stars' I have ever seen. The next night, we were astounded to see nine or ten of these 'stars' moving about in the sky, in what was now becoming a familiar pattern of behaviour.*
>
> *On the third night running, we counted seventeen stars (!) involved in a display lasting for about forty-five minutes. I contacted the Police, at Rubery, near Birmingham, to report what we had seen. I was surprised to learn from the Police Officer that many other reports of similar objects had been brought to their attention. The Officer suggested I contact Brize Norton United States Air Force Base, in Gloucestershire. I telephoned the Airbase and spoke to the Duty Officer, who took note of what I said, and told me, 'We are very interested in these things'."* **(Source: personal interview/*Sunday Mercury*, 12.11.72)**

At 10.21am on 13th November 1972, an object, described as either *'disc-like, or sphere'*, wobbling slightly, and flashing occasionally, was seen heading in a north-west to south-east, direction by Mrs. Margaret Buxton, who was hanging out the washing, at Brown Edge, Staffordshire. **(Source: Mr. Derek James, BUFORA)**

An intense yellow light, with a smaller red light on top, *"like a cherry on a cake"*, was seen over Cold Ash Hill Road, Newbury, Berkshire, at 10.10pm on 14th November 1972, by John Drawbridge - then Secretary of the South West Aerial Phenomenon Society. He attempted to 'give chase' to the object heading away at a speed, he estimated to be over 100mph. **(Source: Trevor Whittaker, BUFORA)**

On 17th November 1972, Mrs. P. Parks, of Highgate Road, Chesterfield was walking home from work over the bridge at Ham Shades Lane, at 6.10pm, when she sighted a glowing object in the sky, described as:

> *"...changing colour from red to white, to green, and revolving. It made no*

noise and was moving at treetop level, at about 10mph. I saw it head away over Thanet Way, towards Chesterfield, and then zigzag over Herne Bay."

In the same month, a couple walking on L'Ancresse Common, in Guernsey, sighted an object they described as:

> *"...about the size of a Viscount aircraft, resembling a circle, imposed onto a triangle, showing a white light at the front and two at the rear."* (**Source: Guernsey UFO Club**)

Towards the end of the month, more than thirty shipyard workers at Faversham, in Kent, watched an object as it zigzagged across the sky, changing shape from circular to cigar, which discharged a number of red lights. Details of this incident were reported to RAF Manston, who promised to forward a report to the MOD. (**Source:** *Faversham Times*, **30.11.72**)

UFO over Kent

On 5th December 1972, an object, described as resembling a *'beautiful flashing diamond in the sky'*, was seen over Oare, Kent, at 9.45pm., by Joan Patching and her husband, while exercising the family dog.

Joan Patching said later:

> *"We were on our way back to the village, after walking Simba, our dog, when l noticed a beautiful blue coloured object, pulsing with light, over some nearby elm trees. I pointed it out to my husband, remarking what a beautiful star it was, although l had never seen a star in that position in the sky before and wondered if it was a new planet. We kept our eye on it as we walked home when, all of a sudden, it began to move towards us, making a feint whining noise, attracting a comment by my husband, who wondered if it might have been a helicopter. To our surprise, it shot up into the sky at terrific speed, and was gone in seconds, proving this was no helicopter."* (**Source: personal interview/***Faversham Times*, **7.12.72**)

UFO display, Warwickshire

On the late afternoon of 9th December 1972, Brian and Olive Langford from Dumblepits Lane, Ullenhall, close to the Wythall border, (just outside Birmingham), next to the busy Birmingham to Redditch Road, noticed two 'bright lights' moving across the sky, which they believed, initially, to be an aircraft on its way to Birmingham (Elmdon) Airport, until they saw:

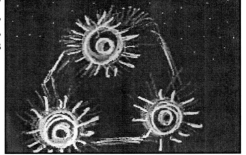

> *"...an object, resembling a lampshade in appearance, displaying three lights, passing overhead and drop down over the Beoley area, where we lost sight of it."* (**Source: personal interview**)

Two days later (11th December 1972) Mrs. Rouffignac was driving along an un-numbered road, which runs past Chobham Common, near Chobham Clump, between the villages of Longcross and Burowhill, when she sighted an object in the sky to the east, described as, *"rectangular, with what looked like a rudder part on the end",* visible for about 15secs., as she turned right onto the B383 road, heading north-west. **(Source: BUFORA)**

UFO over Yorkshire

Mrs. Lorna Butterfield of Eastwood Avenue, Illingworth, Halifax, caught sight of a bright object through the window of her home, at 4.40pm on 14th December 1972.

At first she thought it was a star, but then realised it was heading slowly in a south-east direction. It then changed from a single point of light to *'three lights forming a triangle'*, with the top light and bottom left silver-gold in colour, while the bottom right was a definite blue in colour. The object then moved away and reverted to a single point of light in the sky and was eventually lost from view. **(Source: Trevor Whittaker, BUFORA)**

At 6.15pm on 15th December 1972, Mr. Norris – a resident from Basildon, Essex - was stood outside his house, looking up into a perfectly clear sky, when he saw:

> *"...three large, extremely bright, orange objects, looking like a cross between*

*an arrowhead and boomerang, with defined leading edges, showing
blurred red trailing ones, suspended in the sky, at an angle of 80° off the
horizon. Ten seconds later, they moved quickly away in a V-shaped
formation."* **(Source: Edward J. Woods)**

UFO over Northumberland

At 12.30pm on the 18th December 1972, over twenty members of staff in Northumberland, employed at
a specialist school for people suffering from physical and metal deficiencies, including teachers,
physiotherapists, and psychologists, were called to look out of the window by another member of staff.
They saw an object drifting across the sky, about half a mile away, which they all described collectively, as:

> *"...a dull grey or black cylindrical-shaped object, showing convex top and
> flat bottom, from which smoke trailed. It was about 2-3ft in diameter and
> some 5 or 6ft high, resembling a domestic dustbin in image."*

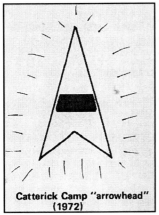

**Catterick Camp "arrowhead"
(1972)**

The object was seen to continue westwards, silently, until out of sight.
The headmaster, who had also witnessed the event, contacted the Police,
who sent an officer to the school; he later informed them he had been unable
to explain the origin of the object. **(Source: Peter Bolam, BUFORA)**

In December 1972, two young soldiers from Catterick Army Camp were
taking a break, while on a map reading exercise, when they noticed an
object, shaped like an arrowhead, red in colour, with a rectangular
darkened middle section, moving across the sky.

As it continued on its passage, they saw it change colour to orange and
finally brilliant white as it passed overhead. About a minute after they had
seen it, the object vanished from view.

At first we thought this connected with a similar incident near Catterick,
which took place in 1973, but from the times and description given, we are talking about two separate
incidents. **(Source: David Almond, BUFORA/Jenny Randles,** *FSR,* **Volume 22, No. 4 1976 –
'British Reports Old and New')**

ADDENDUM FOR 1972

If a person was asked to supply details of English UFO sightings from the early 1970s, it is unlikely that he or she would be able to offer few, if any, examples at all, taking into consideration the difficulties which would be experienced in tracking down these reports, now 40yrs ago. Fortunately, as a result of liaison over the years with many individual UFO enthusiasts, who bothered to catalogue an astonishing number of UFO sightings covering this period, we can now see for ourselves the extent of many hitherto unpublished UFO reports, the majority of which will not be found in declassified Top Secret files made available by the MOD.

FEBRUARY 11ᵗʰ 1972
A horizontal band of intensely bright lights, with a shorter vertical line in the middle, was seen in the sky, at 8.00am, over Stockport, Cheshire, by a Manchester businessman, who was driving to work between Prestbury and Wilmslow.   (Source: *Manchester Evening News, 11.2.72*)

OCTOBER 15ᵗʰ 1972
A self illuminated object, described as a bright star, was seen above the setting sun from Harting, in Hampshire, by Helen Sturm (55). According to Helen, within a short time, it changed shape to that of an elongated star, with a silvery tail, to reddish in colour, before heading towards the North direction,

> *"...where it turned eastwards, and then dropped down to Earth.*
> *As it did so, it assumed a saucer shape and disappeared from*
> *view."* **(Source: Mr. R.J. Nash, BUFORA)**

NOVEMBER 4ᵗʰ 1972
At 4.00am, a former RAF Pilot, with 2,000 flying hours, awoke early. On looking through the bedroom window, he saw a bright, circular object, showing a white and yellow centre, which became blurred at the edges, heading across the sky, towards the east-south-east direction. After about ten minutes, the object vanished in a flash of light, leaving behind a grey cloud. **(Source: Mr. G. Baker)**

1972
Some years ago, during a trip to Anglesey on a rain swept day, we met Mrs. Mair Jeffery and her friend, Mair Williams, to hear about what Mair had sighted in 1972. This was not the only time that we were to hear of UFOs seen. Mrs. Williams, who was a schoolteacher at Rhosybol School, also told us of an incident when she and her pupils sighted a UFO in 1977, during a dramatic increases in UFO activity for that year - now often referred to as the 1977 'Welsh Wave'.

It is difficult to ascertain the purpose of the 'signalling' which occurs between UFOs, if any, but we presume that it may indicate some form of intelligence and communication (not necessarily of an advanced order). While the reason and purpose escapes us, we should be very careful about jumping to the wrong conclusions.

Although we cannot say there was a connection with what Mair saw from the A5, and an intriguing photo taken over Tyn Rhos Caravan Park, near Anglesey, at 5.00pm on the 29ᵗʰ March 2005, by Alex Mera his son, Steve, and two daughters we felt it was worth introducing into the book, especially as we knew both men, and had no qualms about accepting it as genuine.

Steve Mera, the current head of MAPIT and a highly respected member of the UFO community, had this to say:

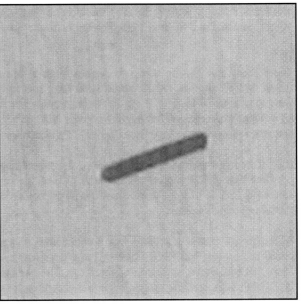

"It was black in colour and tilted at a constant angle. We were looking out to sea at the time when we saw it. The wind sped was 8knots, and cloud cover was 12,000ft, with 6/8ths cloud cover."

The caravan park is situated on a working farm, between Betws-y-Coed, Bala, and Llangollen, at the edge of the Snowdonia National Park.

Margie Jeffreys Ayn

Thursday 18th September, 2003.

Received your phone message ~~Thurs~~ Wednesday evening.

1972

Please bear in mind that nearly 25 years has elapsed since my sighting of the U.F.O's, but I still "see" them vividly in my mind. I didn't make copies of our correspondence in the past, but I'll TRY to recall the circumstances surrounding the incident.

1. It was definitely before 1980 - my Mother died that year.
2. It was after she visited me that Sunday and I'd driven her home approximately 18 miles away to Holland Arms, now known as PENTREBERW on the A5 road. I'd left Penysarn about 5 p.m after tea. The journey would have taken me about 1 hour, there & back. So we are talking approx. 6 p.m when I took the dog for a walk.
3. It would be Septemberish because it wasn't dark and I could see everything clearly i.e traffic etc etc.
4. My ex husband usually came home at 6-30 p.m - I was really hoping he'd come home then, but on hind-sight had taken an alternate route. I just wanted to tell someone or show someone else.
5. I stood there just watching - the one over the lake by Parys Mountain stood absolutely still - no noise at all (so it was a clear evening). It was cigar shaped or a submarine shape and had this huge "spot-light", very, very bright signalling "on + off" to another UFO to its left over DULAS BAY, which was signalling back - when one stopped the other responded immediately.

I didn't go straight home - I went past my house to a neighbour/friend 3 doors away. Philip who had been in the RAF and I asked him what planes could stand still, have no noise and have a bright spotlight. He mentioned a Harrier could hover, but I would have heard the blades of a helicopter while it hovered. Anyway what I saw was at least 4-5 times the length of a helicopter!

I then came back home, told my ex and children then aged approx 14 + 16 years old - everyone laughed - I remember being told I'd imagined it all! - I wished at that time the dog could talk!!! he watched it as well.

I didn't wait to find out how they left, by then I was afraid - Next thing, my daughter's then boyfriend, Peter Farmery arrived at our house - he was quite excitable and blurted out what he'd seen - over Dulas Bay - his father's rented farm borders on Dulas Bay - behind the PILOT BOAT INN - I had had no contact at all either verbally or by phone with Peter to discuss what I'd seen - but still my ex wouldn't believe us. If you ever write a book I'll send him a free copy, SPECIAL DELIVERY!! ha ha.

Over the years MRS MAIR WILLIAMS, who taught at RHOSYBOL SCHOOL at the time of her sitting and the pupils, talk about it - it felt good that someone/anyone else had "seen things".

The young lad Elfed Roberts who used to live next door has left his partner, although he'd told me he'd seen some odd things in the sky. His home, FELIN BACH, DULAS, also overlooks the bay.

My friend EIRIAN HUGHES, she too was adamant, she'd seen UFO's has moved away. This was before I'd met her.

CHRISTINE HUGHES, ABERLEINIAN, Llaneilian also had her experiences - not necessarily the same sighting but there was a lot of activity around here in the late seventies.

Now tell me after nearly 25 years how and why can I remember so much so vividly? - The time/ the day all the circumstances surrounding the incident/ - My daughter was lying on the sofa recovering from German Measles, covered in spots/ the T.V. was on, my ex sitting in 'his' chair/ Peter walking in the sitting room - everything is CLEAR, whereas now I can't remember what I did yesterday!

I worked on a farming estate at the time. The following day I rang RAF Valley to ask if any planes had taken off or landed at MONA or Valley and the first thing he said

4

Do you want to report an UFO incident!

So, there you are - that's my story and I'm sticking to it for ever!

Mair (Jeffery)

Homestead,
PENYSARN,
NR. Amlwch
Anglesey,
Gwynedd
L699AJ.

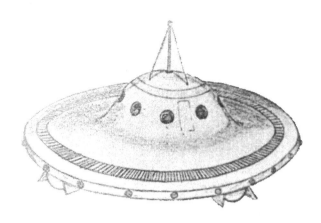

1973

In England, during this year the average house price was £9,942, a gallon of petrol was 35pence, and the speed limit on motorways was reduced to 50 mph from 70 mph until further notice. Arab members of the Organization of Petroleum Exporting Countries (OPEC) announced they were going to restrict flow of crude oil to countries supporting Israel, causing price of oil to increase by 200%. The World Trade Centre in New York becomes the tallest building in the World. Watergate Hearings begin in the United States Senate and President Richard Nixon tells the nation, *"I am not a crook"*. Skylab, the United States' first space station, is launched and Princess Anne marries Mark Philips at Westminster Abbey.

just a bit of info!
on JOHN.
he was one of 6
children. the eldest
his family was at

muning stock. his
father was down
Kngsbury Colliery her.
all his working life. and
John was down to
pit - Fro. until his 20's.
as from school.
We went to Lichfield
To live. As a farm.
Labourer. before moving
To Baddesley Ensor. when
he got a job at
Dunlops. B'ham. he was
just 39. when he died.
Suddenly - he was very
down to earth. and certainly
didn't believe in UFO's

P. 114: Mr. John Spencer who witnessed a UFO while on the way to work along the A5 as depicted on the front cover of _FSR_

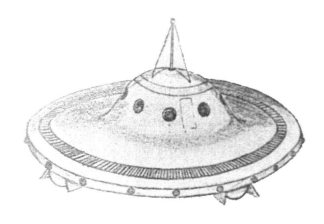

CHAPTER THREE
JANUARY-JUNE 1973

UFOs over East Yorkshire

At 2.35pm on 2nd January 1973 Jonathon Hill, aged 14, of Lime Tree Avenue, Sutton, near Hull, was sat in the back of the family car, being driven by his mother, who was talking to his grandmother sat in the front passenger's seat, when he saw, out of the back window:

> *"...what I thought were two kites, high in the sky, above Sutton Hospital, near Hull, East Yorkshire. At a second glance I saw that they weren't, in fact, kites but two disc-shaped objects, standing out clearly against the overcast sky. I estimated roughly that the objects were about 500ft above me.*

> *Both objects were about 15-20ft in diameter, translucent, showing six darker spoke like areas, with dark or black outer rims. The lower and nearer object was floating lazily in a clockwise direction around its companion, which was completely stationary.*

> *There was a light wind blowing, but it seemed somehow 'locked' tight in the air around it. I watched the objects for about half a minute, until they were out of sight."*

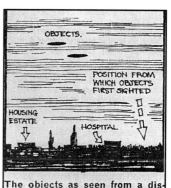

The objects as seen from a distance by witness (sketches based on originals by J. Hill)

The next day, Jon told his father - a teacher by occupation - what he had seen. He suggested that it was more likely his son had seen two seagulls, or even a reflection in the car windscreen! **(Source: *FSR* Supplement, 15 June 1973)**

UFOs over Essex

On the 21st January 1973, David Gregory - a Radio One disc jockey, 'standing-in' for Tony Blackburn – brought the listeners' attention to reports of UFOs seen, following a number of telephone calls made to the BBC Radio Station, by members of the public; they included not only David's sighting, but a housewife from Barking, in Essex, who told of seeing, *"a red ball, with wings"*, (attracting, inevitably, some good humoured scepticism) which landed in her garden and then took-off.

DAVID GREGORY

In 2011 we spoke to David Gregory, who is still involved with the media. He remembered, with great clarity, the sighting which was brought to his attention by his mother. Interestingly, he told us that, following the broadcast, he was warned by the BBC to discontinue any further discussion on the subject on air, *"...effectively gagging me to keep quiet."*

At 7.15pm on 24th January, Barry Watts, of Deal, was travelling along the Deal to Dover road, in Kent, near to the turning with St. Margaret, when he sighted:

> *"...an amber flaming 'ball of fire' flying across the sky, and land in a nearby field. It then took off and was last seen heading out to sea, like a rocket, over St. Margaret. I've never seen anything like it before. It was unbelievable and weird."* (**Source: *Dover Express*, 9.2.73**)

At 6.30pm on 2nd February 1973, Mrs. Edna Huxtable, and Mr. and Mrs. H. Davidson - residents of Umberleigh, in Devon - sighted a large, round, fiery object in the sky, just after two aircraft had just passed each other.

The object, which had a tail and trailing flames, was seen to dash across the sky, and disappear in mid-air, followed by a muffled explosion.

A spokesman at RAF Chivenor suggested it was a meteorite. It sounds like a fireball to us, but even natural phenomena can frighten people, especially when it is out of the normal.

In addition to the UK sightings, it is worthy of mention that during the same period in America, Police in Cherokee County, South Carolina received so many UFO sighting reports that they stopped sending Police cars out to investigate! The sightings, according to police, were in the hundreds and described as *"cylindrical, cigar-shaped"*, *"triangular"*, and *"round, like a saucer, with a cabin on top"*.

By the end of February, according to police, UFO watching had become so popular that on one night more than 50 cars were parked along the side of a road in the county, in hope of catching a glimpse of the object. (**Source: UFO INVESTIGATOR, April 1973, page 3**)

UFO near the M10 Flyover

At 3.00am on 5th February 1973, Jim Sutcliffe was driving home to Howlands, Welwyn Garden City, along the A.414 Hemel Hempstead to St. Albans road, near the M10 flyover, when he noticed a number of cars pulled up at the side of the road.

> *"I stopped and saw that they were looking at a big glowing yellow 'ball' hovering above the ground, 20-30ft above the junction, a few hundred yards away. As one of the watchers went for the Police, the thing shot straight up into the air and vanished."*

According to the *Evening Echo* newspaper, they told of being contacted by an anonymous caller, who told them his car had cut out near the bridge, but started after the 'light' rose upwards into the sky. **(Source:** *Evening Echo,* **Hemel Hempstead, 12.2.73)**

UFO over London

At 5.10pm on 10th February 1973, John Williams, and his two friends, sighted a cigar-shaped object, showing two lights on its body, stationary in the sky over Gunnersbury Park, London while out walking After visiting a local café, they made their way home 20mins later, when they saw the object once again now low down, in the sky. Could it have been a crane, they wondered?

> *"It then slowly turned and became cigar-shaped - now showing three lights. We estimated the dull, dark, coloured object to be 60-70ft long, at an altitude of one mile and at an elevation of 30° in a south-east direction."*

A few minutes later, it suddenly rocketed forward and flashed silently across the horizon, at extremely fast speed, and was gone. This was no Crane! **(Source:** *BUFORA Journal,* **Volume 4, Number 1, Winter 1973)**

UFO Display over Bournemouth

During the early hours of the 11th February 1973, Carl Whiteley - a reporter for the *Bournemouth Evening Echo* - was on duty as an auxiliary coastguard, at Hengistbury Head.

> *"I was looking through binoculars, powerful enough to pick out cars across the bay at Swanage. I was looking towards the westerly direction at the star-studded sky, when I noticed, through the mass of twinkling lights, a light moving high over the Purbecks.*
>
> *At first it gave an impression of a luminous tube, but as it moved southwards, its circular shape became apparent. I watched this object, which appeared to be rotating in the sky, for 45 breathtaking minutes. It was not an aircraft, nor was it a cloud or weather balloon. It returned later, westwards, against the wind, and banked at an angle, before disappearing from view."*

Carl wasn't the only witness. His colleague - auxiliary coastguard Mike Parker - corroborated what had been sighted. It was said that Mike and his brother, Charles, had also seen a cigar-shaped object in the sky while out night fishing, at Mudeford, approximately 20yrs ago! (1953)

Eileen Buckle - assistant Editor of *Flying Saucer Review* - wrote to Mr. Whiteley at the time, hoping that he could clarify details of another sighting made at about that time, involving a group of scouts at Ferndown Common. They reported having sighted four lights in the sky, hovering close together. It was also alleged, on another occasion, that a mysterious object, resembling a flying 'Polo Mint', was seen by other scouts on the common.

Father and son

We contacted Carl's son, Ian, who was kind enough to send us three photographs of his father.

> "*I am forwarding three photos, emailed to me very kindly by Scott Harrison, chief librarian at the* Bournemouth Daily Echo *(note the present name is slightly different to the original name of* Bournemouth Evening Echo, *when my father worked there and wrote his UFO story).*
>
> *The first one shows my father receiving an HM Coastguard Long Service Medal, awarded for 20 years' service as an auxiliary coastguard, in June 1979. He continued as an auxiliary until his death, while on duty, in April1982.*
>
> *The next one shows him in an earlier shot, in 1973, at the Southampton Boat Show, and the third is with me, when I joined him at the* Echo, *in 1970. I am very fortunate to receive these, since Scott has unfortunately become a victim of redundancy and leaves the* Echo *tomorrow.*"

(Source: *Bournemouth Evening Echo*, 12.2.73/*FSR*, July/August 1973, Vol. 19, Number 4)

The following day, a triangular object, resembling an arrowhead, was seen moving northwards, over Newport, South Wales, by two schoolboys, at 11.15pm - possibly connected with later reports of UFOs, described as: *"...clusters of multi-coloured lights"* seen over the Exe Estuary, in Devon. **(Source: *Weston Morning News*, 19.12.73)**

UFOs over Warwickshire

Nancy and Bill Wilson - an elderly couple from Baxterley, Warwickshire - described a frightening experience, during early 1973, whilst driving through the village of Baddesley Ensor, towards their home, accompanied by another couple.

Bill, an ex-Japanese Prisoner of War, holder of the Burma Star, survivor of the infamous Japanese 'Burma Railway', or 'Death Railway' who, in his own words, had 'brushed with death' many times over, told us what happened:

> *"As we neared the top of Dordon Hill, we saw an object, as big as the full moon, hovering, motionless, over the A.5. The car then began to falter and came to a halt. We sat there in the darkness, wondering what to do. Suddenly, the car was bathed in a beam of bright light, projected outwards from the object. To our horror, the 'ball of light' began to move towards us.*

Just as we thought it was about to strike us, it split into two separate luminous fragments of light and raced across the sky, returned, and merged into one, before heading towards the direction of Middleton." **(Source: personal interview)**

At 5.00am on 16th February 1973, Mr. John Spencer from Baddesley Ensor, Tamworth, Staffordshire, was travelling to work along the A5, towards Tamworth, with the village of Dordon, on his right. As he passed the entrance to Birch Coppice Colliery, on the opposite, side of the road he happened to bend down to throw away a finished cigarette through the window it was at this point he noticed something strange in the sky to his right, at 5.05am.

The brightly-lit object then approached his position, apparently on a collision course with his vehicle, causing Mr. Spencer to fear that this was, indeed, going to take place.

"I reduced my speed to about 20mph and watched, with astonishment, as a cigar-shaped object passed overhead, at treetop height, about 20yds away, at an angle of some 150ft in diameter, trailing a 'cone of flame', pinkish/ yellow on the outside, white in its centre, about 12ft away from the UFO - rather than being discharged directly from an exhaust, as one may have expected if it had been an aircraft."

Sadly, we were unable to speak directly with John, who was then a Dunlop worker in Birmingham, as we learnt he had died in the early 1990s, although his wife told us that:

"After having had the courage to report the incident, he was subjected to such a degree of ridicule that he regretted having brought the matter to the attention of the Newspaper in the first place."

Thank goodness there are people like Mr. Spencer, who had the courage to report just what he had seen. He never mentioned any alien craft - just what he saw! **(Source: *Tamworth Herald*, 28.2.73/ *FSR Supplement*, 14.4.73 - 'Low Pass UFO over the A5')**

At 7.45pm on 17th February 1973, Auxiliary coastguard, Mr. Carl Whiteley was to witness another example of UFO activity, when he sighted an object.

"I had my binoculars on another luminous 'wheel' coming over from the west, over the sea, when suddenly, I was aware of an orange movement. It seemed to come from the wheel. I fixed my 124x binoculars on the orange object and it was clearly the shape of a 'flying saucer', complete with dome and what appeared to be portholes. The bottom section - the circular section beneath the dome - appeared to rotate. It hovered and then moved slightly upwards, and disappeared from sight. The object was about a quarter of the size of the moon."

On this occasion, Mr. Whitley chose not to report the incident to the newspaper he worked for, fearing he may be discredited. **(Source: *FSR*, Volume 19, No. 4, July/August 1973, 'World round-up')**

UFOs over Portsmouth

At 6.50am on 22nd February 1973, John Enderby from Copnor, Portsmouth, Hampshire, was getting ready for his newspaper round, when he heard a noise like a loud refrigerator. On going to investigate further, he saw:

"...an orange disc-shaped object, about 30ft in diameter showing yellow and black lights around it base. There were about ten of these working their way around the base of the object, flashing on and off in continuous sequence (not rotating).

The object was hovering about 50-150ft away over the garden of the house. I wasn't in the least bit frightened and rushed back into the house to tell my sister. It was in view for a total of 25secs and my sister saw it as well. As it moved away it took on a cigar shape, showing a rounded dome on top and a smaller one underneath.

It disappeared like a dot on a TV screen when you switch the set off." **(Source: Richard Nash/*BUFORA Journal*, Volume 3, No. 10, Spring 1973/personal interview)**

At 7.55am on the same date, Portsmouth resident - Mrs. Stimpson - was waiting for a bus in Goldsmiths Avenue, when she sighted a glowing, flickering, flame red object:

> *"...like the glow of a magi-coal fire coming from behind trees in Milton Park, moving very slowly across the sky. It and then climbed to a point roughly about 2,000ft in the sky and gently descended, until lost from view."* **(Source: Nicholas Maloret, WATSUP)**

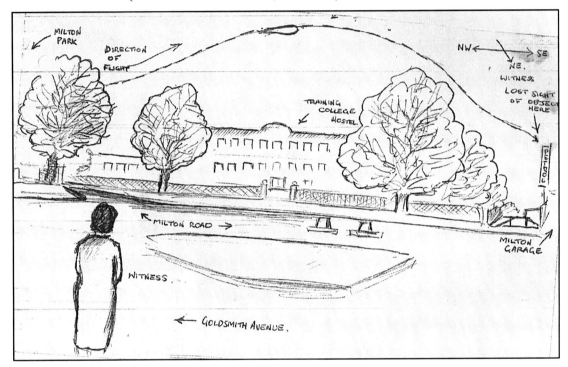

In March 1973, a cigar-shaped object was seen by pupils and staff arriving at Treleigh Comprehensive School, Redruth, Cornwall, They reported that they saw it, moving silently across the sky.

It was quite possibly the same object seen hovering over Carn Brae (an ancient Iron Age site) by motorists, travelling between Redruth and Camborne.

At 9.00pm on 5th March 1973, Martin Bodle (12) and his sister Susan (8) were in their garden at Torrington Road, North End, Portsmouth, when they saw a strange object crossing the sky.

In an interview later conducted by Nick Maloret, they told him:

> *"We saw a perfectly round, luminous orange object, heading north to south. It was slightly smaller than the Moon, and had a hazy blue edge trailing a fiery trail. Then it changed its path from north to south and moved eastwards and appeared to slow down. It then diminished in size and changed in shape to oval, with a slight lump on the top, its tail appearing to shorten, and disappeared from view, when in line with a small star under the Moon."*

Susan claimed she heard a noise like a rocket after the object had disappeared from view. Both children confirmed the length of the sightings was about 30secs. Martin told Nick that at about 11.30pm, he saw what looked like two orange lights, joined together, showing several smaller lights on the surface, moving across the sky through his bedroom window.

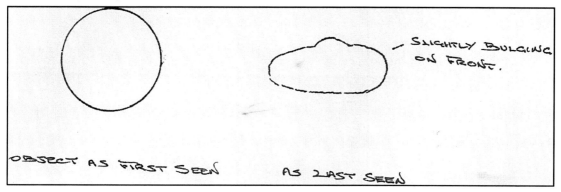

At 3.45am on 30th March 1973, Southsea resident - Royal Navy electronics engineer employee, Ken Elliot - was walking close to Lennox Road North, when he felt a 'vibration' in the air, and heard a faint *'whirly humming noise'*. He looked upwards into the sky and saw:

> *"...some pulsing lights (about three times the size of Sirius or a bit larger) moving in a linear fashion but wavering a fair bit in the air, moving northwards. I made my way to Elm Grove, where I was surprised to see a friend of mine, Chris, who watched the object with me for a few minutes, which, by now, were well over the central area of Portsmouth. My friend commented on its pulsing and swirling motion, accompanied by colour changing.*
>
> *I then went in to my house and picked up a pen and paper and, using the frame of the window, was able to monitor its movements. At this point I noticed another object, about 8,000yds away from the main one, moving in unison. Underneath the two 'bodies' could be seen small objects moving between the two larger ones, about three at a time and every ten minutes or so. Its motion and speed was about one inch of the sky per one quarter of a mile in an easterly direction, its course having altered after being seen stationary over central Portsmouth. At 5.00am the objects had passed the point of reference on the window frame, so feeling tired I went to bed."* **(Source: Malcolm Handley, WATSUP)**

At the same time and date, Mrs. Ludford and Mrs. Windsor - nurses employed at St. James Hospital, Milton, Portsmouth, were leaving the Hospital near to the Warren Avenue gate entrance, following the end of their night shift. They noticed an object that appeared cigar-shaped and was shiny silver in colour (although they think it may have been a 'disc', sideways on, and completely featureless) hovering in the sky above hospital buildings to the east.

Mrs. Winsor alerted a porter and a patient to their sighting. The group then watched the object, which was motionless, at an angle of some 60° with an apparent length of 1-2ft, hanging in the air, at an estimated height of about 10-15ft above the building and about 150ft away from them. Mrs. Ludford told UFO researcher, Nick Maloret:

> *"Emanating from the object was an intense white light, which hurt the eyes when looked at directly. Around the area of illumination, which was roughly circular, was a dark grey indistinct ring, although this may have been caused by the intensity of the light."*

Mrs. Windsor agreed on the shape of the object, but described seeing:

> *"...a dark grey smoke-like area completely surrounding the UFO. It was roughly circular and had around its perimeter a scalloped effect, which I found beautiful."*

Within a few minutes it began to slowly move eastwards, travelling approximately fifty feet above the ground, and was then seen to cross Furze Lane and head out to sea. **(Source: WATSUP [The Wessex Association for the Study of Unexplained Phenomena], Peter A. Hill & Nicholas Maloret)**

The Wessex Assn. for the study of Unexplained Phenomena - (WATSUP)

Another source of assistance with regard to reported UFO activity was Nick Maloret, born in Portsmouth, Hampshire, who has worked in various forms of printing and is a published artist, having illustrated several books and submission of artwork for many small press

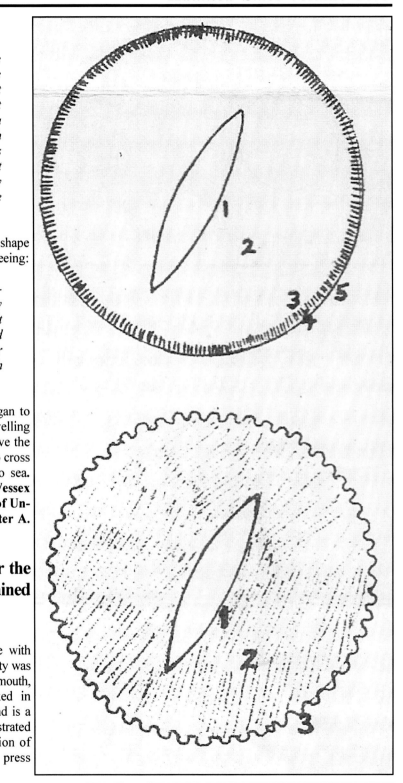

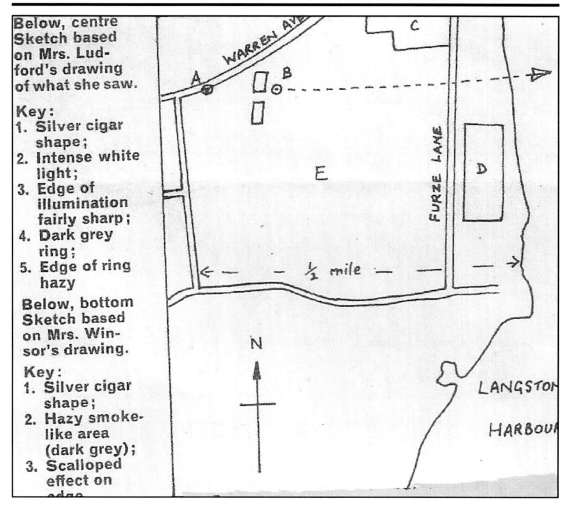

Below, centre Sketch based on Mrs. Ludford's drawing of what she saw.

Key:
1. Silver cigar shape;
2. Intense white light;
3. Edge of illumination fairly sharp;
4. Dark grey ring;
5. Edge of ring hazy

Below, bottom Sketch based on Mrs. Winsor's drawing.

Key:
1. Silver cigar shape;
2. Hazy smoke-like area (dark grey);
3. Scalloped effect on edge

publications. He described how he got involved with the subject:

> *"My enthusiasm was initially fired by the discovery of* Flying Saucer Review *Magazine in the late 1960s, and this great Journal became my mentor, until I eventually took an active role in investigating UFOs in the early 70s. Following an application to join BUFORA, in 1973, I decided to join a local group, which had just been formed in Southampton, by Peter Hill - District Medical Records Officer for Southampton and SW Hampshire.*
>
> *Soon after introducing myself to Malcolm and Brenda Handley - the Chairman and secretary of the Portsmouth branch of the group - I was allocated the task of Journal Editor. Although initially reluctant, it was a role that I came to relish and I ended up editing nine issues and printing them myself. During this time I discovered* Fortean Times, *and sent them many news clippings about local news of interest to them, sometimes following it up with my own investigation.*

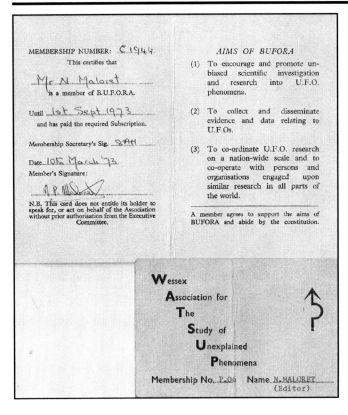

I produced an article for them about big cat sightings on Hayling Island, entitled Swamp Cat Fever, *and sent Jon Downes, of the CFZ journal* Animals & Men - *an article describing my investigation into a report of frog or toad fall, which occurred in Portsmouth, in 1954. Apart from that, now being retired, I enjoy the* Fortean Times, *science fiction, fossil hunting, photography, rambling and natural history."*

Silver 'Rods' over Hampshire

At 7.00am on 31st March 1973, Elizabeth Thomas - a midwife sister from Fareham, in Hampshire - was looking out of her bedroom window, when she saw:

> *"...two bright silver 'rods' hanging vertically in the sky, at an elevation of 45° to the east, towards the direction of Portsdown Hill. Both objects were 'cloud like', with a fuzzy outline, and remained stationary for about two minutes, before slowly descending. As they came lower their shape distorted, becoming indistinct and finally disappearing."*

UFO over Cheltenham

We contacted Jenny Scanlon, from Cheltenham, after learning of what she sighted over the town, in 1973, when aged 11, walking to school near the Bafford Industrial Estate, (well-known to the author, John Hanson, who served his apprenticeship as a trainee Chef, at the *Moorend Park Hotel*, during the early 1960s). She told us:

> *"I was with a group of friends when we saw this jet black object, with a flat bottom and semicircular dome, above what I believe was the plastics factory. We watched, as it silently rose upwards into the sky, before disappearing out of sight, behind some buildings. We were scared stiff."* **(Source: *Cheltenham Independent*, 28.9.95)**

On 15th April 1973, a couple from Lincoln were motoring from Lincoln to Caister, on a day out, and decided to stop for a picnic lunch, at 4.00pm., in the gateway of a field overlooking the A46, from Caister to Nettleton, on the Kirton Lindsey ridge - 400ft in height above the Brigg Valley.

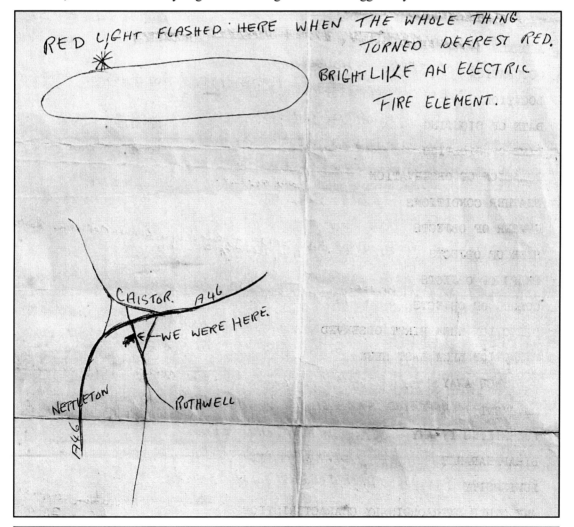

While they were enjoying their meal, they noticed a silver cigar-shaped light in the sky, about 10-15miles away, with a flashing red light on its top left-hand side.

> *"It then changed to pink, then deeper pink and bright red - like an electric fire element - before advancing forward, where it stopped and hovered in the sky, glowing at one end, with a light silver, or grey, colour sheen. After four minutes, it suddenly vanished."* **(Source: Richard Thompson)**

On 24th April 1973, classical musician - Joy Roughton of the *Punch Bowl Hotel*, Low Row, Reeth, in the Yorkshire Dales, near Halifax - heard a mysterious whirring noise outside her bedroom, followedby a vivid red glow that lit up the bedroom. The next morning, she went outside and discovered triangular scorch marks in the garden grass. The matter was reported to the Police, who then contacted BUFORA Investigator man and wife team - Trevor and Doreen Whittaker - from Halifax. In a an interview, later conducted with a reporter from the *Evening Post,* who published details of the incident in their edition of the 10th July 1973, Trevor had this to say:

> *"We spoke to the lady and took measurements and samples of the burnt grass, which was sent to the research centre at the Newchapel Observatory, in Staffordshire. I then contacted the Northern HQ of the Army. They said the red glow was caused by a Very cartridge, discharged in connection with military training. As for the grass the result was burning, caused by pollution from an engine. These two explanations have satisfied us that it was not a UFO."*

Mr. Whittaker disclosed that, during 1967, the organisation had received 40 sightings of UFOs. The average, per year, is between 10 and 12. This leaves one per cent which cannot be explained - statistics that leave us more than a little mystified. **(Source*: Evening Post,* 10.7.1973 - 'A Whirr, a red glow and scorched grass')**

On 30th April 1973, a motorist driving through Slough sighted a dark rugby ball-shaped object with flames coming from the rear pass through the sky. Apparently she wasn't the only one. It is said a number of other motorists stopped to watch the object move over. **(Source: Kevin Hack)**

RAF pilots sight UFO

We spoke to ex-RAF Pilot, Jeremy Lane, who had served with 85 Squadron, flying Canberras, from West Raynham, having logged a total of 1,400 hours flying time, with two tours in Germany. He was on a night-time sortie from RAF Leuchars, together with other aircraft, on 2nd May 1973, flying north, to test the northern Radar Defences.

After reaching an altitude of about 38,000ft, they noticed a strange sight ahead and above, completely stationary in the sky, resembling a Concorde aircraft in shape, with lights flashing around its perimeter, orientated in a North-South direction.

> *"I reported the sighting to the Radar Controller, who confirmed nothing*

was showing on Radar, but he had received other reports from earlier aircraft of a similar object. All of the crew on my flight deck could clearly see the vehicle. As we continued North, I climbed the aircraft with a view to being some 10,000ft higher on the southbound leg, which would give us an idea of whether the vehicle was close, or far away, and its apparent size, depending on how close it was to us. As we came south, the vehicle was still there. I again contacted the Radar operator, who confirmed fighters had been scrambled to intercept, although the Radar had still not picked it up. The lights were still flashing and the orientation of the vehicle was still North-South, but the apparent size of the vehicle remained as it had been, suggesting it was at very high altitude. It was an incredibly clear night and from 46,000+ feet, we could see well into Northern Europe. At some point, as we approached the 'vehicle' from underneath, it became brilliant light and accelerated to the South at an incredible speed; within one to two seconds it had disappeared from view, travelling 500 to 800 miles."

When they landed back at Base, all the crews independently drew what they had seen. A report was submitted to Group Operations, as they understood there was no official channel for submitting reports of such nature, and that was the last they heard. On a subsequent visit to RAF Kinloss, on 25th June in the same year, Jeremy was discussing the incident with a friend of his - then flying Nimrods - when he was told: *"This was a frequent visitor and often sighted by the Pilots."*

Soldiers sight UFO

In May or June 1973, Lance Corporal Mike Perrin, and his colleague - Trooper Carvell, from Catterick Army Camp - were taking part in a regular exercise on Bellerby Moor, at 11.00pm - a lonely and desolate spot on the edge of the Yorkshire Moors - when the radio fitted to their Land Rover failed, followed by the headlights fading and then extinguishing completely.

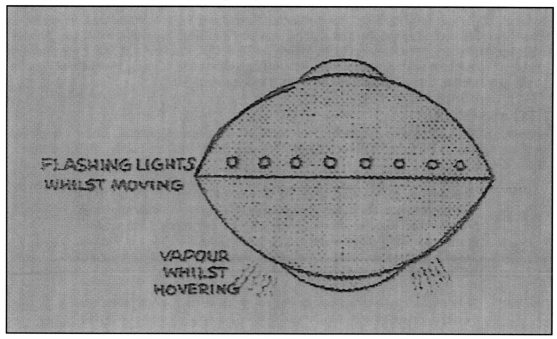

After attempting to remedy the problem they decided to wait, hoping the fault would correct itself, when Mike noticed something approaching in the sky, silently, about a half a mile away. In an interview conducted with Barry King (left), he said:

"It stopped at a distance of, maybe, 100 metres, hovering some ten feet above the ground. It was shaped like a rugby ball, with a row of small circular windows around its middle section. Through these windows shone white lights, which seemed to flash. There was also some form of vapour issuing from the lowest part of the object, together with a slight buzzing sound emanating from it. After it left, the radio and lights came back on."

After arriving back at their base, they reported the matter to their Superior Officer, and were promptly arrested and charged with being drunk and leaving war department property unattended!

The following afternoon, the two men decided to revisit the scene of the encounter and discovered a burnt circle of grass, with a diameter of 30ft. on the other side of some woods.

Mr. Perrin notified his Commanding Officer of the situation and suggested the MOD be informed. He was told it was of no interest to them, although he believes the incident was later secretly investigated. When he asked if he could check with nearby radar and military installations for any information on the UFO that he and his partner had seen, they were refused permission to do so. **(Source: as above/Jenny Randles, UFOIN report/*FSR*, Vol. 28, No. 4, 1978)**

UFO over Northumberland

On 15th May 1973, a number or reports were made by the public, to the authorities, after a silvery disc-shaped object was seen in the night sky, over the Northumberland area. Pupils at Whickham Comprehensive School also took some photographs. The sighting was later explained away as a mock sun. Another suggestion that it was a rocket, launched by the Military, at South Uist, was dismissed, after it was disclosed the rocket had not been fired until some hours later that day. Others told of seeing two 'balls of light' in the sky over Peterlee. One thing is assured we doubt it was any mock sun!

UFO over Wales

In summer of 1973, Jill (known personally to the Authors) - a resident of Redditch, formerly employed by Victim Support at the local Magistrates Court - was on a family camping holiday, in Broad Haven, Pembrokeshire.

"After arriving at the Council-run site, we pitched our tents at the top of the field backing onto woodland, noting, apart from ourselves, there were only two other tents near the main entrance. After retiring to bed, I was suddenly awoken by a loud droning, humming noise coming from above our tent. Puzzled, I tried to reason what could be making this noise, knowing that the noise was unlike any aircraft, or helicopter, I had ever heard before.

Wide awake by now, I sat up, feeling rather concerned, as the noise was beginning to increase in vibration, although the canvas on the tent remained perfectly still, without showing any signs of increased pressure as one might have expected. The only way I can describe the noise is that it sounded like the 'whoosh, whoosh' of some sort of blade. I tried to wake up my husband, but for some reason I couldn't get him to wake up.

I tried whispering to my daughter, who was sleeping in a separate compartment - there was no response. I could now feel the sweat breaking out on my forehead and tried to move my legs to get up, but it was as if they were paralysed. All I could do was lie quiet and hope this dreadful noise would stop.

Suddenly, to my relief, the noise stopped.... all was quiet, apart from my husband's snoring. Eventually I fell asleep."

The next morning, feeling quite exhausted by what had happened and frightened by the experience, Jill told her daughter and husband what she had heard. They laughed at her, suggesting she must have been dreaming. Jill began to get very upset with their attitude, until they unzipped the tent and went outside, where she saw her son emerging from his tent. He asked her, *"Mum, did you hear the UFO overhead in the night?"* following which her husband apologised to her, unable to understand why he had slept through it all.

"To this day, I still cannot answer why I just didn't get up and go outside to see what it was, although at the time my legs felt paralysed. Why didn't I go outside after the noise had ceased?"

Little did they suspect that in four years time, the Broad Haven area was to be the subject of worldwide interest!

UFO over Birmingham

Tony Caldicott – ex member of the Birmingham Group, UFOSIS, during the 1970s, was fishing by the side of the canal, at Parsons Hill, Kings Norton, Birmingham, during Summer 1973.

"It was a clear day. I was occupied with fishing, when a small boat - a cruiser - came towards me, heading towards Birmingham. The man piloting it moored by the side of the canal and got out. He came over to me and said, 'Have you ever seen anything like that before?'

I looked up and saw this object in the sky, quite low. I was flabbergasted to see what looked like an 'Adamski-type UFO', silver, with three globes set into its underside, just hovering silently in the sky. Suddenly, it flew away and was soon lost from sight." **(Source: personal interview)**

At 6.20pm on June 21st 1973, the figure of a hooded monk was seen by three girls, standing close to the entrance gate leading into Coulsdon Common, Surrey, followed by the sighting of a small 'craft' seen hovering over the same locality, a few hours later, which rose up into the air and pursued the girls along the road, before 'flipping over in flight' and disappearing. **(Source: Margaret Fry, Welsh Federation of Ufologists)**

At 11.50pm on June 22nd 1973, Derek Dempster - a former RAF flying instructor (known to the authors personally) who was the first editor of *Flying Saucer Review* - was looking up at the night sky, while waiting for the family Labrador dog, 'Fiddle', at the family home in Kent. He told us:

> *"Apart from a single airliner heading south, there was no other aircraft activity. Suddenly I noticed a pin point of light travelling eastwards. I first thought it was an aircraft, but then realised it wasn't showing any anti collision or navigation lights.*

> *As the light passed overhead it brightened and took on the shape of a star' you would put on a Christmas tree, before fading into a pinpoint of light. The pace of the object reminded me of an Echo 1 satellite I had seen in the 1960s, with two subtle differences; firstly, reflections of the sun should only last for a few seconds this UFO was visible throughout its trajectory.*

> *Secondly, the object did not maintain a steady dead true course but appeared to snake, its oscillations being so small but this may have been an illusion. The object appeared east of Regulus and, disappeared from view south of Procyon - this was no satellite!"* **(Source: personal interview/2011 *FSR*, Volume 19, No. 5, Sep/Oct. 1972)**

Mystery Lights over Warminster

Richard Colborne, whom we had the pleasure of meeting and discussing some of the cases he had been involved with, told of a visit to Warminster, in June 1973, after having been told of a number of sightings of mysterious lights seen in the sky over the southern part of England. On his visit to Warminster, Richard met up with Neil Pike, who is well-known to us. Neil has provided to us, over the years, an overview of not only the UFO sightings themselves, but of the people that gathered on the slopes of Cradle Hill nightly, to watch the heavens, hoping to see a UFO, or as Arthur Shutlewood would have said, *"a glimpse of the 'thing' in all its glory!"*

> *"I was flabbergasted to see a succession of satellite-like lights, heading east to west, across the sky. This took place each night over the course of a few weeks, before it stopped. What I found curious was that Neil was able to predict the appearance of the lights to within less than a minute, which he demonstrated to my own satisfaction.*

> *There were, at the time of the sightings, numerous suggestions that these lights were Skylab, but many who saw them have reservations about this.*

> *These lights followed each other with such regularity i.e. five minute intervals, that it would seem unlikely that they were mere debris. After watching these lights during the course of an evening, it became clear*

that whilst most followed the same trajectory, some were above and some below a very high layer of 'herring-bone' cloud, as some were obscured by certain pieces of cloud that did not conceal others.

What finally convinced me that these were not orbiting objects was when I saw one execute a slow turn and depart over the southern horizon."

In December 2011, we spoke to Neil about the source of his prediction, after dismissing the suggestion of any psychic powers! He told us that, although he would have to check his records for that period, he believed the lights may well have been a spy satellite sent up by the USA, rather than the perambulations of any UFO. (Neil remembered Richard very well and had been an invited guest at his wedding)

THE WARMINSTER SCENE DURING THE 1970S

I had been fascinated by the subject of Ufology for a long time, since having my 'sighting' in the late fifties of a low, circular, and glowing deep red thing in the sky that had a central 'dark' circular area and what appeared to be sections radiating from it. So, it was a natural progression for me to visit Warminster at a time when similar objects were being reported by local people. I had been editing my own newsletter for CUFORG (Coventry UFO Research Group), which then morphed into *Syntonic* magazine. Contributors to that periodical included researchers and visitors to Warminster. I had also completed a book that I was attempting to get published. I wanted Arthur Shuttlewood to give me his opinion on it before I sent it off to the publishers. So I took it down to Warminster and passed it to him, one night, on Cradle Hill. As I remember he was a softly spoken gentleman, with one of those 'craggy' faces that reflected years of journalistic experience. There was an air of depth and intrigue when he told me of some of his encounters on the hills around his home.

The book, which I naively titled *The Flying Saucer Revelation*, was never published, although there were offers by one publisher, in North Devon. I made several trips down to the slopes in Wiltshire, travelling by Black & White coach, as I didn't drive at the time. I always sensed a magetism and magical atmosphere to the place. I have fond memories of staying at the *Farmer Giles* guest house, but mostly of my times 'kipping' on the floorboards, along with many other researchers, at Maureen Butler's flat in the town centre. Maureen was a local nurse, who was interested in the mysterious happenings around Warminster.

I met lots of like-minded people during those visits, and especially recall a visit to Heaven's Gate, at Longleat, with Mike Oram. There had been a sighting in that area, as I remember. A chap called Chris Trubridge from Bath (or was it Bristol) told compelling tales of secret testing going on around Warminster of a device ominously called the 'Infra-Sound Generator', which was apparently capable of shattering whole structures, at a great distance, with low frequency sound waves – could this experimentation be at least partially responsible for some of the 'rattling' roofs reported at the time, or the cause of mice and birds being found 'riddled' with tiny holes? One can only wonder. These questions fuelled my continued interest in the subject and the area.

I remember fleeting glimpses of orange oval shapes above the army barracks in the valley below Cradle Hill, the spooky walks in the pitch black, the deep tank tracks which I navigated by foot in the dark on the 'range', and the moments of wonder, laughter, and goodwill shared by all . . . and wondering why most of us were standing in the cold air, with necks aching from craning at the sky, while members of BUFORA were sitting snuggly in their 'official' van, at the bottom of the field!

There were tales of a tall entity that was seen in the copse atop Cradle Hill... they say it had glowing, red eyes. There were tales of footsteps of an unseen 'something' that scared courting couples, and - of course - there was the 'thing' that hovered over the golf course clubhouse.

Of course, this was many moons ago now, but I am still deeply fascinated with the mystery of strange sights in the sky and all the many related phenomena that seem to be woven into the fabric of life by the same hand. I don't think, however, we are any closer to a comprehensive solution to the mystery of what had been occurring around Warminster. Perhaps this volume offers - at least - *some* insight into it though! **Bob Tibbitts**

CARTERTON
OXON.
4/4/77

(20)

Dear Sir/Madam
                You asked for
anyone who had seen a U.F.O to
write in.
                Four years ago
near Lee-on-Solent, Hants. I spotted
what I thought was a very bright
star. As I watched, it moved
towards me at a terrific rate of
speed. and hovered above me
making a deep humming noise.
It stayed for a minute of or
two then moved off as quickly
as it came.
                I have told several
people of this but they think I
am nuts, so I never bothered
reporting it.
                from
                Mrs Linda Ince.

This letter was sent in to the producer of *Friday's People,* an ATV production broadcast during the 1970s, discussing UFOs, presented by Val Lewis, who we met a few years ago. Val showed us a number of letters sent in by members of the public, including a sighting by the driver of a tram, who told of seeing a re d light appear in front of him.

The letter sent in by Linda Ince is typical of the way in which many people then (as they still do now) expect to be ridiculed for having the courage to report only what they have seen. Scepticism is a healthy prerequisite to matters such as this, but only after investigation *and not before.*

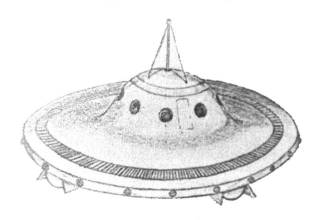

CHAPTER FOUR
JULY - DECEMBER 1973

UFO at Cradle Hill, Warminster

During early July 1973, Bob Boyd - head of the Plymouth-based UFO Group PUFORG - was in the Warminster area, enjoying a week's holiday. The visit had been arranged over a year previously, following conversation with Arthur Shuttlewood, who had suggested he stay at the BUFORA caravan for the princely sum of £4! Bob, a thoroughly likeable man and dedicated researcher of the UFO subject, had this to say:

> *"I must point out that I have never seen a 'Flying Saucer'. I have never seen a UFO that looks like it is a machine that has flown from another place. Nothing I have ever seen looks like a 'spacecraft'. It wasn't until I started studying the literature, after I got married, that I realised some of the early things I had seen were, in fact, UFOs - not Mars, satellites, or very fast boats, (that's another sighting)"*

Bob believes that there is a mystical significance to life and that we are given 'clues' (some more than others) as to the existence and reality of 'the other side of life'. He looks upon these signs as mystic 'prods', which draw attention to an alterative reality, and that we have the free will to pursue or ignore these 'prods' that can come in a variety of ways, including good fortune, psychic capabilities, coincidences, visions, prodigious gifts, or the ability to recognise the gifts of others, ghosts, mysterious events, miracles of nature, UFO sightings, religious miracles, etc. Bob said:

> *"I read a very old book, called* Hindu Thought, *and came across a passage, 'God appears close to them that wish to know Him, yet far away from those that do not wish to have knowledge of Him This is a profoundly true statement and I think should be considered by all involved in UFO thinking; even if it is thought to be just another religious platitude it won't hurt anyone, as an experiment to put it to the test. As an eliminatory exercise it seriously poses the question, if UFOs have anything to do with God, can I please have a sign of this?"*

During his stay, Bob found time to visit Avebury and Glastonbury, but spent most of his time on Cradle

Hill, 'sky watching' with local UFO enthusiast Ken Rogers, and had a number of minor sightings of UFOs. On the morning of the 7th July 1973, Bob made his way up Cradle Hill for the final time, before making his way to the railway station, where he telephoned the wife of his colleague, Ivan, who had originally dropped him off at Warminster a week ago, wondering if Ivan was going to pick him up for the return journey. Much to his surprise, Ivan arrived and Bob suggested they go and have something to eat at the 'BUFORA caravan' and then have a look at Cradle Hill, as Ivan had not been there himself.

> *"It was then that I had a strong feeling we should visit the hill. This strong intuitive feeling increased - something I have not always followed up, but when I do they invariably turn out to be correct, although I would not say I am psychic."*

As the two men pulled up at the bottom of Cradle Hill, at 3.00pm, they immediately saw, in the far distance, over Salisbury Plain, an upright, white cigar-shape, and became excited - until they realised it was a glider banking, which was followed by others. As they sat there laughing about this, Bob saw:

> *"...a bright white oblong emerge from behind the second copse, and very slowly float towards the top of Cradle Hill. I waited, expecting to see an aeroplane, but realised it was too close to be this and not show more detail. I jumped out of the car and saw that the object was now midway between the two copses that line the top of Cradle Hill, and took a photograph with my Zenith 3 M manual camera, using setting as suggested on the film.*

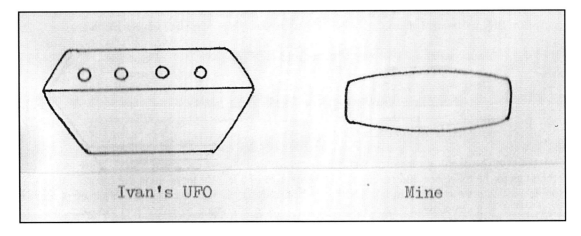

> *By this time Ivan, who had been looking at the gliders, jumped out. He was amazed and said he could see the object spinning, with windows on it. He told me to take a photo, but I told him I had already taken it. The object then went behind the copse at the top of Cradle Hill and out of sight. We then jumped the gate and ran up the hill. Halfway up, we saw a tractor approaching Ivan's car, so he had to turn back, thinking he may have been causing an obstruction. I continued up to the top and spoke to a young couple; they told me they hadn't seen anything. At this stage Ivan joined me. We looked up into the sky and a couple of black dots (similar to the ones we had seen earlier in the week, and failed to photograph) and I took another photograph.*

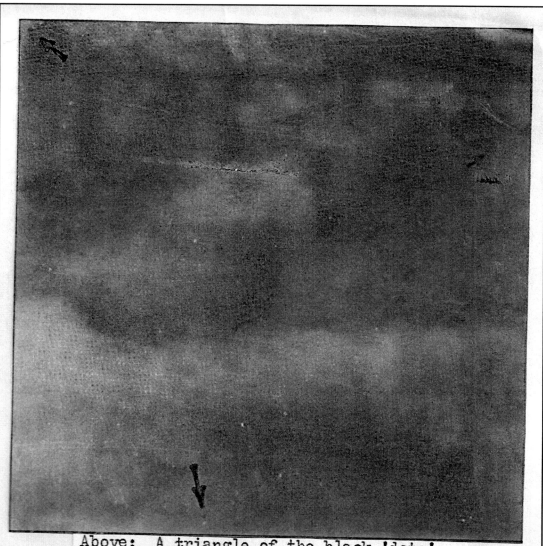

Above: A triangle of the black 'dots'
photographed over Cradle Hill. Below: An
object, resembling a barn or something,
that was not seen at the time.

In the distance we could see an airborne black triangle approaching, and wondered if it could have been a Vulcan Bomber, and took a couple of photographs, although it was still too far away to identify."

Incredibly, during their journey back to Tyneside - a distance of some 300 miles - a number of UFOs were sighted. They included *'black dot things', 'lights' , 'star like objects'* and a *'magnesium like object that left a trail behind, with sparks emanating from either side',* when approaching nearer home. **(Source: *My Warminster UFOs*, Bob Boyd/*Probe*, Ian Myzglod/Peter Tate)**

UFOs over North Cornwall

On the 8th July 1973, UFO researcher Tim Good received a telephone call from his mother - then living at Porthcothan Bay, North Cornwall, who told her son about something strange she and another witness had sighted the previous evening, at 10.05pm. Following further conversation, Tim was able to obtain the following account from his mother:

"I went to draw the curtains; there was a lovely sky of banded colours and some clouds. To my utter amazement I saw three stationary objects

in the sky over the sea. One was a perfectly symmetrical disc apparently reflecting the last of the evening sky, on each side of which was an extremely black object, roughly like a cigar in shape, but of indefinite outline (like a black, furry caterpillar); that on the right being larger than the one on the left.

While watching this phenomenon to transfixed to alert my friends - one of them joined me to see why I was still at the window. After a few minutes the disc entered or went behind the object on the left, and the two sped off at fantastic speed, out to se. I had my eyes on it as one follows the path of a golf ball, until I could see it no longer. After a few more moments the object on the right also shot away at the same speed, in the same horizontal position, and on the same trajectory leaving absolutely no trace of smoke."

Following the matter being brought to his attention, Tim wrote to RAF St. Mawgan, explaining what had taken place, wondering if his mother had seen an example of some rare type of temperature inversion, and asking them if any anomalous ground or airborne radar returns had been brought to their notice. He received a letter in reply, signed by the Flt. Lt. on behalf of the Commanding Officer at the Base:

"Our check of the various operational and radar records revealed nothing out of the ordinary during the period in question. However, our senior Meteorological Officer states that the Duty Officer, on the evening of Saturday, July 7, did observe bright mock suns and halo phenomena, which as you will know, are produced by refraction of light through ice crystals, which are present in cirrus clouds. The alert observer noted, in the daily register, the following technical remarks:

Two bright mock suns, partial 22° halo, part parhelic circle from both mock suns, upper circumzenithal arc of contact to 22° halo; Further mock suns to left of primary and 120° from it on parhelic circle.

The Senior Meteorological Officer was unable to comment on the flight path comments, or the alleged disappearance into the distance at a phenomenal speed. It is, however, in little doubt that what your mother saw was the vivid mock suns. It is hoped that this information will be of some assistance to you in dispelling your mother's apprehension."

According to Tim, his mother was highly dissatisfied with the explanation proffered - an explanation, by the way, which was later dismissed when Tim established that the Duty Officer had witnessed the appearance of the mock suns one to two hours previous to his mother's sighting.

This was not the only time we were to hear of a UFO sighted over this location. On the 23rd July 2009, a couple, out camping, were looking up at the stars, at 2.00am, when they saw:

"...around 20 glowing white lights that moved up and down and faded, then glowed brighter. They appeared to be in a line, with a triangular formation at the front and curving up at the back, and stayed there for several hours. On the way back from the toilet we saw a much closer light, hovering near the

*lighthouse. It was an orangey light, rectangular in shape. It then dropped silently down, out of sight to the beach."***(Source: *FSR*, Volume 21, No. 2, 1975,**

Timothy Good - *Strange Phenomenon at Porthcothan Bay*)

On 9th July 1973, an oval object, with flickering lights and slightly raised middle section, showing a bank of red lights, was seen crossing the sky, over Weston Park, Leicestershire. (**Source:** *Leicester Mercury* **9.7.73**)

Factory worker - Mr. M. Barker - was taking a tea break with a number of other men, at 3.00am on the 26th July 1973. As they looked into the night sky, hoping to catch a glimpse of the American Skylab satellite as it passed over Westwood, in Kent, they were surprised to see:

> *"...four glowing orange 'cigars' which appeared in the sky, one behind the other"*

They watched them move slowly towards the direction of Cliftonville; seconds later, they were gone from view. Mr. Barker contacted RAF Manston, but they were unable to offer any explanation for what the men had seen, and promised to forward a report on to the MOD. About a fortnight later, the MOD sent Mr. Barker a letter, explaining that the objects may have been,

MINISTRY OF DEFENCE
Main Building Whitehall London SW1A 2HB

Telephone 01-930 7022 ext 7035

G N Pike Esq
"Poco"
14 St Johns Road
WARMINSTER
Wilts

Please reply to Ministry of Defence
Your reference

Our reference AF/7464/72/Pt II/S4
(Ai

Date 26 July 1973

Dear Mr Pike

Thank you for your further letter dated 19 July 1973.

If you wish to report a UFO sighting, the branch involved is ourselves (S4f(Air), at the address given above). We co-ordinate all
action taken to investigate reports of UFOs and deal with correspondence on the subject with members of the public.

We are pleased to receive first-hand reports provided they are
forwarded soon after the sighting has occurred and give a reasonable
amount of detail. The most essential information in any observation
is probably:

> Time and date of sighting
> Exact location of observer
> Azimuth bearing or direction of sighting
> Approximate angle of elevation
> Some description of what was seen.

I would like to emphasise that all reports received within the
Ministry of Defence and RAF Commands are examined solely to see if
there are any defence implications connected with the sighting in
question. We cannot, therefore, undertake to pursue our research,
other than for defence implications, to a point where positive correlation with a known object is established, nor do we advise observers
of the probable identity of the object seen. I should add that since
the Ministry of Defence interest in the subject is limited to defence
aspects, a study of the scientific implications of UFOs has not been
carried out.

Yours faithfully

MISS G J JAMIESON

"...a sun shadow, cloud formations, reflections, or possibly, space-junk"
...neither of which was accepted by Mr. Barker as being an explanation for what he and the others had seen. (**Source:** *Kentish Times, 29.7.73*)

During the same period Mr. Pike, a resident of Warminster, wrote to the MOD, asking them about the reporting structure with regard to sightings of UFOs, and received the following answer:

Close Encounter, Scotland
Margaret and Christine had just left Lochore Country Park, Scotland, at 9.00pm in August 1973, following a visit, and were travelling in the rear of the vehicle as it pulled-up to a junction where the green ended and a housing estate began.

A car drew up quietly behind them, at which point the radio went dead and the car engine cut out. As if drawn by a magnet, Christine and Margaret looked to their left, across an area of open ground, and saw, heading towards them:

> *"...two veritable giants, moving in a rather mechanical manner - like machines, rather than living beings - wearing one-piece silver suits, emphasising their over large heads."*

Christine cannot be sure how long it took the entities to cover the space that separated them, but she does have a vivid memory of the strange beings getting closer and closer to the car, and the car simply refusing to start. When the two beings were almost up to the window, within yards of where Christine sat frozen and unable to move, she experienced a choking sensation and, it seems, passed out.

What happened next is a mystery. When Christine came to, she saw the backs of the two giants as they returned in the direction they had come from.

Moments later after they disappeared from view, a cone of light spread around the trees at the edge of the field, as if marking the path of an object, heading skywards. At this precise moment, the car engine roared into life, as did the radio, and the driver of the vehicle behind them rushed up and shouted:

"What the bloody hell was that?"

When Christine arrived home, she noticed a considerable time lapse. **(Source: Ron Halliday)**

KAREN (left) and Fiona . . . " We were frightened "

THE TALL VISITOR

A GANG of boys rushed past schoolgirls Fiona Morrison and Karen McLennan. They shouted: " A flying saucer's just landed."

The boys pointed to a wood opposite the building site where the two girls were playing.

Just at that moment, Karen's mother, Mrs Caroline McLennan, was in the front garden of her home in Elgin, north-east Scotland, when she heard a loud, whirring noise.

Her next-door neighbour joked: "Sounds like a flying saucer."

Fiona and Karen found the boys were right. Terrified, they stared across at a mysterious object hovering in the wood.

Fiona, 10, says: " It was like a silver-coloured saucer, with a bump on top. It flashed with a reddish-orange light.

" It looked just like something out of Dr Who."

Karen, who is also 10, says: "There seemed to be someone standing beside it. He was tall and wore a silver suit."

"The figure disappeared when the saucer shot off into the sky. We were frightened. But when the saucer took off, it was as if it had been a dream.

" I forgot about it until the next morning, when I told my mum."

Mrs McLennan said: " I remembered the whirring I'd heard. It was such a weird noise.

" A patch of grass in the wood had been flattened as if something had landed on it. The tree beside it had dry, scorched leaves."

At 11.15pm on 5th August 1973, a number of people on the cliff top at Portloe, Cornwall, heard the sound of rushing wind, followed by the appearance of:

> *"...a rotating round, slightly glowing, object, which appeared over the cliff top."*

It then passed silently overhead, before disappearing over another cliff top.

Was there any connection with the now famous sighting that took place over the cliff tops of Moign Downs, in Dorset (see Volume 3) by Angus Brooks in 1967? **(Source: *BUFORA Journal*, Volume 6, No. 3, Sept/Oct. 1977)**

Close Encounter, Northampton

In December 2006, we spoke to Diane and Peter Shepherd from St. James, Northampton - head of the Northamptonshire UFO Forum - about what they witnessed, during the late evening of the 8th August 1973.

Peter later said:

> *"We were just leaving a friend's house, at 3.00am, when we saw this saucer-shaped object, the size of a football pitch, resting on the ground in a nearby field. I was stunned and climbed onto the roof of the car to get a closer look. It was dark grey in colour, showing a perfectly smooth exterior, with seven rectangular amber coloured windows, or lights, facing us. It*

was beautiful to behold, and was as solid and real as the car I was standing on. The object was accompanied by a number or red spheres, which hovered over nearby trees and the road.

I decided to approach closer, so got into the car and drove a few hundred yards towards the object, believing I would be in a good position to see more of the object as it passed overhead. Suddenly, one of the red spheres appeared in front of us. The next thing I remember was driving down the road, about 300yds away, with the dawn now coming up. When we looked at out watches, we realised we couldn't account for forty minutes of lost time."

During conversation with the couple, interjected by Diane's irrepressible bubbly laugh and sense of humour, we were told they had received a visit from the BBC, who interviewed them for a documentary, *but suggested the incident hadn't happened*! Sadly, Diane - an authority on the UFO subject - was to later pass away from cancer. Her bubbly laughter and adorable sense of humour is sadly missed.

In autumn of the same year, former mechanic Richard Smith of Piccadilly Road, Swinton, Manchester, was walking along Greasbrough Road, accompanied by his brother, David, on Carr House Hill, at about midnight, when they saw:

"...An object, about the size of two single deck buses, hovering by the side of an electricity pylon. It was showing a row of green lights, or windows, along its dullish outline. It never moved or made any noise in the time we watched it. We both felt it was somehow watching us. It is strange but the more I try and remember, the more puzzling it becomes. I am not claiming that what I saw was an alien spaceship, because I'm sceptical about things of that nature, but I have an open mind. I'm just curious and would like to know what it was." **(Source: Philip Mantle, Yorkshire UFO Society)**

UFO over Cheshire

At midnight on 18th August 1973, two teenage girls - Patricia McDermott and Sharon McManus, from Ellesmere Port, Merseyside - were walking home along Sutton Way, when they noticed an object fly across the sky, flashing red and orange lights. At first they took it to be an aircraft, but were astounded to see a dome-shaped object passing overhead. They stood rooted to the spot in terror.

As soon as it had gone out of view, they ran home in panic. Mrs. Mary McDermott confirmed that they were very scared and *'as white as a sheet'*. When they contacted the Police, they were asked if they had been drinking! Other explanations offered to them was that they had seen the American Skylab - hardly likely, bearing in mind the girls told of having seen the object, which appeared to be 10ft across, flying close to the rooftops. **(Source: *Ellesmere Port News*, 22.8.73)**

Encounter with Ghost, Portsmouth

Stanley Pitt, from Portsmouth, had occasion to contact Nick Maloret of the Portsmouth-based UFO group (WATSUP) with regard to a UFO sighted by him and his brother in 1974.

Whether there are certain people that are more susceptible to sighting strange phenomena than others is, of course, open to speculation. Another reason could be the locality where Stanley Pitt lived, understanding the close proximity to what has been regarded as the most haunted house in the UK nearby Wymering Manor .

The eerie Grade II* listed building in Portsmouth is featured in the 1086 Domesday Book and was once home to Edward the Confessor. Its current structure dates back to the 16th century when it was used as a vicarage and monastery. The building still has two 'priest holes' where Catholics hid to escape persecution.

Paranormal Investigators claim to have sensed the presence of between 20 to 30 spirits in the home, including those of children laughing and whispering. The building has gained a reputation among ghost hunters for high levels of paranormal activity, including sudden drops in temperature and strange apparitions.

3

Bearer
Tittulaire

HAROLD TAN

"At about 10.30pm, I was walking near a cemetery, opposite the Church, at the southern end of Old Wymering Lane, when we saw what I thought was a drunk leaning on the cemetery wall. Moving closer to the figure, we felt unaccountably cold and then noticed the man was dressed rather oddly. 'It' was wearing what looked like a cape that concealed its arms, which were secured at the neck with a length of cord, tied in a bow. The 'man' had, on his head, a tall hat with wide brim, similar to the type worn by the puritans, for the Stuart period. The face was dark and indistinct with no features present. Despite this, I had an impression that the 'man' was smiling at me. At this point I was about 10ft away from him. Below the level of his cape trousers were visible, which appeared to be tucked into shiny boots. I stood rooted to the spot, for a number of minutes, feeling almost hypnotised. Suddenly the figure began to fade away, until it disappeared completely. Frightened, I ran home."

According to Nick Maloret, who investigated this matter, Stanley told him he had seen the 'ghost' on other occasions, at the same time and place, for about a week afterwards. Nick was to discover that another UFO sighting had taken place in Old Wymering Lane, during the 1950s, involving Portsmouth resident - Mr. Harold Tamplin.

Close Encounters at RAF Alconbury

Marc Uptergrove contacted us by email, from Los Angeles, in 2005, enquiring whether we had any knowledge of strange happenings, which included ghostly children's voices and the appearance of a bizarre 'leaping man' - which was apparently witnessed by a number of servicemen at RAF Alconbury, Huntingdonshire - a curiosity triggered by conversations held with his father, Wesley, who served at the Airbase in the early 1970s.

We knew of no such incidents, other than previous UFO sightings that had taken place at Sawtrey and Godmanchester, and spoke to Wesley:

"On the third day of duty, at RAF Alconbury, I was instructed to take over the night G shift for a member of the Security patrol, who had gone sick. This involved keeping watch over the Airbase from a 25ft concrete tower - one of six, that lined the inside of a corridor encircling the perimeter of the Airbase. After being transported to the site, I climbed up the ladder and settled down for the night. As night descended I stood there, unable to even see the next tower, due to the dark and foggy conditions. I became aware of an area of clearing that stretched out from the fence bordering a dense forest, which I found, for some strange reason, very unsettling, although I cannot identify why I felt like this. At about 6.00am, I was sat on the floor inside the tower, reading a book by flashlight, when suddenly, I heard the unmistakable sound of happy children's voices, rising and falling, as if borne on the wind, rather than a fixed source. Puzzled, I went out onto the 'cat walk' and peered into the darkness, feeling perplexed rather than frightened.

All of a sudden, the voices stopped. I was about to re-enter the tower when, in that split second, the voices were all around me - so close and so

loud, as if I was in a school playground. With my heart racing, I made my way down the ladder to the ground. The voices were just as loud. I felt surrounded ... then they began to fade away, leaving me struck and amazed by what I regarded as a privileged experience."

Wesley paid a visit to the local Library in an attempt to discover the folklore of the area, hoping to find a clue as to what had happened. He was surprised to learn that a number of children had been killed in a train accident that had occurred, close to the Airbase, some years previously, and wonders if the two are connected.

It would appear that the incident to which he refers took place near to Abbots Ripton, when three trains, including the *Flying Scotsman*, collided as a result of signal failure (caused by ice) on 21st January 1876. This resulted in the death of thirteen people, seven of them children, as shown in a sketch on the

THE RAILWAY ACCIDENT AT ABBOTS RIPTON, HUNTINGDON: GENERAL VIEW OF THE SCENE OF THE ACCIDENT.

front page of the *Illustrated News* (29th January 1876).

We were contacted by Roger - another ex-Serviceman, previously at the Airbase - who confirmed ghostly stories were rife, although he had never personally spoken to anybody that had witnessed something for themselves, first-hand, and took them with 'a pinch of salt' - a situation which was to change when a close friend of his witnessed something, or someone so frightening, he refused to discuss the incident with Roger, telling him:

"We were carrying out some routine work to an F-5 Aircraft, parked on the runway - a job that should have been completed in an hour. When he failed to make the telephone call, requesting a lift back from the Hangar, a search went out to find him. They found him sitting in the aircraft, as white as a sheet, with the canopy closed. Although I asked him, many times, what it was that he had seen, he declined, saying that it had frightened him so much he refused to go anywhere near that location again."

We discovered, from another source, that the man had seen a terrifying hairy humanoid, which had walked past the aircraft.

Roger wondered if the talk of ghosts seen near the Hangar, close to the F-5 flight line, could have been connected with an accident taking place during the Second World War, when a number of people were killed after a 500 pound bomb, being loaded onto an aircraft, exploded for no apparent reason.

We received a number of emails from Dennis Prisbrey, who was stationed at RAF Alconbury, between 1973 and 1975. He told us of rumours, widespread at the time, about some of the airmen having sighted a 'creature' near the north side of the Airfield, but attributed it to tall stories. Like Mr. Uptergrove, he was involved in a variety of security tasks. They included Tower Guard, and monitoring an alarm panel covering the main bomb storage area.

Dennis told us:

"The SAS (Special Ammunition Storage Area) was a high security nuclear bomb storage facility, surrounded by a double row of wire fences, with concertina wire coils on top, dating back to the 1950s. Around the perimeter were a number of small elevated guard towers, spaced at intervals, manned by a single guard. In late 1974, a new alarm system was installed, involving the use of motion detectors that would eliminate the need to post guards to these towers. Unfortunately, due to problems and their frequent activation, with no visible cause, it was decided to 'man up' two of the three towers. A friend of mine, Sergeant Baker, Airman First Class, who was working at the Airbase before I arrived, told me in conversation, one day, he had heard the voices of children, whilst working one of the towers, and it was believed these children's voices were the ghosts of children killed in a railway accident near to the Base, at the turn of the Century.

I also heard about an incident involving two mechanics, who were working on an aircraft parked on the North side of the Base, one of whom was so frightened by the appearance of a 'strange hairy creature' that he jumped into the cockpit of the aircraft and refused to get out for some time. I took such stories at face value, purely because I never encountered this 'leaping man', or spoke to any of the witnesses.

My attitude was to change, following a conversation with my two regular partners, Sergeants Randi Lee and Jackson, after learning of their involvement in an incident, which happened prior to my arrival at the Airbase. One night, while on patrol with their two dogs, they saw some movement near the towers and called the Main Gate to check if any workmen were still on site. When told not, they asked for a truck response team to assist with searching the area. As they approached a tower, they came face-to-face with a hairy figure.

The dogs stopped in their tracks, absolutely terrified, frantically trying to get away. One of the handlers urged the dog to attack the intruder, but was bitten by his own animal – that's how frightened the dogs were.

The truck arrived just in time to see the creature, whatever it was, climbing over the security fence, where it was last seen entering North Woods."

Another witness to this event was Wesley Uptergrove. He found himself in a terrifying situation, according to his son, Marc, who described what his father saw.

"He was the NCOIC of a group of three men and their dogs, charged with guarding bunkers, underneath which were stored, I believe, nuclear warheads within a large, fenced area.

One foggy night, my father received a radio call; there was an intruder within the perimeter and shots had been fired. He tore out in his truck and sped towards the location of the shooting. Seeing a figure in the fog, he pulled over, thinking it was one of his guards. He rolled down his window and was screamed at, full in the face, by what can only be described as a man-like, bipedal creature. My father nearly wet himself in fear. In an instant the thing ran off at incredible speed and my father drove after it. Within moments it had sped past another of the guards, who also fired upon it; he missed due to the fact he was practically dragged backwards by his guard dogs that were yelping and straining to flee in the opposite direction.

The third guard and his dogs were running towards the scene when they turned the corner of a bunker, only to be intercepted by the creature running at full speed. As his dogs wailed, the thing hit the taut leashes and pulled them away from his grasp, lacerating a good deal of skin from the unfortunate man's forearm in the process. My father and these men witnessed this creature make fantastic, running bounds across the grounds before leaping over two tall, well-spaced barbed wire fences in a single bound. It disappeared into the surrounding woods.

My father's description of the creature is a little vague, but in his defence he only saw it briefly and, as he puts it, the whole situation was fast, confusing, and difficult to process. 'It was hairy, approximately 5ft 9ins. in height, and had intelligent, human-like eyes, a flat nose, and large ears. The teeth were large but not fanged. The lower face was rounded in a way that suggested the look of a walrus. The face was narrow around the eyes, but the head flared out again at the top. It had very muscular, frog-like thighs, with what appeared to be reversed articulated legs like a horse'. Incredibly, he and his fellow airmen also witnessed a floating apparition on the very same night they encountered the weird 'man'.

We visited the area in 2006, and saw for ourselves the remains of the towers, now demolished, marked by heaps of rubble along the perimeter of the Airbase - still under the control of armed USAF guards. We then made our way to Monks Wood, approximately a couple of miles away, which lies adjacent to where the watch towers were, next to Bevel's Wood (no doubt connected with Sir Robert Beville, Lord of the Manor of Chesterton) and spent time talking to the security guard at the Centre for Ecology and Hydrology (CEH) - the UK's centre of excellence for integrated research in terrestrial and freshwater ecosystems, situated in Monks Wood. We were surprised to hear from him that:

> "...a number of employees had seen monk like figures walking through the corridors. On one occasion, much to the shock of the employee, the figure vanished through a wall."

We examined old maps, hoping to find clues as to the reasons why these manifestations had occurred, and found a tumulus to the west of Monks Wood but nothing in the adjacent woodland, opposite to where the control towers had been situated, apart from discovering the wooded area - now known as Park Farm (closest to the airfield) - was called Long Coppice. Monks Wood had been known as Boulton Hinich Wood, prior to RAF Alconbury being constructed, but we were unable to identify from where the name had originated. Research conducted into the surrounding area revealed some interesting information. We discovered ghostly children's voices had also been reported at Hichingbrook House, Huntingdon, built around an 11th Century Nunnery - a building after the reformation, given to Thomas Cromwell as a reward for overseeing the dissolution of the monasteries, which later became the home

A strikingly similar story comes from Cornwall, about a quarter of a century later. Julia 'Jools' Quinn - now living in Bodmin, Cornwall decided to go out for a drive to Davidstowe Airfield, one evening, with a friend, hoping to see something out of the normal, bearing in mind its 'spooky reputation'. After locating the Davistowe lookout tower, which was constructed in World War 2, she had this to say:

> *"We had the car lights on and there was a full moon. All of sudden about ten or twelve sheep came running up, close to the right-hand side of the tower. I thought what has frightened them? Without any warning, something on two legs appeared and ran past us on the left-hand side of the tower. I can still see it in my mind's eye to this present day. It was a couple of hundred yards away. It was taller than a man, probably 7ft I would estimate. It had big pointy ears and had dark brown wiry hair covering its body. It stood there for at least ten seconds - not all fours, but on two legs. The sheep then ran away, and were quickly followed by the creature. It had a strange face like a wolf, rather than the popular illustration of the Beast of Bodmin. The jaw was very long."*

During a visit to Bodmin Gaol, she saw a picture on the wall, which she believes was identical to what she had seen. Unfortunately, after the company managing the gaol went into receivership, the whereabouts of that picture is not currently known.

of the Earl of Sandwich, i.e. formerly the home of the 9th Earl of Sandwich, whom it was said, (as well as having once heard a werewolf) according to local myths and the internet, had demolished:

> *"...the west wing of the house because he thought it was inhabited by a Werewolf, in 1947."*

We contacted Huntingdon Archives, in 2009, and asked them if they would examine personal papers once in the possession of the 9th Earl, to see if there was any information in support of this extraordinary statement. They told us, in a guide, published in 1970, by Philip Dickinson, that:

> *"During the Second World War, the house had become too large to maintain and the family moved out for the duration of the war, when it was used by families from London and elsewhere as a recuperative home. After the War, the Earl set about a programme of general restorative work on the house to make it habitable again with the architect Marshall Sissonto, and it was as part of this process that the wing was demolished."*

In 1832, two stone coffins were found containing the remains of two nuns, during repairs carried out to the house by architect Edward Blore. Was there any connection with modern day sightings of ghostly nuns seen at Nun's bridge, over Alconbury Brook, reputed to be haunted by one of the nuns who lived at the old convent - now Hinchingbrook School? This was formerly Huntingdon Grammar School, the site of which is now Cromwell Museum, dating back to 1565. One of its students was none other than Oliver Cromwell - not to mention the rumoured secret tunnels supposedly connecting the house to the local railway station. It is alleged that 2005 builders renovating the house refused to work during the night, after apparent sightings of the Monk.

We also learnt from a retired USAF Colonel, who had been stationed at RAF Alconbury, of sightings of a *ghostly black dog* seen on the aerodrome, which rumour had it belonged to the Old Duke's house before the runway was built. Apparently, the animal had to be shot before the Duke's body could be removed after he died, and that the officers' mess was haunted. In 2012, as this book neared completion, we wrote to the school, and received a prompt reply from Mr. Wheeley, at Hinchingbrooke History Department

> *"I have had a look at the extract you sent and what you have fits with the oral histories re: ghosts at the House. The explanation given by the Records Office for the reasoning behind the destruction of the west wing is by far the most believable. The only difference I would now point out is that the bones under the stairs are not now thought to be nuns. One is certainly a man, and whilst the other may have been an elderly nun, it is now thought that they were benefactors of the medieval nunnery. This rather undermines the oral histories which describe the haunting of the staircase, under which the bones lie, as being the ghosts of nuns. I can confirm that children voices have been reported coming from an empty room upstairs at the School"*

Bizarrely somewhat as footnote to this matter are the ongoing claims made by John Hanson's niece Mary Whitsitt who lives in Gravesend Kent that she is related to the Earl of Sandwich, we wish her every success in establishing this line of ancestry. She writes:

LORD SANDWICH
MRS PROBY
STANLEY BALDWIN
PRIME MINISTER
MRS BALDWIN NURSE.
LORD MONTAGU
MAJOR PROBY
AT HINCHINGBROOK ABOUT 1926

My Great, Great, Aunt Ella Corbin was one of a large number of children and was bought up on a farm in Somerset. She managed to get herself in a position where she saved up enough money to go to America to sell cosmetics. Bizarrely, while over there, she joined a Hindu cult and renamed herself Amiya. She met the Earl of Sandwich, who was then in his 50s, and fell in love. They married, making her a Dowager Countess, and returned to live in Hinchingbrook Castle. My mother remembers my great Aunt arriving at the house in a Bentley. She had a tape-recorder with her, which was quite a rare and expensive item in those days of the 1960s. Ella died in 1984. There was a big dispute over some paintings. My mother has spoken to the current Earl of Sandwich, Lord Montague, who is in the House of Lords. He told my mother, who is currently writing a book: 'You do realise that you aren't owed anything?'

Warminster - a personal view

Warminster - a Wiltshire market town - considered, by many, to be the 'Mecca' for UFO enthusiasts, following a plague of UFO reports and strange sounds that struck the area in late 1964, is now deemed synonymous with the books written by Mr. Arthur Shuttlewood - a local Journalist living in the town. Eloquently described by Mr. Shuttlewood, as 'it', 'them' and 'The Thing', he captured the imagination of the reader with phrases such as, 'flickering fireflies of bejewelled radiance', 'silvery giants', 'glittering starships', and 'slithering invisible serpents', immortalised within the pages of his books, which were to fire the imagination of many 'sky watchers' assembled on the hill during those halcyon days.

One of them was Neil Pike, who kept a diary covering the events that took place between July 1971 and 1976, which included both his and then wife Sally's sightings. Neil told us:

"I always found Arthur a very amiable character - exceedingly enthusiastic and very helpful in guiding me along the right road, at least initially. I knew him well, even to the extent of ferrying him about on his frequent lectures. His mind was open to any thoughts on the subject, and he frequently promoted whatever had last been imparted to him. Even after some years, he had not really formulated a position based on his own analysis.

This I found to be strange. He began to accept, without reservation, any reports, however outlandish, particularly if they supported his current line of belief, and I felt he was prone to exaggeration - a tool of the journalist's trade. I told him as much to his face, at the time, because we were good friends. My own opinion is that he came to believe in his own legend in a lifetime status and lived, in part, in a world of his own. Because of this, I did not consider his second and third books to be worthy of real merit.

As regards Bob Strong I found him very prone to mood swings, which he blamed on his UFO experiences. He was quite secretive and his practical interest seemed to end after his experience at Heaven's Gate, Longleat (when he was attacked by a lion) *but I felt he did hold the key to much of what subsequently became the Warminster mystery, although I never got anywhere to reaching a conclusion. Another man I knew well was Ken Rogers.*

He was a frequent guest at my home and did much to advance the Warminster reputation, but he was subject to bouts of paranoia.

He was not a man whom I would class as a close friend. He and Arthur were on the opposite sides of the fence and they had many violent disagreements.

Ken's real value was that he did a lot to set down witnesses accounts of UFO sightings in the town, and also set up his own magazine."

(Source: personal interview)

Another frequent visitor to the location was Bob Tibbitts, who is pictured (then and now) left.

Encounter on Cradle Hill

Who or what was it that was seen at Cradle Hill, Warminster, on the 8th September 1973, by Mr. and Mrs. Ron McClure from Bournemouth? The couple had been walking along the top of the path, when they noticed a 'man', dressed in a dark green denim material, with an anorak-type hood almost covering his face. After greeting him, they were rewarded with a deep gruff groan, but chose to ignore it.

Ron said later:

> *"A little further on, we were astonished to see the same 'figure' standing by the gate in front of us, knowing he had not overtaken us. At 2.00am, I was talking to some other 'sky watchers', about the odd 'figure', when three people came rushing over to our group in an excited state, unaware of the previous conversation, and spoke of an incident that had just occurred, involving a strange 'man', described as six and-a-half to seven feet tall, wearing a two-piece garment of dark green denim material, with an anorak-type hood covering his face. When one of the 'sky watchers' shone his torch at the 'man', who was holding a silver object (similar to a torch, but odd in shape, with a red piece on the end) the man shouted at them, 'Move on, Go Away'.*

> *One of the 'sky watchers' shouted out, 'Are you going to harm us?' Back came the answer, 'Yes'. One of the 'sky watchers', called Rob, went to confront*

the 'figure', a few yards ahead of him, who promptly vanished into thin air."

Ron presumed they were obviously talking about the same 'figure' he and his wife had seen earlier, except the person they had seen was only five and-a-half feet tall.

With a sighting of this nature, one is bound to wonder whether this was a 'set-up' by hoaxers, rather than the appearance of a ghostly visitor, or 'Alien' occupant, but if one accepts the validity of what Rob told Mr. and Mrs. McClure, then clearly this could not have been the work of any hoaxer. **(Source: Leslie Harris,** *Scan* **Magazine)**

On the same evening, Robert Birkett - a member of Kettering UFO Group - was taking part in a 'sky watch' held at Harrington Airfield.

> *"Just before 1.00am, a saucer-shaped object, projecting a number of beams*
> *of light, downwards, was seen moving silently across the sky, heading*
> *towards the south-west, at a speed of about one hundred miles per hour. I*

Evening Courier, Thursday, September 13, 1973

Investigating those U.F.O. reports

SKY MYSTERIES EXPLAINED

CASE HISTORIES

managed to take a photograph before it disappeared."

We contacted Mr. Birkett, over thirty years later, hoping he could supply us with a copy of the photograph. Unfortunately, with the passing of years, he had mislaid the negative, although he was adamant the photograph was genuine in nature.

UFO over Wales

During the same month a luminous cloud, approximately 100ft in width, by 200ft in length, was seen slowly drifting through the sky over Pensarn, Abergele, at 2.00am, by two young men out walking. The cloud was seen to stop in mid-flight over the local Police Station, and then moved back towards the beach.

A few minutes later, a huge black oval object was sighted flying along the coastline from the direction of Rhyl, accompanied by two other identical objects - no more than 500ft off the ground.

As these gigantic objects passed over Pensarn Railway Station, the 'lead one' halted in mid-air, allowing the others to merge into it, showering the darkness with dull green, blue and red colours. The two youths were to complain, later, of having sustained sunburn to their faces and the tops of their hands. These symptoms were also experienced by a third youth, who had been asleep at the time.

According to Margaret Fry, who brought this matter to our attention, she discovered a similar incident had taken place years previously.

Many miles away in Olton, Solihull - a small suburb, just off the A41, on the outskirts of Birmingham - a UFO was seen hovering over the locality, by a number of residents. Sadly, all of their sightings reports, later sent to BUFORA, could not be traced. This was a source of irritation to Margaret Westwood - head of the Birmingham UFO group, UFOSIS - who investigated this and many other incidents. Admittedly, she should have made copies, but in those days it was easier said than done.

We contacted Brian James - then a representative of BUFORA (who appears to have mysteriously vanished off the face of the Earth!) He was unsuccessful in his attempt to recover these files, which Margaret had given us permission to look at. Despite further enquires to trace these documents, their current whereabouts remain unknown. Margaret sadly passed away in 2009. **(Source: Birmingham based Group, UFOSIS)**

UFO over Kent

Steven Dadd (now in his 50s) from Hythe, in Kent, contacted us in September 2010.

> *"Sometime in the autumn of 1973/1974, I was on my way home from school at about 5.00pm, when a large ball/light bulb-shaped object descended through the sky and hovered approximately 60ft above my head. I was terrified and unable to move through fear. Suddenly it shot away into the sky and was gone.*

When I arrived home my parents saw the distressed state I was in and, when I told them what I had experienced, they just laughed at me in disbelief. I'm not sure exactly when this happened but, within a week or two, I saw, on the front page of the Hythe/Dover Adscene newspaper, a photograph of the same UFO I had seen, taken over Dover Docks, and remember the derogatory opinions expressed by the editor, at the time. Unfortunately, I haven't got a copy of the paper but I'm sure it is in the library somewhere."

UFO over Orpington, Kent

During 1973, Graham Brooke and his then girlfriend, Julie Taylor, had been to a party held at Orpington Hospital, but left early, at 8.15pm. They were walking towards Sidcup, along the Orpington Road, as darkness fell, when they saw something moving through the sky, above the road.

"It stopped in front of us, at an angle of about 50-60°. It's hard to say how big it was, because there was nothing nearby to compare it with - it could have been small and close, or huge but further away.

I would say it may have been 300yds away and was as big as a football pitch. It was a 'flying saucer'. It had a round panel underneath, which turned slowly, and about seven illuminated panels that gave off a glow, rather than a beam. It stopped in front of us, as we stopped walking, and just stayed there for a few seconds. It must have seen us. It then altered its direction by turning left and away, over some trees. We ran across the road and stood on a small brick wall, but it disappeared over the trees.

We were flabbergasted and really excited; we couldn't wait to tell someone – anyone - so we flagged a car down and two guys stopped. We told them and asked for a ride to Sidcup. They didn't believe us and made fun of us, but when we asked them the time - it was now 11.10pm.

We only left the nurses' quarters at 8.15pm, which seemed like less than half an hour ago. We were as shocked about the time as we were the sighting."

We tried to contact the couple and left messages, but received no reply. Whilst in all cases like this it would have been beneficial to talk to them about the matter personally, we were unable to do in this instance but felt it seemed to be a genuine sighting. (**Source: www.uk-ufo.co.uk**)

Close Encounter, Northamptonshire

In September 1973, a male resident (23) of Bedford, of Italian descent, who was employed as an engineer, had been to a dance held at Northampton, approximately 23 miles from his home.

As he drove alone, along theA428 at 2.00am, just passing the small Church of Little Houghton - the first village on the road from Northampton to Bedford - he slowed down, on seeing what he took to be the headlights of an approaching car.

"Suddenly I was blinded by this light, heading straight for me; the next thing I knew was finding myself walking along the Bromham Bridge road, about

two miles out of Bedford. My coat and shoes were wet, as If I had been walking through long grass.

I felt very refreshed and wide awake, as if I had rested well. I made my way to a friend's house and asked him to drive me slowly back along the Northampton road, as I could not remember where I had left the car. Near a turn-off from the main road, signposted to the village of Olney, we found the car locked up in the middle of a ploughed field. (The keys had been in my pocket) The gate was shut and there were no tracks seen in the soil near to the car. A farmer later towed the vehicle out of the field. There were no marks, or scratches, found on the car."

According to the researcher - Miss E.C. Hargreaves - whom the witness had confided in, he decided not to tell his parents what had actually happened, but told of having stayed with his friend after the dance. He didn't, in fact, tell Miss Hargreaves what had taken place until 12 months later, feeling that he just wanted to block out the incident from his mind.

Understandably, this was a matter that caused him much concern and led to outbursts of moodiness and confusion, not forgetting the fear, as he tried to come to terms with something completely out of the normal. What had happened along that quiet stretch of country road that evening and where had that missing five hours of time gone? Even if he had subconsciously driven the car without any specific memory of having done so, why were there no wheel marks or traces of the car having been driven along the ploughed field?

One senses that there was an awful lot of information tied-in with this incident that we shall never know about, particularly bearing in mind we do not know the identity of the person concerned, and that this matter took place now nearly 40years ago. What a pity we were unable to track down Miss E. Hargreaves, who was living in Copper Cottage, Ravensden, Bedford, and knew the identity of the man. **(Source: as above, Letter to *FSR*, Volume 22, No. 1, 1976)**

UFO over Derbyshire

It the early hours of September 1973, a woman living in the small village of Harpur Hill, which lies south-east of the town of Buxton, in the county of Derbyshire, contacted the Police, after having sighted an object she described as resembling a helicopter rising out of part of the excavated site, at the nearby Hillhead Quarry.

Another witness to this event was Simon Crowe - a security guard at the quarry. He told of having sighted the same 'helicopter' earlier in the night, at 10.00pm and midnight. Although he couldn't positively identify it as a helicopter, he confirmed it had hovered and made a sound similar to rotor blades.

"The first time I saw it, the craft was hovering about 50ft from the ground and shined what appeared to be spotlights onto the quarry floor, as if searching for something. When I approached it in my Land Rover, it flew towards the part of the quarry designated as Mines Research. On the second occasion, it rose out of the quarry with its lights on and disappeared in the direction I had seen it take previously."

This was not the only time we were to come across reports of UFO activity around this area.

On the 17th September 1973, Mr. Desmond Boddington from Sidcup, in Kent, was walking home at 11.00pm, when he noticed orange coloured lights flash across the sky parallel to the Thames and out of view in ten seconds. Interestingly he pointed out that: *"The lights were arranged in a 'V' formation."* (**Source:** ***Kentish Times*** **[Sidcup and Bexley] 20.9.73)**

Sighting from Sky Lab 3

At approximately 4.35pm on 20th September 1973, astronauts Alan Bean, Owen Garriott and Jack Lousma, sighted what they described as a red 'satellite', of which they took four photographs, while aboard Skylab 3, at 1645-1646 GMT, while over Madagascar Channel, at the extreme western edge of the Indian Ocean.

The sighting was logged in Alan Bean's personal diary of the flight, written a few hours after the event.

SKYLAB-3 SATELLITE SIGHTING DATA   compiled 1977 June 08
                                          James E. Oberg
-
EVENT: SIGHTING OF 'BRIGHT SATELLITE' BY ALL THREE SKYLAB-3 ASTRO-
       NAUTS (ALAN BEAN, OWEN GARRIOTT, JACK LOUSMA).
DATE: SEPTEMBER 20, 1973 (DAY 263) AT APPROXIMATELY 1645 GMT
LOC.: S.W. INDIAN OCEAN
REV: SKYLAB REVOLUTION 1863
ORBIT: ASCENDING NODES (8 REVS APART)
       NBECL   027.3W   0806:18GMT
       NBECT   216.7W   2031:25GMT
          period= 93.134 MINUTES
          WS/R = 23.67 DEGREES

THE SECOND MANNED SKYLAB VISIT WAS WITHIN FIVE DAYS OF RETURNING TO
EARTH AFTER A RECORD-BREAKING 59 DAY EXPEDITION. CREW HAD AWOKEN HAD
0700 GMT AND WOULD GO TO SLEEP AT 2300. THEY HAD EATEN LUNCH IN THE
WARDROOM AND WERE DOING A 'PROCEDURES REVIEW' IN THE WARDROOM PRIOR
TO BEGINNING A NEW SERIES OF EXPERIMENTS IN THE AFTERNOON.

DURING THE SIGHTING, THE CREW WAS OUT OF CONTACT WITH THE GROUND.
THE ON-BOARD TAPE RECORDER WAS NOT TURNED ON. THE FIRST RECORDED
MENTION OF THE INCIDENT WAS ON AN AIR-TO-GROUND LINK SOME 4.5 HOURS
AFTER THE EVENT. GARRIOTT LOGGED FOUR PHOTOGRAPHS TAKEN OF THE OBJECT.

DEBRIEFING COMMENTS ARE ATTACHED. IT SHOULD BE NOTED THAT THE
'A-CHANNEL' TAPE RECORDER WAS NOT ON. TAPE 263-05/D-550 HAD RUN
OUT AT 1547:56 AND THE NEXT TAPE, D-551, WAS NOT ACTIVATED UNTIL
APPROXIMATELY 1811:20.

AIR-TO-GROUND TAPE 263-10/T-671 Page 9 of 14/5207 (excerpts)

approx 2103GMT
LOUSMA   DID YOU TELL HIM ABOUT THAT SATELLITE WE SAW?
BEAN   YES, WE SAW A GREAT SATELLITE. WE DIDN'T KNOW IF WE TOLD YOU
             ABOUT IT.
LOUSMA   THE CLOSEST AND BRIGHTEST ONE WE'VE SEEN.
BEAN   HUGE ONE.
LOUSMA   WE'VE SEEN SEVERAL. IT WAS A RED ONE.
CAPCOM   NO, YOU MAY HAVE TOLD SOMEBODY, BUT IT WASN'T THIS TEAM.
             I DON'T REMEMBER HEARING ABOUT IT.
LOUSMA   I GUESS WE DIDN'T REPORT IT. IT WAS REFLECTING IN RED
             LIGHT, AND OSCILLATING A4,OH, COUNTING ITS PERIOD OF
             BRIGHTEST TO DIMMEST, ABOUT TEN SECONDS. IT LED US INTO
             SUNSET. THAT WAS ABOUT THREE REVS AGO, I THINK. SOMETHING
             LIKE THAT, WASN'T IT, OWEN?
(NO ANSWER) Other topics then were discussed.

> *"Out the wardroom window we saw a bright red light, with a bright/dim period of 10secs. It got brighter and drifted along with us for 20mins or more....it also was moving relative to the stars. It may have been very near. It was the brightest object we've seen."*

The next mention of the sighting was in a radio conversation with ground control, logged in the following document compiled by James Oberg, in 1977: The second manned Sky Lab visit was within five days of returning to Earth after a record-breaking 59 day expedition. The crew had awakened at 0700 GMT, and would go to sleep at 2300 GMT. They had eaten lunch in the wardroom and were doing a 'procedures review' in the wardroom, prior to beginning a new series of experiments in the afternoon. During the sighting the crew was out of contact with ground control. The on-board tape recorder was not turned on and the first recorded mention of the incident was on a ground link, some 4.5 hours after the event. Garriott had taken four photographs. During the taped discussion, the conversation went as follows:

LOUSMA: *"Did you tell him about that satellite we saw?"*
BEAN: *"Yes, we saw a great satellite. We didn't know if we told you about it."*
LOUSMA: *"The closest and brightest one we've seen."*
BEAN: *"Huge one".*
LOUSMA*: "We've seen several. It was a red one."*
CAPCOM*: "No, you may have told somebody, but it wasn't this team. I don't remember hearing about it."*
LOUSMA: *"I guess we didn't report it. It was reflecting in red light and oscillating at, oh, counting its period of brightest to dimmest, about ten seconds. It led us into sunset. That was about * three revs ago, I think. Something like that, wasn't it Owen?"* (No answer by Owen)
LOUSMA: *"Things we saw out the window".*
GARRIOTT*: "For example we saw that satellite about a week before splashdown. That was one of the most unusual things that we saw and I guess Jack noticed it looking out the window. This bright reddish object was out there and we tracked it for about 5 or 10 minutes. It was obviously a satellite in a very similar orbit to our own. It was rotating and had a period of almost exactly 10 seconds because you could see the brightness vary with that period. We followed it until sunset and it went out of sunlight just 5 to 7 seconds after we did. It held its position nearly the same in the wardroom window for that 10 minute interval. It was reddish in colour, even when we were well above the horizon. As we approached sunset it turned more reddish, presumably because of the sunlight change. What satellite it was and how it happened to end up in such a similar orbit no-one ever explained to us. And I would like to hear a few words from someone about that satellite."*
BEAN: *"You bet. We never saw it again. You'd think we would have seen it the next night, or it would cycle by another time. Maybe it did and we weren't looking out the window."*
LOUSMA: *"You might point out that it never did take the shape of an object, but it was always brighter than any other star or planet in the night sky. It was much brighter."*
BEAN: *"We tried monitors and everything on it, but we could never make it into anything other than a bright light."*
LOUSMA: *"In doing T002 (manual navigation sightings)I had, on other occasions, at least once or twice, seen other satellites, although they appeared as star points of light."* The debriefing then switched to other topics.

---

* "Three revolutions ago", at about 1.5 hours per revolution = 4.5 hours before. Garriott said, later, that the object did not lead the Skylab into sunset, but rather *followed* the Skylab into sunset. During the debriefing, there were two sections in which the 'red satellite' was discussed. The first discussion is presented:

On page 20-1, during the debriefing on visual sightings, the 'red satellite' was discussed again:

GARRIOTT: *"Do you want to talk about that satellite?"*
LOUSMA: *"I saw a couple of satellites that appeared like a satellite would on Earth. I saw one that was not like one you would see on Earth, so why don't you mention it?"*
GARRIOTT: *OK. About a week or 10 days before recovery, we were still waiting for information to be supplied to us about the identification. Jack first notices this rather large red star out the wardroom window. Upon close examination, it was much brighter than Jupiter, or any of the other planets. It had a reddish hue to it, even though it was well above the horizon. The light from the Sun was not passing close to the Earth's limb at the time. We observed it for about 10 minutes prior to sunset. It was slowly rotating because it had a variation in brightness with a 10-seconds period. As I was saying, we observed it for about 10 minutes, until we went into darkness, and it also followed us into darkness about 5 seconds later. From the 5 to 10 second delay in its disappearance, we surmised that it was not more than 30 to 50 nautical miles [35 to 58 statute miles or 56 to 93 km] from our location. From its original position in the wardroom window, it did not move more than 10 or 20 degrees over the 10 minutes or so that we watched it. Its orbit was very close to that of our own. We never saw it on any earlier or succeeding orbits and we'd be quite interested in having its identification established. It's all debriefed in terms of time on channel A, so the precise timing and location can be picked up from there. Soon after this debriefing, Garriott told one of us (Sparks) during an interview, that his best estimate of the time interval between the Skylab going into sunset and light's disappearance was about 5-6 seconds. Garriott explained exactly how he counted out the seconds, "one thousand one, one thousand two, etc." Alan Bean wrote in his flight diary that the red satellite 'drifted along with us for 20 minutes or more'."*

They were not the only astronauts to see something highly unusual on their missions. While we should be careful about forming any interpretation of what these things are and where they come from, Buzz Aldrin has disclosed he and other astronauts saw a UFO, which paced them for a time during their journey to the Moon. This information was kept secret by NASA for all of these years.

Buzz said: *"There was something out there, close enough to be observed, and what could it be? Now, obviously the three of us weren't going to blurt out, 'Hey, Houston, we've got something moving alongside of us and we don't know what it is', you know?"*

According to present information, it has been alleged that the object seen from Skylab 3 was similar to what the three Astronauts of Apollo 11 saw. It is clear, from the intriguing image seen, that this was no satellite, and it remains unexplained to this present day. Was it some alien debris en-route to another destination, a structured craft, or just space junk not of this World? We shall never know what it was. However, what we do surmise is that it is still out there!

There have been a number of images, both still and moving, of the Astronauts on the Moon and other NASA missions, which seem to show UFOs, and, as we know, Astronaut Gordon Cooper was open about seeing 'unknowns' on numerous occasions. According to a taped interview by J.L. Ferrando, Major Cooper said:

> *"For many years I have lived with a secret, in a secrecy imposed on all specialists in astronautics. I can now reveal that every day, in the USA, our radar instruments capture objects of form and composition unknown to us. And there are thousands of witness reports and a quantity of documents to prove this, but nobody wants to make them public."* (**Source: Robert Emenegger,** *UFOs, Past Present and Future,* **1974/Bruce Maccabee and Brad Sparks,** *wwwhttp://brumac.8k.com/Skylab3/SL3.html/NASA)*

In late September 1973 (exact date not identified) Richard Stolley (11) of Heath Avenue, Halifax, reported having sighted a UFO flying south over the town, at 6.00pm. In an interview, later conducted by members of the South Lincolnshire UFO Study Group, he said:

> *"It was long and thin, with a thin wedge on top. It was in sight for about two minutes, travelling slowly, before it vanished behind a cloud."*

Close Encounter, Somerset

At 11.00pm on 16th October 1973, Italian born Mrs. Gabriella Versilli, was driving along the B3187 road to Wellington (A 38) and had just passed the turn-off (on her right) to Langton Budville, some six miles from Taunton, when she glimpsed a very bright light in the fields ahead and to the right of her. At first she took no notice of it, although she was sure there were no buildings in that locality. All of a sudden, the car's headlights began to flicker and dim and then went out, accompanied by the engine spluttering and finally cutting out, the car then coming to a stop at the side of the road.

Gabriella tried to start the engine, without success. Glancing around her she noticed a half-moon, or hemispherical shape, flat on the top, with a rounded dome still at ground level, illuminating the grass with its dazzling light. Getting out of the car she opened the bonnet, hoping she may be able to sort out the problem, when she became aware of a humming sound - not unlike a generator - apparently emanating from all around her. She put the bonnet down and was about to open the driver's door, when she felt:

> *"...a strong hand fall on my left shoulder, pushing my body down a few inches"*

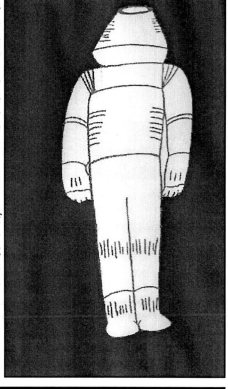

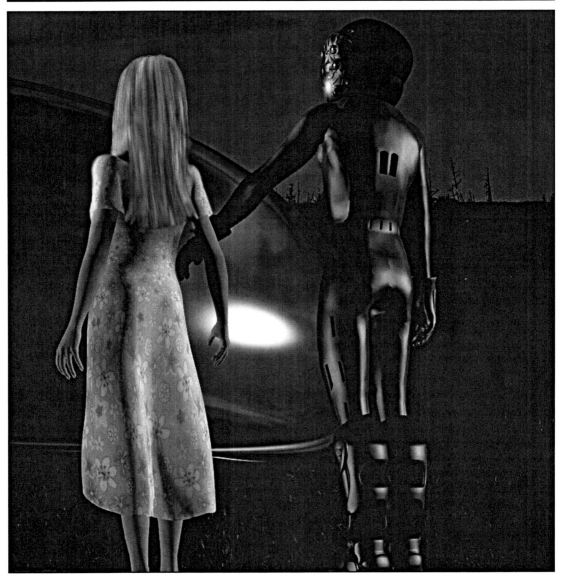

Turning around, she was confronted by the sight of a tall, dark coloured, metallic 'Robot'!

In an interview later conducted with Barry King and Andrew Collins, she described the 'Robot' as:

> *"...tall, over 6ft, perhaps 6ft 6ins. and seemed to be composed of some sort of shiny, dark blue metal. Each time it moved, it made a knocking sound. On its head was a small oblong box device, with a glass panel on the front, containing a small velvet coloured light, which flashed not on and off but across the panel lengthwise, about a flash a second; the head, or helmet, had no human features - just vents, or openings, on the side. Similar vents were seen on the side of the body. It had glove like coverings on its hands, with a chain mail type thing - like on suits of*

armour - on its palms. The 'Robot' had big boots, with thick soles, and walked with a stiff movement of the legs, with arms at its side, and then I passed out."

She then became aware of standing in the field next to the 'Robot', in front of a large object, in what appeared to be half rounded moonlight, its light having subsided, allowing her to see what was clearly some sort of machine, silver grey in colour - not unlike aluminium in appearance - supported by thick legs, about two and-a-half feet high, by two feet across. (Two were seen, there may have been more.)

The size of the object was estimated to be 20ft by 40ft and had large oblong windows around the middle, from which emanated a yellow light. She then passed out for the second time.

When she gained consciousness, she found herself lying on top of a sheet of smooth rubbery substance on a grey table, about 4ft wide by 6ft long, bordered on the sides by a 3ins in diameter shiny, smooth, tubular rail, terminating in a flat end at the side of her head, in the middle of an icy cold circular room, covered by a light blue blanket.

Her clothes had been removed; her wrists and legs were secured against the table by what looked like rubber bands. The floor was completely covered in 3ft square sections of what she presumed was black rubber matting - like the sort used in cars, with the 'pimples' uppermost. On the walls could be seen a collection of wire coils - bits of metal. Over to her right was a grey console, with red, yellow, blue and green, controls.

Above her head could be seen two transparent tubes, plastic like in appearance, pointing down towards her head, the upper parts being fixed to the curved ceiling.

> *"...then three human looking men came into view, all about the same height, 5ft 6ins – 5ft 8ins, fair haired and slim. All wore similar garments - a skull cap, ending just above the eyes, tied behind the head, facial masks from the top of the nose to the chin, light blue tunics, with a grey metallic edging, long gloves reaching to the elbows, with the normal complement of fingers that we possess on their 'hands', with a long apron going down to their ankles, with thick sole boots on their feet. Two moved over to the left-hand side of the table and occasionally nodded their heads. They didn't appear to breathe at all and at no time did I ever see their eyes blink."*

The 'Examiner' explained, after he had seen her looking at the 'Robot' still in the room, that he was a:

> *"...trained retrieval device to perform manual work outside the ship, and bring specimens in for study."*

Three red, green, and probably white, 6ins boxes, or cubes, were placed on the rail of the table; one near her feet, the other by her stomach, the last next to her head, which began to glow one by one.

The blanket was then removed. The 'Examiner' took several small grey instruments from the far end of the table and obtained a small nail paring from her right index finger, whilst a small plastic bottle with tubes and wires was used to take a blood sample from her right arm. A miniature, round device, held in the palm of his hand, was passed over her body, glowing brighter and dimmer as he did so.

> *"He also used a thin pencil like instrument for probing and a large black rubber suction object, which had a row of glowing lights, used mainly around the groin area, causing me discomfort."*

At this stage a black blanket was placed over her, as she was shivering from the cold. The cubes were then removed and placed on the floor, followed by all three men leaving the room.

> *"I lay there for several minutes, looking around, unable to move. My throat was painfully sore and I felt sick.*
>
> *The 'robot' stood immobile by the wall, its light flashing. One of the men then re-entered the room, walked over to the far end of the table next to the cubes, and lifted the blanket, staring, without any visible emotion. I tried to struggle but could only move my head. The man then placed a small pin like device to my thigh, which made me feel numb and semi-paralysed; then he raped me."*

Afterwards, he produced a small blue cloth of sponge like material to wipe her body, and left the room, after pulling the blanket down. The flashing light on the 'Robot' had stopped. The three men came back into the room. One removed the pin from her thigh, whilst the other two lifted up the blanket, folded it, and placed it on the floor near the console.

The bands were removed from her wrists. She then blacked out for a third and last time. Her next recollection was finding herself next to the car. Shaken, dazed and nauseated, she started up the car and drove away. She arrived home at 2.30am in a very distressed state, and went to bed.

The next morning, she told her husband what had occurred. After much discussion, they decided to try and forget the whole incident and say nothing to anyone, for perfectly understandable reasons. One cannot even imagine the level of ridicule and embarrassment a complaint of this kind would have attracted if the matter had been brought to the attention of the media.

If things were not bad enough, worse was to come (if that's possible), when shortly before Christmas 1973, the family began to receive a number of peculiar telephone calls and anonymous postmarked letters, all addressed to Gabrielle - all in the same ink and handwriting, just a few lines only, written on ordinary notepad paper - instructing to *forget what happened to her in October*, signed *'a friend'*.

Unfortunately, each of these (up to 25 separate letters, up to April 1976) was burnt.

Visit from the 'Men in Black'
According to Barry King, right up to the time of the investigation made by him and Andrew Collins into the matter the couple received a number of visits from two sinister men, described as looking like father and son, both wearing thick black spectacles, who usually appeared in a black 'diplomat style car', which had darkened windows, often seen cruising slowly around the area.

> *"The younger was about 25, tall and slim build, and he had short dark hair, with a beatnik beard. He nearly always wore a roll neck sweater, black jacket, jeans and moccasins. The older was about 50, tubby, balding, and about 5ft 6ins tall. He wore a brown overcoat, navy trousers, and*

*boots. They never identified themselves, or answered any questions put
to them by us."*

The appearance of these two men, and their unwarranted intrusion into the home of Mr. & Mrs. Versilli,
may seem difficult to understand, especially after the husband threatened them with the Police, to
which they replied:

"It would be very unwise, as there would be unpleasant repercussions."

The sole topic of conversation, held with the husband and wife during these numerous visits, appears to
have consisted of repeated warnings from the two men that they should forget about the matter for the
sake of the couple's health, welfare, and sanity - a threat the couple obviously took seriously.

According to Barry the strange visitors, who would now be referred to in today's UFO climate as the
'Men in Black', continued to keep in contact with the family right up to when he and Andrew Collins
became involved, advising the couple they would be discontinuing their visits because the matter was
in the hands of the investigators, and was being officially recorded, which doesn't appear to make
sense, but of course, nothing about the UFO phenomena rarely does!

Since 1974, Gabrielle was to be the subject of various examinations by several Doctors and Psychiatrists,
who suggested she was hallucinating. We tried to find out the current whereabouts of Gabrielle, who
had been given various pseudonyms by other authors over the years, but were unable to find her, and
believe she has either emigrated or changed her name. **(Source: Barry King/Andrew Collins,** *UFOIN
report/New BUFORA Journal***, April 2003, Issue no. 8)**

UFOs over Luton

At midnight on 18th October 1973, six brilliant white 'lights' were seen floating downwards through the
sky over Luton, Bedfordshire. They were then seen to drop to the approximate height of an aircraft
after approaching from the London area, and then change into a 'V'-shaped formation - now orange in
colour, and apparently rotating, or pulsing - before disappearing over rooftops. **(Source: Mr J. Cowley,
BUFORA)**

Was there an Alien Incursion at Marconi Defence Centre?

We spoke to Hilary Porter from Farnborough, Hampshire - Vice chairwoman of BEAMS, (British Earth
& Aerial Mysteries Society). The group is run by her and partner, Ken Parsons, contributor of many
published articles and numerous appearances on various TV programmes - with regard to a number of
personal experiences that occurred, while working as an Engineer for Marconi Space and Defence,
Frimley, Surrey, during the mid 1970s, who decided, after 31 years of service as an Engineer, to 'blow
the whistle' on a number of chilling accounts, involving matters which should raise some concern.

*"Right from the outset, I knew there was something odd about this day.
For a start, the security guards were not on duty, and parked in the personnel
department car park was a large black MOD car. Something was up, I
thought to myself, as normally, when the MOD visits the establishment
they spruce the place up.*

*I went through the entrance to the old Victorian building, known as the
'Haunted House' because of all the strange things that had allegedly*

happened there, and was surprised to see a chain had been strung across the stairs, prohibiting entry, marked 'Strictly No Admittance'. I asked my colleagues if they knew what was happening, but they had no idea. Something was definitely up, as I kept encountering groups of people huddled together, whispering and behaving in a covert manner.

After receiving a call from Security to collect some work, I made my way to the designated area, and was near the security hut, when I heard agitated voices coming from inside, as if someone was very worried. I overheard someone exclaim words to the effect that they were not going to work on the night shift after what had happened to their colleague, the other night.

Still not knowing what they were on about, I made my way back to my office, noticing how strict security was. When I knocked on the door to gain admittance, the security guard allowed me in, but instead of walking back the usual way, decided to see what was on the other side of the 'No Admittance' signs, curiosity getting the better of me."

Hilary made her way along the corridors that led to other engineering sections, but found the place bizarrely empty of employees. Mystified, she found herself coming up against another warning sign and chain prohibiting entry. A flood of realisation swept over her. Something very serious breaching this Top Secret storage facility had clearly happened, but what?

"I know I cannot prove what the nature of the security breach was but, bearing in mind the initial conversations I heard from those security guards, I have often wondered it there was a connection with a story circulating, afterwards, that a grey coloured 'Alien', wearing headgear, illuminated by a blue light, was discovered looking through Top Secret documents, kept in a secure area, by an armed guard, accompanied by his Alsatian dog, who was so shocked by the experience, he required psychiatric treatment in a special MOD Hospital. One evening, I remember looking out of my window and seeing two orbs of brilliant white light heading from West to East.

One veered off towards Farnborough, the other took up a hovering position, over the Frimley complex, before inexplicably extinguishing from view. On another occasion, I saw a hexagonal object flying over the base. This was to be just some of several strange events and experiences which befell me over the years."

Halloween Mystery

Ronald Stone - now living in France - described a very odd experience, which happened to him and his colleague, while driving between Countesthorpe and Foston, on the evening of the 31st October 1973.

"Just south of Leicester we narrowly missed hitting a fallen tree in the road, which gave us quite a shock, and decided to stop for something to eat and drink. After travelling some miles, we saw a sign for 'The village', on the main road. Despite it being a main road, it was a small metal sign, about 8-10ins wide, by 20ins long, attached to an old unlit lamp-post, painted a dark colour blue, with faded red lettering, pointing down an unlit lane.

We turned right and came to a junction, where we noticed two figures walking towards us. Peter, my colleague, wound his window down, in order to speak

to them. As they grew closer, we saw they were identically dressed in black long cloaks, with a loose hood framing a long neck, showing small bald white heads, with black trousers and shiny black shoes.

I shouted in alarm and drove away quickly, feeling frightened. It got stranger. We drove down the road for a couple of hundred yards, and turned into a well lit pub car park. It was a most charming pub, but devoid of customers, it was full of glowing polished brass and a real log fire.

I looked at my watch. It was 9.30pm. The barman asked us what we wanted. 'Two pints of Bass', I replied. He poured the drinks and asked us for two shillings. I was taken aback because, even in 1973, the cost of a pint of beer hadn't been a shilling (5 pence) for a long time. Although we had metric money, we did have a few coins of the old silver coinage on us and scraped the shillings together and paid him. After drinking our beer without any sign of other customers, we hastily left, some minutes later, and found our way back through the village to Northampton, where I arrived home at 11.00pm., after dropping off Peter."

Ron Stone and Peter returned to the locality, in daylight, a few weeks after the event, hoping to locate the Public House, but found no trace of the building, or the street sign. He still seeks the answer to what happened, over thirty-five years later. Who were the strange figures?

Were they dressed up for Halloween? Why could they never find the missing pub? Were they, in some way, catapulted back in time, or was there some other rational explanation? (**Source: personal interview**)

In November 1973, Marjory Gammack from Gainsborough, Lincolnshire, employed as a care assistant at a local Nursing Home, was carrying out checks on the residents, at 6.00am., when she saw a large mushroom-shaped object hovering in the sky, flashing orange, red, and yellow lights, underneath which could be seen smoke, or mist, billowing out of the base. (**Source: Richard Thompson**)

At about 10.30pm on 12th November 1973, Mr. John Spalding of Lincoln Road, Washborough, sighted an unusual light heading towards the direction of Lincoln, across the southern sky.

"It then stopped in the sky and was still there when I went to bed, at midnight. It was much too high to be a plane; I thought it was a satellite until it stopped dead. People may think I am barmy, but I know what I saw. The only explanation for the object is that it came from an outside intelligence."

This wasn't the first time John has seen something strange in the sky. In 1959, when aged 14, he and his mother were in Portland Street, Lincoln, when they sighted a grey, cylindrical object, heading across the sky. (**Source: South Lincolnshire UFO Study Group/*Lincolnshire Echo*, 14.11.73**)

UFO over Kent

Kent resident Peter Hildebrand and his friend, John, were fishing on the beach at Grain, in Kent, on 24th November 1973, at around midnight. Peter's friend brought his companion's attention to what he thought was a fishing boat out at sea, about a mile away, showing a very bright light. They put it to the

DATE OF REPORT 14/6/1974

NAME Marjorie. ~~H~~ Cammack.   AGE 55.

ADDRESS Gainsborough, Lincs.

OCCUPATION Night care staff, residential home.

LOCATION northend area Gainsborough.

DATE OF SIGHTING November 1973.   METALLIC ?

TIME OF SIGHTING 3 A.M.   NOISE Nil.

DURATION OF OBSERVATION Ten minutes

WEATHER CONDITIONS cold, clear.

NUMBER OF OBJECTS one.   ELEVATION 15°

SIZE OF OBJECTS appeared to me about half the size of the moon.

SHAPE OF OBJECTS "mushroom"

COLOUR OF OBJECTS yellow, Red and Orange blend.

DIRECTION WHEN FIRST OBSERVED Static. "hovering."

DIRECTION WHEN LAST SEEN ?

DISTANCE AWAY

MOVEMENT shadows, and or smoke from beneath it.

PULSATIONS IF ANY

DISAPPEARANCE not seen.

LUMINOSITY

ANY OTHER EXTRAORDINARY CHARACTERISTICS

PSYCHOLOGICAL EFFECTS "pleasant shock" and amazement.

HAVE YOU HAD ANY SPECIAL TRAINING No.
OBSERVATION

PLEASE WRITE THE SEQUENCE OF EVENTS WHICH LED UP TO THE OBJECT
BEING OBSERVED:

I was doing a round of the building at 3 A.M. on ~~took~~
passing a large window, I observed the object in the sky,
to me it looked about Tree high (the largest tree I have
ever seen) I observed it for about ten minutes. it
moved slightly, but seemed to hover. I had to finish
my "round" but returned to the window and it
had completely disappeared. without sound.

I VERIFY THIS STATEMENT TO BE CORRECT.

PLACE OF EMPLOYMENT, I OBSERVED THE TIME TO BE 3 AM. ON LOOKING THROUGH A LARGE WINDOW IN PASSING I STOPPED TO LOOK AT THE SKY, AND SAW, A LARGE MUSHROOM SHAPED OBJECT. HOVERING. IT WAS COLOURED YELLOW, ORANG AND RED. BLENDED, LIKE FIRE. WITH SMOKE OR MIST BELOW IT. I WATCHED, AMAZED FOR TEN MINS. BUT HAD TO GO AWAY TO FINISH MY ROUND, I RETURNED TO THE WINDOW FIVE MINS LATER AND IT HAD DISSAPPEARED WITHOUT SOUND.

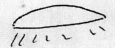

If there is insufficient space for your story above, please continue on an additional sheet.

PLEASE USE BLOCK CAPITALS AND PREFERABLY A BALL-POINT PEN

Name in Full.(Mr.,Mrs.,or Miss)....MARJORIE...CAMMACK.........
Address:..........119..HORTON..TERR.......GAINSBOROUGH.....
Telephone Number:.GAINSBOROUGH.3568..........Age:.....55.........
Occupation.....NIGHT.CARE.ATTENDANT.......HOUSEWIFE.
Professional/Technical/Academic qualifications:....................

back of their minds and continued fishing, but noticed, a short time later, that the light was approaching their position. Minutes later, it was now in line with the beach and about the height of a nearby army lookout tower. Peter said:

"It then turned and came towards us. When it was about 60yds away, we looked at it and were amazed. I have never seen anything like it before. We ran to the bank and lay down while continuing to keep our eyes on the object which had stopped directly above John's Tilley lamp. There was no sound from it - not even a down draught. It resembled a dirty silvery grey giant clay pigeon, with a dome on top, and had oval windows showing a bright light. It hovered above the Tilley lamp for about five minutes, before moving away slowly, at walking speed, along the beach, towards Sheerness, and then became lost from view."

There have been many sightings of mysterious glowing white lights and orange spheres reported all along the coast of the Thames Estuary and River Crouch, during the 1970 and 1980s. Groups of strange glowing lights 'flying in formation' were also seen. Does the secret military testing area of Foulness

hold the key to some of the strange objects seen over the Thames Estuary and local areas? **(Source: Southend-on-Sea UFO Group/***BUFORA Journal* **6/6 March/April 1978/Mr. J. Castle/Mr. Larry Dale)**

Close Encounter, Nuneaton

At 6.45pm on 30th November 1973, Nuneaton resident - Michael Currie (16) - reported sighting an unusual 'craft' hovering silently above his house, estimated to be 20-25ft long, pointed at both ends, with five large, oval, windows along its length, brightly lit from the inside, showing no sign of any external lights, propulsion, flight, or control surfaces.

> *"Inside the craft were three occupants; one facing me at the back edge of the first window, apparently looking at the wall between the first and second windows, a second on the far side, in the same position, with his back to me, while a third walked past the front window, towards the front of the object, allowing me to see their top halves. They were wearing gray coloured clothing, had shoulder length gold/blond hair, and were human in appearance."*

The craft, moving very slowly at apparent walking pace, then flew over the neighbour's house at a height of about 40ft off the ground, before disappearing from view. **(Source: www.ufowatch.com/sightings/display)**

At 11.25pm on 2nd December 1973, Fred Graham and his wife, from Cowes, Isle of Wight, were walking the dog near their home in Solent View Road, when they saw what they thought might have been a Comet, but realised this was unlikely to be the case.

> *"It was an inverted, brilliant red, semi-circle, with a straight line running across it, flying towards us from the direction of Bournemouth, before it gradually faded to a faint glow in the sky."*

(Source: Isle of Wight UFO Society/*The News* [Portsmouth] 4.12.73)

UFO over Kidsgrove, Staffordshire

At 6.45pm on 19th December 1973, Mr Gerard (20) was driving to his girlfriend's house in Kidsgrove, Staffordshire, on a clear, frosty night, when he sighted an object drop down from a steep bank, topped by trees.

> *"It moved slowly, hugging the contours. When it reached the road it crossed, it then rose up the parapet of a bridge before dropping down onto the main electric rail line travelling south, towards Birmingham. As it reached the rail, it streaked away within seconds. During the sighting I could hear a faint buzz or hum. The object was a solid looking blue sphere, about 1-2ft in diameter, and approximately 60ft away."* **(Source: *Northern UFOLOGY*, April 1979/Stephen Banks, BUFORA)**

A few days before Christmas 1973, a mysterious array of lights was seen in the sky over Abridge, Essex, one late evening, by resident Caroline Ebborn:

> *"I saw a red pulsating 'ball' next to the moon, which began to rise upwards into the sky, changing shape to a diamond, showing bright yellow lights at each end and neon red ones at its rear. It reminded me of a jet on take-off. After a while, a pale green fluorescent light appeared."*

Caroline was not the only one to see the UFO. Two other Epping residents also described seeing a similar object, later, on the same evening. **(Source: *West Essex Gazette*, 4.1.74)**

ADDENDUM FOR 1973

If a person was asked to supply details of English UFO sightings from the early 1970s, it is unlikely that he or she would be able to offer few, if any, examples at all, taking into consideration the difficulties which would be experienced in tracking down these reports, now 40yrs ago. Fortunately, as a result of liaison over the years with many individual UFO enthusiasts, who bothered to catalogue an astonishing number of UFO sightings covering this period, we can now see for ourselves the extent of many hitherto unpublished UFO reports, the majority of which will not be found in declassified Top Secret files made available by the MOD.

Ivan T. Sanderson in his home office, *circa* 1965.

FEBRUARY 19th **1973 Ivan Terence Sanderson** (b. January 30, 1911) one of the most important Forteans of all time, died. He was a naturalist and writer born in Edinburgh, Scotland, who became a naturalized citizen of the United States. He is remembered for his nature writing and his interest in cryptozoology and paranormal subjects.

Perhaps his most important achievement within Forteana was his work on the so-called 'Minnesota Iceman' together with Bernard Heuvelmans, and his ground-breaking animal collecting expeditions to West Africa and the West Indies during the 1930s. During an expedition to Trinidad he discovered the first bioluminescent reptile; a small lizard. This discovery was so controversial it wasn't confirmed until the 1990s when a documentary team found the same creature in the same Trinidad cave system. He was the author of a number of books including two on UFOs.

FEBRUARY 24th **1973**
Colchester housewife - Elsie Long - got up to put the dog out, at 7.00am, when a bright 'light' caught her eye in the sky:

> *"I looked up and saw a bright object, shaped like a cigarette. It was stationary for about five minutes, then its tail faded and it moved away slowly. It seemed to be spinning very fast by the way the sun caught it. I don't know what it was. I have always been interested in other people's reports of UFOs, but this is the only one I have ever seen. After it had gone, I went back to bed and told my husband what I had seen. He just laughed."*

At 9.45pm, the same date, Garry Gill (27) of Park Avenue, Dover, was driving into Dover along Green Lane, on the Buckland Estate, accompanied by two friends.

> *"We saw this bright object in the sky over the St. Radigund's Abbey area; it was orange/pink in colour. We set off after it and had it in view in about 15mins. At one stage I believe we were about 200yds away from the object. It hovered over thorn bushes, about three quarters of a mile away from St. Radigund's Abbey, and about 100yds off the ground. Suddenly, it began to fade and took on a red colour; within 15mins it had disappeared."* **(Source: *Dover Express and East Kent News*, 22.3.73)**

Another witness was Mr. G. Ennew of the Avenue, Wivenhoe, who had this to say:

> *"I was not surprised when I read of Mrs. Long's sighting of a UFO, around 7.00am. I was in Marks Tey on the same morning. The object I saw was in the east, and I couldn't keep my eyes off it. It was the most beautiful golden colour, which I kept sight of for all of 15mins. When I first saw it, it seemed like a massive saucer, flat on its back - then it appeared to come upright - the sun's reflection making it appear cigarette shape. I know one thing, I'm not laughing."* **(Source: *Colchester Evening Gazette*, 26.2.73/27.2.73)**

MARCH 22nd 1973

Mr. C. Mark - a butcher by trade - and his wife, from Keyingham, Yorkshire, were driving from Hull to their home address, at 2.40am, when they saw a bright orange sphere pass silently in front of them, at an angle of 45°. Seconds later, it vanished from sight - like a light going out. **(Source: Mr. N. Beharrell)**

MARCH 24th 1973

Greengrocer Alan Blades (17) of Hawes was driving over the bleak and lonely Buttertubs Pass, connecting Wensleydale with Swaledale, during the early hours. As he approached the downhill run to Hawes, from the Moorland pass - famous for its limestone formations, which resemble butter tubs - he noticed a red glowing, oval-shaped object, just above his car, and between it and the 2,000ft summit of Stags Fell.

> *"At first I thought the car lights were shining on something, but when I stopped and switched them off, it was still there. I did not dare switch the engine off, in case it would not start again. At first it was upright, but then seemed to cant to one side and move slowly away. As I watched, it seemed that the underneath was spinning. By this time I was scared stiff and set off for home. As I approached the first houses, at Simonside, it had been keeping pace with me, but then accelerated to the south-east."*

When Alan arrived home he was, according to his father, Joe:

> *"...in a terrible state, and as white as a sheet and in tears"*

This wasn't the only occasion when UFOs were seen in the locality. Bizarrely, Alan's brother, Bob, and his wife, Elsie, were driving into Swaledale, a couple of months previously, when they saw a similar object some distance away. **(Source: *Northern Echo*, 26.3.73)**

APRIL 8th 1973

Mr. Glanmor Bebb (52) and his wife, June, of Maes-yr-Haf, reported having watched a saucer-shaped object, hovering over an empty advance factory, towards the direction of the Brecon Beacons, during the early evening of this date. After about ten minutes the object flashed across the horizon, faster than the eye could follow. Mrs. Bebb said later:

> *"It was hovering 300yds away. I did not know what it was, but it definitely was not an aircraft, light, or a star."*

The couple reported the incident to Blackwood Police. **(Source: *Western Mail*, 10.4.73/*South Wales Argus*, 10.4.73)**

JULY 3rd 1973

Trainee dental mechanic Michael Hallowell (16) - then an amateur UFO investigator (pictured below) - was with four friends, outside his home in Beverley Court, at 9.45pm, when he saw:

> *"...a disc-shaped object with a bright yellow centre, white rim and long blue tail, travelling at a height of approximately 600ft over Jarrow town centre. It then disappeared behind a cloud over Jarrow Central School. It looked like a fried egg. Another friend of mine came around to tell me he had also seen it pass over."*

Michael contacted the weather centre at Newcastle, who told him it was not a natural phenomenon. Coastguards at North Shields, said:

> *"We are damned if we know what it was."*

RAF Acklington, was also contacted, and the duty officer took a description from Mike of what he had seen. The Police suggested it might have been something natural, such as a meteor burning up. This was the same day as the object seen over Cradle Hill and the day before the sighting by Mrs. Good. A well-respected Fortean researcher suggested that Mike had also had a successful singing career in the United States during the same period.

In April 2012 we spoke to Mike, who has provided us with assistance, over the years:

> *"I must confess that having read the account in the* Gazette. *I've become somewhat disturbed,*

for virtually every fact stated by the reporter is contrary to recollections of my colleagues and I. It is almost as if two separate sightings are being described. The weird thing is that the presence of a fourth person had completely obliterated itself from our memories, until I read it in the clipping you sent. I have been able to contact her, and she states that the day after the event she could remember nothing about it, other than the fact that 'something had happened'.

She is very reluctant to give a statement, or talk about it, and has specifically asked that her name be kept confidential. Since reading the clipping, I've had two episodes which seem like 'flashbacks' that bear some correlation to the Gazette *account, but not to my original memory of the event. I'm baffled."* **(Source: *Shields Gazette*, 4.7.73)**

JULY 7th 1973

An oval-shaped object, with white flickering lights and a raised central section, showing red lights, was seen hovering in the sky over the Western Park estate, Leicestershire, by eleven year-old Jackie Wilson and Ian Crawford. The boys thought the object was going to land, but it suddenly shot upwards into the sky and disappeared from sight. **(Source: Geoffrey Coxon)**

IN 1973 JOHN KEEL WROTE TO BUFORA :

Dear Norman,

     . . . . We are in the midst of a great wave here.   It started last year and is continuing unabated but is receiving very little publicity.   The innumerable sightings around Piedmont, Missouri this spring, and around Manchester, Georgia in August/September, have gained national attention, however if previous patterns are repeated, and if the flap continues, UFOs may become a momentary sensation again sometime next spring.   In recent weeks there have been many sightings in the Catskill Mountains (where I spend most of my time these days) but I have not seen anything myself here.   As you know from Dr. Schwarz's FSR articles on the " Woodstock UFO Festival " of 1966, this area had quite a wave during the 1966-67 peak . . . .

     . . . . If a new publicity wave materialises I expect it will be quite different from those of the past.   The anti-Air Force/anti-Government propaganda of the Keyhoe era will probably be absent.   There will be greater emphasis on the psychological and philosophical aspects, and a number of sociologists and folklorists will surface with articles and books which will offer new perspectives and new approaches.   A whole new storm will brew between the physical scientists and the behavioural scientists. The reality of UFOs as extraterrestrial vehicles will not only be seriously challenged, but a new set of explanations will be offered. As usual, these explanations will deeply offend the ET believers. The controversy will become more diffuse and certainly more complicated.

Since 1967 I have reluctantly supported Dr. Doel's first possibility (BJ, Vol. 3, No. 11, p. 29) " That in fact saucers don't exist, and we have been duped these many years." And I have been trying to determine exactly how this hoax has been accomplished and, more importantly, why ? I do feel that the Fort/Sanderson viewpoint is the correct one, that all paranormal manifestions are interrelated, and that the core of this thing is the manipulation of human beings through what was known in other ages as magic and " enchantment." Space and Time being distorted, hallucinatory allegorical events are staged to cover up the real meaning and activities of the manipulative force. This is not a " Keel Theory " but is thousands of years old and a basic tenet of all theological concepts. Fort and Sanderson (and Keel and Vallee) attempted to simplify this, never claiming originality. Yet people like Alan Sharp are still grumbling about the " Keel Theories!"

I could cite hundreds of relatively obscure books which deal with the ufological problems in surprising ways (*e.g.* Bentham's THE THEORY OF FICTIONS, 1832) but it is my experience that hardcore ETists are not only poorly read but seem to choose to remain that way. The works of the great thinkers and observers of the paranormal of the past remain remote and even incomprehensible to the armchair ufologists. A scholarly friend of mine once remarked, " Never try to argue with a Marxist or a Hindu. They think they have the answer for everything." We might add ufologists to the list. They presuppose the intervention of extraterrestrials in all events, past and present . . . . just as Von Daniken finds evidence of the gods in every lump of carved stone.

No " Dark Force " turned me away from the ETH. Careful in-depth investigations into hundreds of UFO cases and bizarre events forced me to reject any belief and accept the available facts. The USAF and the RAF apparently underwent the same process in the 1943-55 period.

In one of his last interviews (PSYCHIC OBSERVER, February-March 1973, pp 150-55) Ivan Sanderson said, " It's been known to authorities for forty years now that they do not come to us through our space-time. They don't come from another planet. They come through from another set of dimensions, not another dimension or a fourth dimension, but they come from another whole universe, or whole bunch of universes which are interlocked with ours either in space or time. That's why we can't catch one, because they are not really here . . . . The intelligences behind certain types of them can make them just the way you, being a New Yorker, might expect in our technological age such a thing to be. Whereas for a primitive tribesman somewhere down in the Grand Cheaco they'll make it look a thing probably quite different, more like something he would know about . . . . They don't really *come* from anywhere."

john a. keel,
New York, USA.

We concur with the late John Keel, who believed in the existence of *something* or *someone* who may be just as puzzled as to what we are doing in their plane of existence, as we are about them.

We have nothing but praise for Mr. Keel's views. Dr. Hynek himself suggested that UFO manifestations appeared to owe their origin to something more in keeping with the paranormal, than the visitations of some extraterrestrial species. Apart from that, one is minded to ask what interest an advanced civilization would have in us. While UFOs have been with us down the ages, they have apparently made no direct effort to contact us as a race, if only to explain their presence on this planet. We have always felt that 'they' exist alongside us going about their everyday business, *seemingly* having no interest in the affairs of man. One thing is assured, they won't go away and will continue to be seen in our skies, irrespective of whether we believe in them or not. When we set out to discover if there was any truth to UFO phenomena, many years ago, we never considered how prolific sightings had been. If we had found only a little evidence to support the existence of such phenomena we would not we writing these books (especially bearing in mind that we are constantly being told by those in Authority that they do not exist!)

It is of interest to mention that in addition to a wave of UFO sightings that occurred in America, during October 1973, another wave was reported during November 1973 - this time centred on the Canadian province of Quebec. They included reports of UFO landings, when humanoids were seen, disturbances to vehicles, and complaints of irradiation from some witnesses concerned. It was alleged that in the majority of the humanoid incidents, the entities appeared to be engaged in reconnaissance. Once again we accept that these have not taken place in the British Isles, but they are now, in the main, forgotten cases and well worth bringing to the attention of the reader, if only to see for themselves that this is, after all, a Worldwide UFO phenomenon. Ideally, we would have liked to have covered a much bigger area in the series (approximate) which is staggering in its conceptions. These reports alluded to by Keel, included an unusual 'light', seen apparently scanning the area on the night of the 5th October 1973, which was believed, by the farmer and his wife, at Chambly, Quebec, to be the Police looking for cattle thieves, after cattle had been reported missing. The following morning, the normality of everyday life around the farm was interrupted by the arrival of a thick smoke seen ascending from a field, which was unusual as it had been raining for a short time, and the field had not been ploughed for a number of years.

At 11.35am, a round, yellowish object, resembling a cupola, some 75ft in diameter, was seen from a distance of about a third of a mile away in a field. Although this was very odd it was presumed, by the occupant's at the farm, to be boy scouts, camping, especially after five small people were seen approximately 4ft tall, their legs hidden by the tall grass. What looked like a small bulldozer emerged from the tent and made its way to a small spring, about 200ft away from the 'tent'. According to the witnesses, the 'boy scouts', who were wearing what looked like some sort of yellow helmet on their heads, were continually busy, moving backwards and forwards between the 'tent' and the 'bulldozer'. When a cursory check was made of 'them', about 25mins later, there was no sign of the objects, or the 'boy scouts'. Enquiries made, following this incident, revealed a neighbour had seen a large object take-off from that field and head off towards the nearby Rougemont Mountains. Shortly after midday, the daughter of the farm returned home from work. On hearing what had happened, she went out to have a look and discovered a large circle of burnt and crushed grass, 55ft in diameter. On the ground traces or tracks, 6ins across, were visible proceeding from this circle to a smaller one, 12ft in diameter, close to the spring. The girl returned home but later felt very sick, developing a bad headache, nausea, and symptoms of irradiation. The incident was later reported to Philippe Blaquiere and Wido Hovile - members of the UFO Quebec group - who visited the location on the 4th November 1973. The men took some colour photographs of the circles and track, which were still visible. They also noted the presence of two high voltage power lines to the west, and found a cyclical axis (a fold of rock layers that slope upward on both sides of a common low point. Synclines form when rocks are compressed by plate-tectonic forces. They can be as small as the side of a cliff or as large as an entire valley).

Another Canadian case which excited our interest, apparently paralleling that of John Day, took place during the evening of the 18th November 1973, involving four young women, aged between 14 and 24, who were travelling to Montreal. Near Sorel-Tracy in southern Quebec, they noticed a luminous 'ball', about the size of a water melon, hovering over a pylon, about a quarter of a mile ahead of their position. As the car passed this point, the object - which was described as being white in colour with a slightly yellowish tinge, surrounded by a thin halo, alternately dimming and shining - started to move, from right to left, before flying over the Saint Lawrence River. Within a short time, they realised that the object was now following them.

> *"It seemed to move closer when we were passing through uninhabited districts and recede when driving through populated areas. Sometimes it was ahead of us; other times, it was behind. Its height constantly changed from 30ft to the height of low clouds. Before arriving at Contrecour (area No. 9) a red and grey car overtook ours, at great speed. At that moment, the UFO ascended high in the sky. After leaving Contrecour the object stood still at the Poles height, far in front of us."*

While still discussing the events hotly, and recovering from what had been a frightening experience, they saw the UFO fly towards the river and hover over a field. At that time they were in a line of cars, separated by approximately 6ft and travelling at about 60mph. One of the women later said:

> *"We were forced to slow down, due to the cars in front having to pass a pink cloud, which was lying down on the road. It was light red in colour, similar to sand, and about the same length of four cars, joined together - the width of the road and the height of a car. We had no idea what was causing this cloud to appear and were astonished by what was happening and forgot about the UFO, which was hovering over a field to our left. Everything seemed very quiet and silent; our car was functioning well, and we have not felt any physical indisposition or psychological effect, neither at that moment nor since. In the cloud we had to slow down to 20mph, but when we were clear I accelerated to 40mph, but had to reduce my speed again when we saw a car that had overtaken us, now in the ditch, with its headlights on, aimed at the road."*

Incredibly the story gets even more spectacular, when we learn of the following:

> *"Just before we left the 'cloud', at 6.00pm, we saw the appearance of a small man, standing exactly on the white line of the road. I had to make a sudden manoeuvre, and stopped the car, to avoid hitting him. This little man seemed unconcerned with the passage of the vehicles and appeared to be sweeping or cleaning the road, even if the apparatus he was using seemed very unusual for that kind of job. He (the creature) was moving it back and forth exactly on the white line. 'He' was wearing clothes that were dark green in colour, or black, and was only seen from the side. His head was covered in a peaked cap that hid his face. His legs were very short, as was his outer garment. He was about 5ft tall."*

She drove past, feeling angry that she might have hit the man. She tells of seeing another car stopped by the side of the road, a little farther up, with two or three persons, in dark clothing, stood next to it. On their return journey, at 8.00pm, she says the light red cloud was still there but there was no sign of the car that had been in the ditch, and arrived home at 9.15pm. One might think that this was the end of the story - not so

BELGIUM, DECEMBER 1973

TRACY, QUEBEC
NOVEMBER 18, 1973

RESEMBLANCES BETWEEN THE HUMANOID SEEN AT TRACY, QUEBEC,
CANADA, NOVEMBER 18, 1973, AND THE HUMANOID SEEN AT
VILVORDE, BELGIUM, IN DECEMBER 1973.
NOTE ALSO THE SIMILARITIES WITH THE HUMANOIDS OF THE
BETTY AND BARNEY HILL'S CASE, U.S.A., SEPTEMBER 1961.

- At **9.15pm,** a Police Officer of the Provincial Quebec Police sighted an oval-shaped object, above the Saint Gerard-de-Magella.
- At **10.15pm,** two white parallel bars, resembling beads or globes, joined together, were seen to cross the sky in six seconds, heading in a south-east direction, from the region where Tracey had encountered her UFO.
- Five minutes later, at **10.20pm,** a luminous 'ball' was seen, stationary in the sky over Sorel, some 20° above the horizon. Its colour was seen to change from vivid blue to green, then to red. Fifteen minutes later, it had gone from sight.
- At **10.30pm,** a luminous object, resembling an upside-down pear, with red and green lights on both sides, was seen motionless in the sky over the Boulevard Industrial area, at Joliette, estimated to be 100ft above ground level. It then headed away slowly southwards, before being joined by two other similar objects.
- At **10.46pm** an object, described as looking like a truck's headlight revolving in a clockwise direction, was seen in the sky over Longueuil, on the south-eastern edge of Montreal. Seven minutes later, it moved away towards the Jacques-Cartier Bridge.
- At **11.00pm,** numerous luminous spheres were seen performing an aerial display over Saint Thomas, Joliette and Berthierville (three globes were seen) until the early hours of the next morning.

This was just the start of a heavy period of UFO activity - until now, long forgotten. It seems absurd that people still fight to convince us that the majority of UFO sightings can be explained away. The evidence is overwhelming in its implications and disturbing in nature. **(Source: as above/*The UFO Register,* Volume 7, Parts 1 & 2, Contact International, UK)**

In the same month an ex Royal Canadian Air Force officer, who had just left the force after serving five years - then living on a farm, a couple of miles from Greenwood Air Force Base, Nova Scotia - was looking out of the window, at 8.00pm, on what was a cold, clear, crisp night, with no moon and lots of starlight, when he noticed a bright light above the horizon, but at first paid no attention.

"At first I thought it was landing lights from an aircraft coming in for a landing at the Greenwood base. After a minute or two, curiosity got the better of me and I grabbed my coat and went outside. I saw a white light illuminating the horse coral from above; the horse was prancing around and acting skittish - then the light began to slowly drift towards me. I immediately yelled out to my friend, Paul, to come outside. As the light came closer, I could make out a circular, saucer-shaped object, about 40ft diameter, with a single white light coming from its centre.

By the time my friend, Paul, came outside, the object was still moving slowly towards me. There was no sound, except for a slight whistling noise - the kind of noise you might expect if a large object was passing through the air. It came to a complete stop when it was directly above us, bathing us both in light - bright enough to read a book. The UFO was no more than 100ft above our heads by this time. We were both totally in awe.

Seconds later, a military tracker (CP-121) aircraft came roaring over the roof-top of our farmhouse from behind us. It seemed they were on a collision course. In a blink of an eye, the UFO made an abrupt 90° evasive move, travelling 80ft to the North. Even above the noise of the aircraft, we could both hear the whooshing sound of the object when it moved. The tracker aircraft made a steep bank to align itself with the UFO again, and put on full throttle to its engines, hell bent to intercept this hovering object. Within a matter of five seconds, the UFO had made three quick jolting movements before I saw its lights disappear over the North Mountain, about 6 to 7 miles away. The tracker aircraft immediately throttled down its engines and returned towards the Greenwood Air Force Base."

After collecting his thoughts and realising what he had just witnessed, the man called a close friend, still stationed at the air base, and asked him to contact Greenwood Control Tower and find out what was going on. To his amazement he was told there had been no aircraft in the air at that time. Despite a number of e-mails sent to the website asking them to put us in touch with the person concerned, after explaining the nature of our work we received no replies. **(Source: UFOINFO.WWW, 2012)**

In one of his last interviews (*Psychic Observer*, February/March 1973) Ivan T. Sanderson said,

"It's been known to authorities for forty years now, that they do not come to us through our space time. They don't come from another Planet. They come through from another set of dimensions, not another dimension, or a forth dimension, but they come from another whole universe, or whole bunch of universes which are interlocked with ours either in time or space. That's why we can't catch one, because they are not really here ......The intelligences behind certain types of them can make them just the way you, being a New Yorker, might expect in our technological age, such a thing to be. Whereas for a primitive tribesman, somewhere down in the Grand Cheaco, they will make it look a thing probably quite different, more like something he would know about....they don't really come from anywhere".

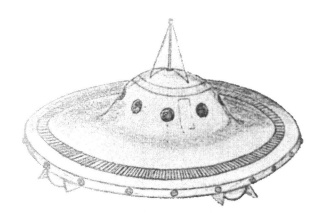

1974

After a record 84 days in orbit, the crew of *Skylab 4* returns to Earth. A Turkish Airlines Flight 981, travelling from Paris to London, crashes in woods, near Paris, killing all 346 aboard. Charles de Gaulle Airport opens in Paris, France. On 10th March, a Japanese World War II soldier, Second Lieutenant Hiroo Onoda, surrenders in the Philippines. March 18 – End of Oil embargo crisis: Most OPEC nations end a 5-month oil embargo against the United States, Europe and Japan. March – The Terracotta Army of Qin Shi Huang is discovered at Xi'an, China. April 6 – Swedish pop group, ABBA, win the 1974 Eurovision Song Contest with *Waterloo*. In Birmingham, England, two pubs are bombed, the *Mulberry Bush* and the *Talk of the Town,* killing 21 people (the Birmingham Six are later sentenced to life in prison for this).

ROY LAKE

Whe wanted to spotlight the commitment made by Barking-based UFO researcher - Roy Lake, whose has been interested in UFOs for over 50yrs. We spoke to Roy during May 2012, and asked him what had sparked off his interest.

Roy Lake, second from right, with Lady Mayoress, and alien (who the other two are, we don't know)

"After reading a book entitled Flying Saucers Have Landed, *by George Adamski, in 1953, which outlined the sighting of UFOs and Alien Beings. Strangely my own father had sighted something, but I didn't know about this until after he had passed away. I couldn't leave the subject matter alone and I was always interested in space travel as well. The first film I saw was* Destination Moon.

I remember my father saying to me, "They will never get to the Moon!" In the 1960s, when I was aged 15, I contracted TB. The Doctors gave me a year to live; I had a hole in the side of my lung, the size of an old penny. I was told I would have to be in hospital for two weeks, but two years later, after treatment and X rays, I was told that I was all clear. When I returned home I began to read books about the UFO subject, and a couple of people who knew of my interest told me about strange things they had seen. As the years passed by, I was to become the butt of ridicule but I carried on with my research. In the autumn of 1967, I was on night duty and came home, one morning, to see the postman stood outside the house, with his mouth wide open, two doors down from where I lived. I asked him what was up and he said to me, "What the bloody hell is that?" I looked up and saw what looked like a chandelier or the star of Bethlehem in the sky - the sort of thing you get on Christmas cards.

All of a sudden it just went out, as if you had turned a light off. I knew it wasn't Venus, satellite, or ice crystals. I had a feeling that I should look up. When I did so, I saw what looked like a lava lamp. It was orange in colour and reminded me of plasma - elongated in shape. It then began to move away slowly and changed shape to perfectly round and about the size of two football pitches. It was silent and headed away towards London. I was so exhilarated and excited I had seen something out of the ordinary that I rushed into the house and awoke the wife and kids. They must have thought that I was going 'round the twist'! During the afternoon, my wife awoke me earlier than usual and told me the news presenter - Kenneth Alsop - was on the TV and telling people about a UFO, chased by two Police Constables through Devon. The officers showed a drawing, which was identical to what I had seen."

Roy, now in his 70s, has met many researchers over the years, including Tony Dodd, who was to become a personal friend, and who advised him how to deal with reports of Alien abductions. Roy has appeared on *The James Whale Show*, Live TV, *The Why Files, London Weekend TV, L.B.C* and *Radio 1*. He is an authority on the UFO subject and has committed himself to the UFO cause not to gain any financial remuneration, but to offer assistance to those who have fallen victim to some frightening experiences, and support to many others

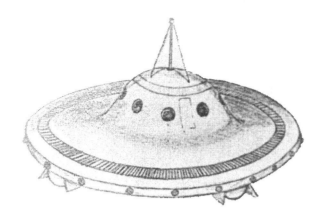

CHAPTER 5
JANUARY-JUNE 1974

UFO over Lowestoft

On 3rd January 1974, schoolboys playing on Beccles Common, near Lowestoft, ran home in fright, after a cigar-shaped object passed overhead, accompanied by a loud noise (from which the boys were to develop headaches) before dropping below the horizon.

Three days later, on the 6th January 1974, a family visiting Ashby Church, four miles north-east of Aldeby, noticed:

> *"...a golden metallic object, motionless in the clear blue sky, towards the south-east, which vanished from sight, a few minutes later."*

To their astonishment, ten minutes later, a dark grey 'cigar' shape appeared from behind cloud over in the south-west, heading slowly towards the south-east, before disappearing and reappearing in a different part of the sky. **(Source: Ivan W. Bunn)**

---

*Authors note: **John:** "I was a police officer on duty, that day, and remember seeing the interior of the Mulberry Bush, following the bombing haven taken place. on the 21st of November 1974 It is an image that I can still picture clearly - steel girders, brick walls and what were humans, reduced to a powder - all this for a cause. I was then working in Sparkhill, which was heavily populated with Irish people, and met one woman, who was in one of the Pubs that night; she was badly injured, but was one of the lucky ones. There was of course a backlash to this with many Irish businesses being target for criminal damage and arson, the situation was very tense for days afterwards. I also remember a lot of bad feeling amongst the Police, when hundreds of us were sent to the Elmdon Airport Birmingham, after ground staff at Belfast International Airport refused to handle the coffin of IRA member James Patrick McDade who was killed in an explosion while planting a bomb at the Coventry telephone exchange on the 14th of November 1974."*

UFO over Hampshire

At 8.30pm on the same day, John Victor Guthrie from Bordon, Hampshire, was driving home with his mother, along the A3, towards Hindhead, along a stretch of new dual carriageway, east of Thursley still under construction, when they noticed a bright 'light' in the western part of the sky, at an estimated height of between 2-300ft, some 400yds to their right.

"I wound down my window and reduced speed, in order to observe this rather strange object which was long diamond in shape, with a cylindrical affair, brightly lit all around on top.

I knew from its shape and the absence of any navigation lights, it was no aircraft.

By the time I stopped the car and got out, it had gone." **(Source: Ivan W. Bunn, The *Lantern* Series/ Frank Marshall, BUFORA)**

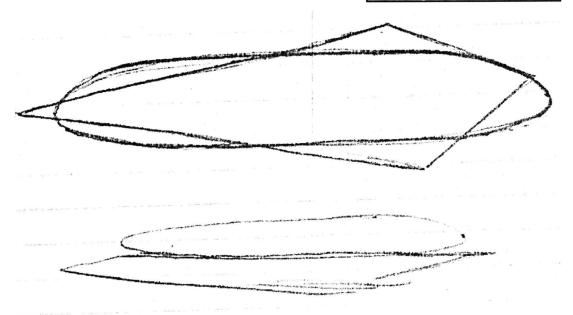

Cross-shaped UFO over Kent

At 5.25pm on 8th January 1974, Geoffrey Coughlin (15) from Buckley Hill Bromley, Kent was looking out of the window through binoculars, when he saw an intense light a long way off. He was accompanied by his mother and two brothers.

"It seemed to be hovering and then turned away slowly, but continued to turn and came about in our direction. It came fairly close to the building, but then changed course to the north and headed away, before being obscured by trees and houses on the horizon. I estimated the 'craft' to be 200ft long by 150ft wide, and was diamond or cross-shaped.

As we were about to leave, we saw in the same place, an intensely bright light. A few minutes later, the second 'craft' left in the same direction taken by the first one - west to north." **(Source: Margaret Fry)**

UFO over Bedfordshire

On the 16th January 1974, Mr. D .P. Daish, who was then employed as an RAF meteorological officer, at RAF Cardington, Bedfordshire, was at home making himself a drink in the kitchen, when he felt the urge to go and have a look outside.

"It was a wild night, with a strong gale force wind; the sky was partly cloudy, with low cloud, at a height of between 2,000-3,000ft and excellent visibility. I saw a red light about as bright as the brightest star in the sky, moving in a most peculiar way. The best way I can describe the motion is to compare it with that of a ping-pong ball on a jet of water, moving up and down very erratically. I was puzzled and called my parents and brothers to come and have a look outside. My brothers and I then made our way to the top of the garden. The light was over the old Warden Airdrome, about 2-3miles away the home of a number of antique aircraft.

We watched the light weaving and bobbing for about ten minutes, before it dropped like a stone and disappeared from sight. A short time later we saw another red light on the western horizon, moving slowly eastwards, towards us, but this turned out to be an aircraft." **(Source: FSR, Volume 21, No. 1, 1975)**

UFO over Derbyshire

Walter Buswell - a retired Police Officer from the Derbyshire Constabulary - spoke of an experience, which was to 'scar him mentally for life':

"I was on night duty, at 11.42pm on 17th January 1974, in the front passenger seat of a Police car being driven along the A50 Trunk Road, near Mayfield Golf Course, a fine dry night, with good visibility, when I noticed a number of unusual lights, low down in the sky, and brought it to the attention of the driver, 'Mo' PC Maurice Barsley, who suggested they were probably the Northern Lights."

Suddenly, without any explanation or further discussion, Maurice stopped the Police car in the middle of the road, got out, and walked to the side of the road, where he stood listening intently.

"I shouted out to him, 'What's the matter?' Maurice replied, 'I don't know, Walter... that noise'. I listened carefully, but couldn't hear anything.

Somewhat puzzled by my partner's out-of-character behaviour, I wound down the window of the car and immediately heard what sounded like the noise of a loud engine coming from the left, together with a noise similar to a child's spinning top and a high powered flame gun. I looked around the bleak landscape, hoping to identify the source of these three strange sounds - unlike anything I had ever heard before in my life."

Walter picked up the radio telephone and contacted the Force Control Room.

After explaining what was happening, they advised him to observe and report back.

"I got out of the Police car and stood in front of the vehicle, the noise still quite loud and continuous. A man on a motor scooter rode past us, stopped, got off his machine and ran over to us in a very agitated manner saying, 'I hope you don't think I'm barmy, but I have been followed by this bright light'. Unsure of how to deal with the situation, I advised him to seek shelter with us and updated Force Control room.

We decided to move from our present position on the hill to flat ground, so as to obtain an uninterrupted view of the open countryside, taking the frightened witness with us. The first thing I noticed was a bright light, low down in the sky that suddenly vanished but reappeared a couple of minutes, later now to the left of its original position, before reappearing at another location. A bright light appeared in the sky to our right, far brighter than the one previously seen, accompanied by an increase in volume. A brilliant thin beam of light either shot upwards from the ground into the sky, or the other way round - it happened so quickly - illuminating the landscape in the near distance, then extinguished. This was followed by a red light, which shot off across the sky. Darkness then returned." **(Source: personal interviews/Jenny Randles)**

Was there any connection with what was seen by the officers and a spate of what became referred to as the appearance of 'mystery helicopters' seen around Cheshire and Derbyshire, during this period? In the *Derbyshire Times,* dated 18th January 1974, it was reported that police were baffled by the same mystery helicopter, as it had been seen in the Macclesfield area, where they had kept it under constant observation before it disappeared towards the High Peak area. The Macclesfield Police Force contacted the Derbyshire Police, and alerted them to the elusive helicopter, which was sighted by patrol men heading over Mam Tor, in the vale of Edale. The police set off in pursuit, but lost sight of it when it changed its heading and disappeared in the direction of Sheffield.

There was another report, at the same time, that the helicopter had made a landing close to Jodrell Bank Radio Telescope, in the small village of Goostrey. A total of seven Police Forces were involved in attempting to identify this mysterious helicopter by January 1974, and although many more sightings were made of this mysterious night flying helicopter, no civilian or army helicopters were found to be responsible to this day.

Oddly (or maybe not) we were to come across a sighting in the 1990's of a saucer shaped object UFO seen over the Radio Telescope by a family retuning home one evening .This was brought to the attention of personnel there who explained it away as a planet!

UFO over Sunderland
During the early evening of the 23rd January 1974, Sunderland housewife Margaret Naylor, and her son, Michael, aged 11, were amazed to see a strange object, hovering over Barnes School. Mrs. Naylor described what had happened:

"After arriving home from Thornhill School, at lunchtime, my son told me he had seen four UFOs. When Michael arrived home at teatime, he told me about another UFO. I didn't really believe him until I went outside and saw a long, black, oblong object, more rounded on the top than under-neath, hovering over Barnes School.

A red light came around it - then green, yellow and orange. It seemed as if it was going to go up in flames; then the lights died down. It became black again, and continued to hover over the School, and then disappeared. I have never seen anything like that before in my life!" **(Source: *Sunderland Echo,* 24.1.74/Eileen Buckle/personal interview)**

UFO over Surrey
Mr. Trevor Duell was heading home, southwards, towards Liphook, along the Guildford by-pass, on

23rd January 1974, at 8.10pm. As he began the journey towards the summit of the hill, with Guildford Cathedral on the left of the A3, he saw some lights in the distance, which he thought might be connected with the construction of the new bridge.

After realising this couldn't be the case, as the lights were now hovering about 200ft above the bridge, he stopped the car and got out, finding he was almost directly under the lights - now visible as two beams of light, projecting downwards from a rectangular shape in the semi-darkness.

At this point several other cars pulled up. The drivers stood, or sat, watching the completely silent object, estimated to be 20ft long by 10ft wide, illuminated by red and green navigation lights, showing no sign of any tail, or wings. Ten minutes later, the 'craft' turned slightly and headed away northwards, towards the direction of Guildford. The following night, a similar UFO was seen over Farnham. **(Source: Omar Fowler, SIGAP/PRA)**

UFO sighted on the Berwyn Mountain

At 8.30pm on 23rd January 1974, a huge explosion shattered the peace of the night sky around the villages of Bala, Llandrillo, and Llandderfel, situated next to the Berwyn Mountain range. Little did anyone suspect, in their wildest dreams, *then,* that this incident was to lead to huge media curiosity, still current over 35years later and attract explanations offered ranging from the rational to the bizarre they included -

- An alleged landing of an Alien craft, followed by the recovery of alien bodies, covertly extracted from the scene by the military.
- Top secret aircraft that crashed.
- Earthlights.
- Misidentification of natural phenomenon.

Over the years, there have been numerous investigations made into this matter and subsequently published, by people such as Andy Roberts (opposite) writing in *UFO Down? The Berwyn Mountain Crash* and Margaret Fry of the Welsh Federation of Independent Ufologists, details of which were published in her book, '*Link to the Stars,* ' in 2009

One of the sources behind the suggestion it was a recovered UFO, was retired Police Sergeant Tony Dodd - then head of UFO investigations for Quest International - who became known to us, after I (John) joined Quest as an investigator in the mid 1990s.

Ironically the only matter I was ever asked to become involved in was offering some support to Janet, from Stourport, who had alleged, through the *News of the World,* that she had been abducted by aliens and wanted to see Tony, who asked me to see her on his behalf .I have to admit I was completely out of my depth, but believed she was a genuine woman, who was clearly still traumatised by what had occurred to her. For some reason what stuck out in my memory was when she told me that after waking up in her bed she discovered some strange marks on her feet caused by she alleged walking up the ramp that led into the craft. Clearly the use of hypnotic regression as an instrument to obtain evidence form the subconscious memory of the UFO witness is one of a specialised nature and are matters well outside our remit. Tony told of being contacted by a high ranking military officer:

> *"At 11.36pm, they made their way to the Berwyn area and decamped in a car park off the above and to the side of the B4391, which cuts through to the top of the mountain before making its way to the village of Llangynog. Soldiers then arrived from the mountainside carrying oblong boxes, which were loaded onto the officer's vehicles.*
>
> *The informant told me he was ordered to take the boxes to Porton Down, in Wiltshire. When they arrived, the boxes were then opened in front of the*

MYSTERY: January 1974...an explosion...fear...UFO?

A QUARTER of a century ago, on a cold, unsuspecting mid–January night a massive explosion shook the earth of the Berwyn mountains. What followed didn't just awaken fears in Corwen and Bala but has proved country–wide intrigue since 1974. Following countless theories about what happened that night at Cader Bronwen, near the village of Llandderfel, many local people believe events were 'swept under the carpet'.

Berwyn alien cover–up?

It WAS a UFO I saw that night

NORTH WALES DAILY POST JULY 2nd 2008
PART TWO OF TWO.

Retired gamekeeper breaks silence over 'the Welsh Roswell'

Retired gamekeeper Geraint Edwards speaks out about an incident in the Berwyn Mountains which he insists was a close encounter

Believers in UFO crash are limited in their research

2374

YOUR piece about the alleged Berwyn Mountain UFO crash (*Leader*, February 8) was interesting in that it demonstrated the research limitations of those who believe in the physical reality of a UFO crash.

Scott Felton rails against me for my theory that one of the lights seen that night was that of a poacher's lamp.

I did hold this theory for many years, based on documented evidence about the times and location of the poachers on the hillside, the type of lamp they were using and what Nurse Pat Evans saw.

But good research never stagnates and when, two years ago, I came across further information about the poachers and their whereabouts at the relevant time, I altered my theory to fit the facts.

In my book about the Berwyn events, *UFO Down* (CFZ, 2010) which Scott clearly chose not to read for fear of being exposed to documentary evidence, I detail all the relevant theories and twists and turns of this most unusual event.

There is no evidence – but much wishful thinking – to suggest an 'alien' spaceship crashed on the Berwyn Mountains on January 23, 1974.

But the huge light Pat Evans and her daughters observed for 15 minutes remains unexplained and as such the mystery of the Berwyns continues.

**Andy Roberts,
Caerwys.**

■ An artist's impression of the UFO crash.

staff. They were astonished to see what appeared to be two dead Alien bodies. They were 5-6ft tall and thin and looked almost like skeletons covered with skin."

It was brought to Tony's attention that the incident had not happened until the 24th January, 1974. He suggested the possibility that a second UFO had gone to the assistance of the first one, which had crash-landed on the Berwyn Mountain. A similar account, involving the recovery of alien material from off the Berwyns was given to Bristol based UFO researcher, Terry Hooper, in 1990, by an army Air Corps officer of Flight Lieutenant Rank, who contacted him by telephone (referred to as 'K.M'). He told him (from Margaret Fry's book, *Link to the Stars*) :

> *"That he and a colleague, who were then members of an operational unit (unnamed but still in existence today), were instructed by their Commanding Officer to take part in an I.O (In and Out) job, in 1974."*

The man said he was part of an army unit that travelled up past Birmingham, and arrived at Llangollen on the 20th January 1974. He claimed they had escorted a number of oblong boxes to Porton Down, Wiltshire, and that he his companions were warned that if they opened the boxes, they would be arrested. If they resisted arrest, they would be shot! The man also claimed that:

> *"...a pilot friend of his had flown Army men to Berwyn Mountain, with containers, in three army helicopters, to the mountains, which they filled with wreckage and flew to Porton Down!"*

The informant then sent Terry four silvery shards claiming they had been given to him by the anonymous RAF man, who said that they had been taken covertly from the debris. The rest of the object had allegedly been taken to Porton Down, (now the Defence Science and Technology Laboratory, an Executive Agency of the Ministry of Defence) in Wiltshire - a place that, to the layman, is sinisterly synonymous with germ warfare. Terry gave the samples to two separate parties, who promised they would analyse them, but these were never returned. The fourth, some 2ins x 2ins, in size he sent to UFO researcher - Margaret Ellen Fry. This arrived at her house on the 23rd January, 1997. Margaret said:

> *"I gave this fragment to Roy Winch, a family friend, who was knowledgeable with aircraft components, both in the UK and the USA. He told me that it was not aluminium, lithium steel, iron, and wasn't magnetic. The silver fragment was slightly pitted and scratched and was light as a feather, yet impossible to bend, flatten, or scratch. When we first had the fragment, we noticed it showed complicated patterns of circles and at one time four, three dimensional florets, which have now faded."*

Over the Christmas period of 2011, we contacted Terry, who confirmed having sent the material to Margaret, but told us he had now proved to his own satisfaction that the information obtained from 'K.M' was:

> *"...proven to be a lie, and that I (Terry) believed the fragments to be a mix of*

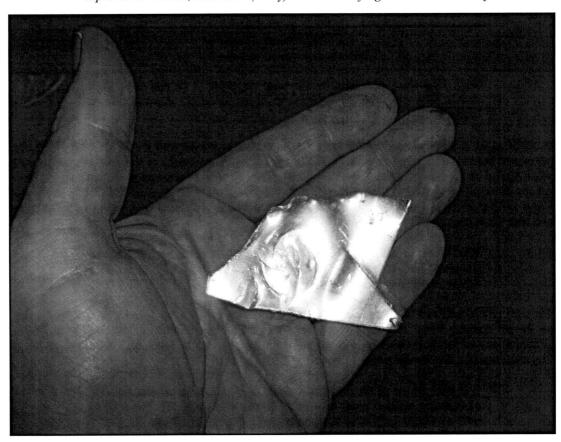

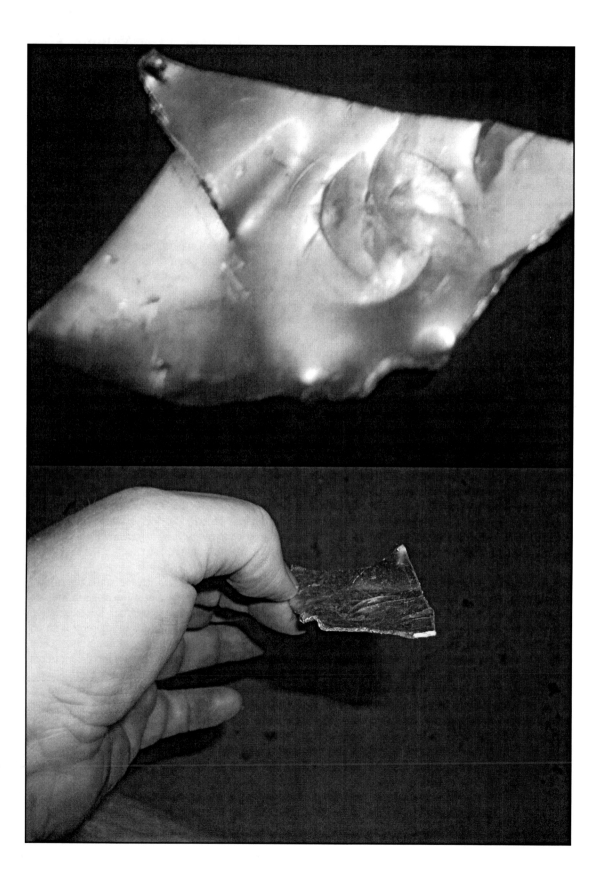

alloys, rather than anything of Alien origin. Furthermore, I do not believe there was ever any UFO crash on the Berwyns at all."

Whilst we have no reason in disbelieving accounts of saucer-shaped objects and their occasional perceived occupants on the ground, their physical detention by the authorities are matters that invariably usually rest on unreliable sources of information, probably because we have never come across anyone that has claimed they have detained the occupants of these machines! We have always been wary of information involving the crash-landing of alien ships and the recovery of alien bodies. One would presume that if this scenario had taken place, the Public would be none the wiser. An example of the way in which the truth is stretched to suit the individual belief system of the researcher took place some years ago, and involved an interview with a USAF Captain, who claimed he had filmed UFOs over a Lincolnshire Airbase. When we eventually tracked down the source of this information (the editor of a Newspaper) he admitted that all he had ever received was a letter, with scant details about the incident. Needless to say, the information contained in the letter did not support the lengthy article which followed, later published in a UFO magazine that told of covert meetings with the 'informant' on a lonely rain swept railway platform in Yorkshire, and a story which was, to put it bluntly, embellished out of all existence.

Perhaps the reader can understand our reticence in accepting versions of events like this, rather than listening to people of honest and reliable background, who have nothing to gain but much to lose by coming forward and just telling what they saw. Common sense dictates that, within the fabric of our defence forces, there exists a specialised team of people, who would be called out to recover debris that has either been found or landed on this Planet, this would of course include virtually anything either man made or not! One would presume that such a team would be highly trained and fully aware of the dangers to the public, through contamination and radiation, and that a thorough forensic examination would be made of the locality concerned. It would be fair to say that this presupposition would appear to have been given credence, bearing in mind the instances we were to come across involving what appeared to be visits by government officials, following a report of a UFO seen in the locality. We appreciate that things may have been a little more rustic in 1974, but the very suggestion that soldiers of the lowest rank could interfere with secure containers, whether stone or metal aboard the lorry, while *en route* to Porton Down, seems impossible to believe, *not because it may or may not have happened during recent history,* but about the way in which we are told it happened that's the subtle difference!

What concerns us is that while we would not be surprised if an alien craft had landed and alien bodies recovered (a scenario which, for all we know, may well have already taken place at some stage in modern history), the sequence of reported events seems, in this instance, to be too good to be true. The suggestion 'they' were moved by army vehicles and driven down the motorway sounds more in keeping with an episode of *Dr. Who!* But, of course, this is what the newspapers adore. They enjoy nothing else than a 'flying saucer' yarn, dished out with lashings of covert operations and aliens, who may have conquered the vastness of space with their far more advanced technology, only to crash-land on Earth! Terry Hooper claims that in 1979, *the true events of that night* were revealed to him and his colleague, Franklyn, by a Senior Police Officer, following communication with the Home Office. We asked Terry if he was prepared to tell us more information about what was, after all, a rather startling statement, but he declined, which of course, is his prerogative. We asked American scientist Nick Reite to have a look at the photos submitted to us by Terry, after having sent a copy of the 'material' photos (as shown and described in Margaret's book) which, for all intent and purpose, had come from the same source, as far as we knew.

"The metal seen in the manuscript pictures may be similar to the ones held in the hands in the Berwyn 1 through 4... But they are not the same pieces that

are for sure. The text of the story claims that the UFO metal was super-light and super tough? Not so tough as to defy tin snips, which left their mark? What I will do is take the one picture. I am talking about, circle the area of interest and re-attach it here.

Again, I really can't say for sure what the metal is. In the Berwyn 001 through 003 pics, it looks like either stainless steel or aluminium. In Berwyn 004, it looks almost like galvanized (zinc coated) metal of some sort. If it truly is lightweight, it could be a magnesium or aluminium alloy. Good God! I hope it's not beryllium (a toxic metal, though only nasty in dust, shavings, or ingestion) If you can get some, John, I can get you a definitive answer."

We spoke to Terry, who assured us that the sample sent to us was from the same batch of metal sent to Margaret Fry. The fact that it appears different in description and visual image is something we are unable to explain. Perhaps there was some variation in what was supplied to Terry by his contact. The answer eludes us both.

On the 9th January 2012, we received a sample of the material from Terry Hooper for analysis by Nick Reiter. The metal was first of all photographed before being cut into two. One piece was then posted on the 13th January 2012, to Nick. The sample was received by Nick on the 23rd January 2012, who had

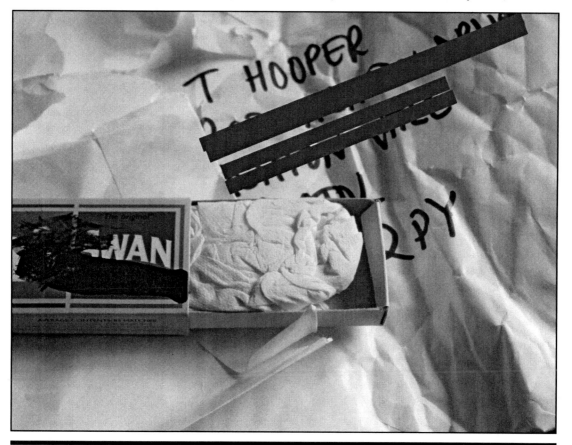

this to say:

> *"Well just in some simple tests I did myself, I can say that it is NOT magnesium. So I rather think it is not the same metal that was indicated in the "cropped" older EDS graph that was published (the one I was able to identify the un-labelled partial peaks for). Still won't know for sure until I have some EDS done on it - looking into that right now. My prediction is that it's an aluminium alloy."*

In a personal email, sent to us on the 18th February, 2012, Nick explained that due to reasons beyond his control he had been unable to arrange the scientific examination of the sample using the SEM and EDS work, because of recently implanted restrictions now currently in force at the University he uses. Unless he was prepared to pay, $500 which wouldn't be cost effective bearing in mind that we believe this to be aluminium.

Nick being the sort of man who appears to thrive on dogged determination to get the job done, gave us his findings in March 2012:

> *"One of my first impressions of the Berwyn metal (below) was that it looked like it had a conventional sheet metal "mill finish" surface pattern - in other words a very fine pattern of lines (generally less than a micron deep)*

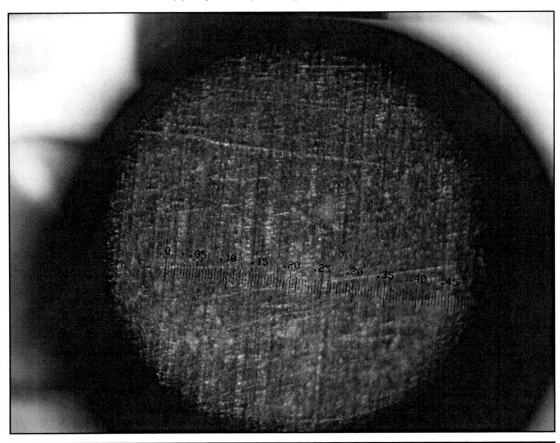

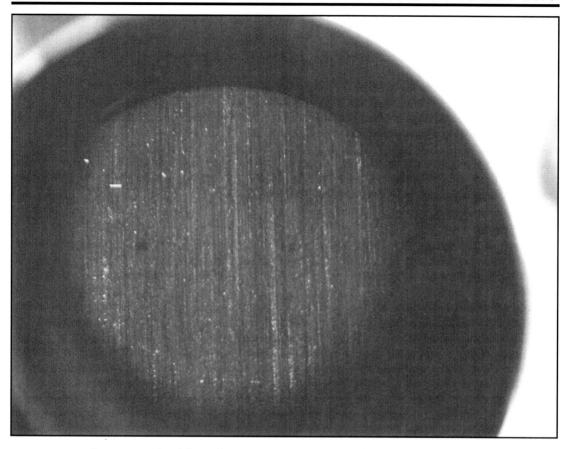

that is a result of the milling rolls the hot sheet metal is extruded between when it is made. On both sides of the Berwyn sample, this mill finish is in the same direction, indicating that it was indeed made by a typical roll process. I used a small inspection microscope to get a couple of photographs at about 30X magnification. I took a photograph of the surface finish of the Berwyn sample, and one of a piece of 6061 alloy aluminium sheet metal of the same thickness (commercially obtained). As you can see, both have a similar finish and texture, although the Berwyn piece has lateral scratches and pits, indicating simply that it has been handled quite a bit. The control piece (above) is a new piece of metal obtained from McMaster Carr Company in the US.

I used a micrometer to measure the thickness of the Berwyn metal in several spots. It is a very neat .050 inches thick - a common industrial thickness for aluminum sheet of many grades.

I then used a flame test for magnesium on a small shaving of the Berwyn metal. Negative results - it is not a magnesium alloy. I then used a calibrated NaOH solution to look for solubility with another small shaving. Yes, in this case, the shaving of metal dissolves like aluminium. It appears to be an aluminium alloy. It is my hope that EDS spectroscopy will be able to *pinpoint what alloy.*

The alloy is neither ferromagnetic, radioactive, or fluorescent.

EDS will be the most definitive arbiter of the composition of the Berwyn metal. However until that time, my engineering opinion is that the sample is a small cutting of a common thickness (.050") of aluminium sheet metal, showing a coherent surface finish from common dual roll extrusion."

Although some people might wonder why on earth we would go to these lengths to establish that this was highly likely to be aluminium, it seems only right that one should do so, rather than allow speculation and conjecture to continue by those that would believe differently.

The Event

At 8.30pm on 23rd January 1974, a ten mile stretch of the Berwyn Mountain range, between the B4391 Bala to Llangynog road, that included the villages of Llandderfel, Llandrillo and Cynwyd, were shaken by a strong Earth Tremor - its epicentre being some 5,000 metres below the town of Bala.

Edinburgh University seismological department recorded an earth tremor at 8.39pm, following the explosion at 8.39pm. One would assume that this was caused by a large meteorite, entering the Earths atmosphere?

As a result of this tremor many people came out of their house, curious as to the cause of the loud 'explosive noise'. Some saw beams of light over the ridge of Cefn Pen-Llety, which rises steeply above Llandrillo, towards the peak of Cader Bronwen Mountain; thinking it might have been an air crash, some telephoned the Police. They set up a major incident log and instructed Police Officers to make their way to Llandrillo, to conduct a search and rescue, where they were joined by a three man team from RAF Valley.

The Officers arrived in the yard at Garthiaen Farm, (situated below the lower pastures of Cader Bronwen), at 9.10pm, and spoke to Huw Lloyd - the teenage son of the occupants. He then agreed to drive them along the farm tracks above Llandrillo in his Land Rover.

A few minutes into the journey, they found their passage partly blocked by a car, which was known to belong to locals, who were engaged in occasional poaching, known as 'lamping' - shining a large, powerful, beam along the field, to disturb rabbits and hares before setting dogs on them, illuminating the area seen by some of the villages from below.

Despite a drive around by the party concerned, who chose to stay inside the vehicle, rather than conducting any search on foot, which would have been impractical at that time of night, understanding the terrain of Cader Bronwen, nothing was seen out of the ordinary, apart from a brief white glow in the terrain to the south.

The only other vehicle seen was a Police car, on their way back to the farm. Another witness to the mysterious sound and tremor felt was District Nurse, Pat Evans, from LLandderfel who, thinking that it might have been caused by an aircraft crashing to Earth, contacted the Police at Colwyn Bay to offer medical assistance, just before 9.30pm.

Due to the telephone lines being inundated with calls, she was told to *'go and have a look'*. (Despite

GWYNEDD CONSTABULARY

Form No. 162

DIVISION <u>Llandudno</u>

POLICE STATION <u>Dolgellau</u>

Date <u>30th January, 1974</u>

To: The Chief Superintendent, Llandudno

From: Inspector G. O. Evans

Subject:

Institute of Geological Sciences

Sir,

I have to report, with reference to telex serial No. 43/29/1/74, that the following information may be of interest to the survey team.

At 9.5 p.m. on Wednesday the 23rd January, 1974, I was informed by Inspector Vaughan, Operations Room, Headquarters, of an incident at Llandrillo.

Having regard to the substance of that information I feared an aircraft disaster in the vicinity of Llandrillo and, having made the necessary local arrangements for such a contingency, I left Dolgellau by car immediately, for Llandrillo. On the way I stopped in Bala where I consulted briefly with P.S. E. W. Roberts and together we set off from Bala for Llandrillo in the Bala G.P. van which Sergeant Roberts drove.

It was a dark, cold, wet and windy night.

We reached Llandderfel turn off on the B4401 about 9.35 p.m. and arrived in Llandrillo about 9.40 p.m.

Whilst travelling along the B4401, at a grid position which I now estimate to be 014370, I saw, first through the top nearside part of the windscreen and almost immediately thereafter through the nearside door window, a green light which appeared to me at that time to be a Verey Light signal. This supposed signal lasted for approximately 5 seconds before it extinguished or became hidden from sight by rising ground. From my position it was at an angle of about 45° high from the road. It was some considerable distance away as its' light was not reflected on our position. It was travelling and seemed to be from ground to air. It travelled in an arched trajectory. I cannot, with any degree of certainty, estimate its' direction of travel, but it seemed to be travelling east. I associated this light with the supposed aircraft and in fact Sergeant Roberts and I discussed its' significance especially as a green light would not normally be used in such circumstances.

We were at this time travelling at high speed and visibilit: through the windows of the G.P. van was somewhat reduced due to raindrops and misting. In addition the road was not very well known to me.

It will be observed that position, on grid reference 014370, would give, in daylight, a good view east along the Dee river valley and the land on each side is fairly high. It is possible, and not at all a certainty, that the light came

from behind the southern range of hills, across the valley
and became hidden from view behind the hills on the northern
side of the valley.

   Having regard to the fact that the incident was not
connected in any way with a crashed aircraft, the bright
green light seen by Sergeant Roberts and I, an hour after
the time of the reported explosion, assumed an entirely
different aspect which is unexplained so far as I am
concerned. That night, and the following day, I spoke
with several of the villagers. Some said that on feeling
the very severe tremor and hearing a sound, described by
many as a train rushing through the village, they ran out
into the streets and saw lights coming from a position south
of the village and beyond the range of hills in that area.
To my surprise not one of them mentioned the green light,
although most of them must have been out in the village
streets at that time as they were on our arrival about five
minutes after the light was seen by us.

.... Inspector.

It is worth bringing to the attention of the readers another incident that took place in December 1966,
when a vivid flash was seen in the sky over Warwickshire, followed by an explosion, which was reported
over a 50 mile radius. The culprit was discovered to be a 2lb (910g) rock, previously part of an asteroid
belt, orbiting Mars and Jupiter - dating back 4.5 billion years - which came to Earth at the tiny village
of Barwell, near Leicester.

We learnt that if a meteorite is sufficiently large, and compresses enough air in front of it (bearing in
mind it would have been considerably larger when it hit the outer atmosphere, possibly three times that
size) you will get a sonic boom. When this happens they are called a bolide. The noise from that
explosion can cause a bang as well

OPERATIONS ROOM -- INCIDENT/MESSAGE FORM

Form ◯

CONSOLE No.	RECEIVED BY	DATE	TIME	FROM (NAME, ADDRESS, TELE. No.)	MESSAGE N°
3	173.	23	2054	MR. BISCO. 7 TYNYGROES. Llandeilo. 279	4-9

TEL.	P.F.N.	V.H.F.	VERBAL	999		TELEX No.
				✓		

INCIDENT AT ½ml. S.E. Llandeilo.

PREVIOUS ?

NATURE There has been a tremendous explosion and I can see lights on the mountain. I think it's a crashed aircraft. My wife states there are

CLASSIFICA?

999/1

OFFICER I/C INCIDENT AND/OR REPORTING: lights flickering on the mountain

ACTION TAKEN (INDICATING RESULT) — My neighbour thinks it's a man made explosion. He saw a Land Rover making its way up the mountain earlier this evening There is nothing to be seen on the mountain now

2100	Carmarthen Ambulance — informed
2107	Llanelli Ambulance & Fire Service informed.
2115	Pc 192 - 717 in WA 023 directed to scene
2149	Insp Hughes Holywell - The first report was recorded here at 2035 - I am going out to investigate
2150	Insp. G.O. Evans - reqd further info - en route to scene

Passed To	Received By	Sent By	Time	Copy
C.C.				
D.C.C.				
A.C.C.				
TRAFFIC				
C.I.D.				
ADMIN.				
DIVS				

INSPECTOR – DUTY OFFICER

OPERATIONS ROOM — INCIDENT/MESSAGE FORM

CONSOLE No.	RECEIVED BY		DATE	TIME	FROM (NAME, ADDRESS, TELE. No.)	M
8			24·10·4	0910	P.S 592.	

TEL.	P.F.N.	V.H.F.	VERBAL	999	TO Seismological Dept.	TELE
T					Edinburgh Observatory.	

INCIDENT AT Llanavillo.   PREVIOUS

NATURE   Have you any information on the readings
from your seismograph yet please.   CLASSIFICAT

OFFICER I/C INCIDENT AND/OR REPORTING: Not yet. However J. with the

ACTION TAKEN (INDICATING RESULT) trigonometrical distances involved we
will be unable to pin-point its location but we should
be able to say if it is an earth tremor or an impact
tremor and from the energy dissipated some idea of the
mass of the object can be assessed.

10.50   The seismograph readings indicate a tremor of
RESULT   magnitude 4 which is of earthquake proportions.
We are unable to state if it is of impacts origin
or natural earth tremor.

INSPECTOR — DUTY OFFICER

Passed To	Received By	Sent By	Time	Copy
C.C.				
D.C.C.				
A.C.C.				
TRAFFIC				
C.I.D.				
ADMIN.				
DIVS.				

OPERATIONS ROOM – INCIDENT/MESSAGE FORM

Form 326

CONSOLE No.	RECEIVED BY	DATE	TIME	FROM (NAME, ADDRESS, TELE. No.)	MESSAGE No
	[illegible]	[illegible]	[illegible]	Mr [illegible] Dudlock, [illegible] Place, [illegible] Road, [illegible] 810	[illegible]

TEL.	P.F.N.	V.H.F.	VERBAL	999	TELEX
✓					

INCIDENT AT

PREVIOUS RE

NATURE At about 10pm, last night I saw a bright light, hovering & then falling North of [illegible], vertical from the East; between the North Pole Star

CLASSIFICAT

OFFICER I/C INCIDENT AND/OR REPORTING: [illegible] Constellation.

ACTION TAKEN (INDICATING RESULT) thought that I would inform you because of the reports of tremor in Wales.

[illegible] none was heard.

This light was well clear of North Wales area.

Passed To	Received By	Sent By	Time	Copy T
C.C.				
D.C.C.				
A.C.C.				
TRAFFIC				
C.I.D.				
ADMIN.				
DIVS.				

[illegible signature]

INSPECTOR – DUTY OFFICER

OPERATIONS ROOM — INCIDENT/MESSAGE FORM   Form 326

CONSOLE No.	RECEIVED BY	DATE	TIME	FROM (NAME, ADDRESS, TELE. No.)	MESSAGE No.
C				Alan Lewis,	C.1

TEL.	P.F.N.	V.H.F.	VERBAL	999		17 Industrial Terrace	TELEX
				✓		Llanrwst	

INCIDENT AT — Llanrwst

PREVIOUS REF
HQ 5154(?)
07
CLASSIFICATE

NATURE — Explosion   MH 075 345.
              (LLANRWST (CADER BRONWEN))

OFFICER I/C INCIDENT AND/OR REPORTING: There has been a terrific
ACTION TAKEN (INDICATING RESULT) — explosion somewhere, all
the houses in the estate have been shaken.
All the village are out but we don't
know what it is

(other 999 calls being received at same
time).

2056 - contacted duty crew Sgt Vassey RAF Valley to
to investigate possible crashed aircraft (?)
2058 - ?? Sgt Vassey, inf. (will investigate)
2100 - ?? (on duty at Llandudno) there was
a terrific explosion I heard it. There is
a flashing light on on CADER BRONWEN it
could be a crashed
aircraft. (   )
'999' received

	Passed To	Received By	Sent By	Time	
	C.C.				
	D.C.C.	.			
	A.C.C.				
	TRAFFIC				
	C.I.D.				
	ADMIN.				
	DIVS.				

P.T.O.
INSPECTOR – DUTY OFFICER

Pat Evans
District Nurse, Llandrillo

knowing Officers were searching land above Llandrillo, and a major log being opened, Mrs. Evans was not given any specific location.)

Mrs. Evans decided to make her way up to a vantage point on the B4391 Road, which leads up and over the Berwyn Mountain range, some 15 minutes travel time from her home, accompanied by her teenage daughters Diane and Tina - both of whom possessed basic first aid training.

When they arrived at the road summit, the mother and two daughters were astonished to sight:

> *"A massive full moon sized object, glowing and pulsating on the dark hillside. We didn't see it land, or take off. We saw some vehicle lights in the distance and small torch-like twinkling lights around the object itself, which we took to be rescuers lights. We judged the object was about a mile away and impossible to get to easily on foot, so we decided to return home. However, we did hear that something loud had taken off about ten minutes after leaving the scene."*

After watching it for a few minutes, they drove along the road, turned around, and continued to observe it for a little longer.

Unknown to the women, the same object was seen by several other witnesses, one of whom told of

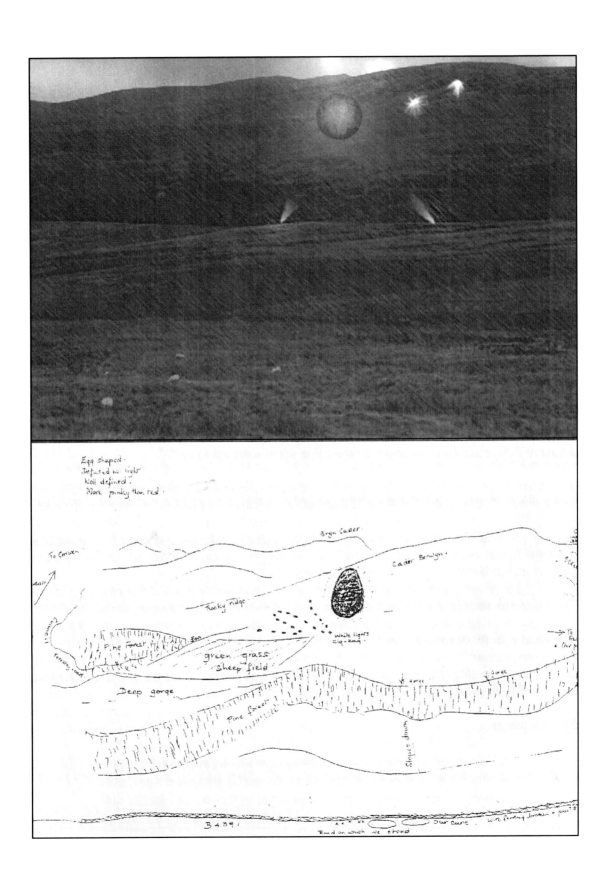

Egg shaped.
Defused no light
Well defined.
More pointy than rest.

To Corwen

Bryn Cader

Cader Berwyn

Rocky ridge

Pine Forest

White lights zig-zag.

green grass
Sheep field

Deep gorge

Pine Forest

Slopes down

B 4391

Road on which we stood

seeing it initially at 8.40pm, and then later watching it slowly descend onto Cader Bronwen by 9.25pm.

The next day, after an unsuccessful search was made of Cader Bronwen by Police and the RAF team, despite no aircraft having been reported missing, this search being officially completed just after 2.00pm, on the afternoon of the 24[th,] contrary to popular belief, there is no evidence of them having conducted any search of Cader Berwyn. Huw Lloyd, who guided the Police up Cader Bronwen on the 23rd January, claimed the RAF team (only) was spotted searching Cader Berwyn later in the afternoon. This probably resulted in gossip circulating locally. Pat Evans, and her daughters, was the subject of humour directed against them, of having encountered: *'Dynion bach qwrydd' - 'little green men'*.

An example of this was a televised documentary, produced from interviews with several non-primary witnesses made by *Firefly Productions,* on 2nd July 2008. Unfortunately, the programme contains many inaccuracies. Both testimonial and material evidence was not broadcast and, in our view, failed to offer a balanced account of what had taken place. The researcher in this matter was Scott Felton a man we had met up with up some years previously, who had showed us the scene of the incident. Scott is a friend of Margaret Fry and the couple have been working together on this matter for some time now.

Scott Felton said:

> "Firefly Productions *and* Channel 5 *programme failed to deliver a fair and balanced production, despite having promised me differently. I am very disappointed with their coverage of this event, and am surprised they had the opportunity to finally put the record straight, knowing that not one single newspaper article or other documentary has ever managed to convey the true information known at the time. In fact, this is probably the worst and most prejudiced programme ever to be shown, giving large amounts of air time to those opposed to the event and absolutely none to those for the event.*
>
> *With hindsight I now believe that this particular documentary and the series as a whole was commissioned with the deliberate intention of debunking Britain's best known UFO event in the light of the release of hitherto classified files and public interest in a spate of UK UFO sightings earlier in 2008. Several other UFO Investigators involved in other cases were asked to take part and it seems the purpose was to learn the extent of their evidence with no intention of whatsoever using it. This would be of no value to a TV Company, so I believe it will have been passed on to persons or agencies unknown."*

This was the same company that contacted us and Margaret Fry for information relating to various investigations carried out by us, including a spectacular incident in July 1955, involving Margaret Fry, when she and her companion witnessed the extraordinary landing of a UFO at Bexleyheath, in Kent, details of which can be found in *Volume 1.*

After emailing them copies of our 'write-up', which included corroboratory evidence from other witnesses, they inexplicably changed their mind about using the material.

Another case we discussed with them was the Zygmunt (some spell it Zygmund) Adamski incident. This was reinvestigated by us and Doncaster based UFO researcher, David Sankey. Despite it being patently obvious to all and sundry, there was no connection between this man's death and UFO activity, we were advised they were still going to link Mr Adamski death with UFO activity rather than referring to our investigation into the matter which showed nothing of the kind had taken place. The reason why they decided on this course of action, as outlined in an email sent to us, was because:

"It would help the viewing figures."

Scott Felton points out that while he would consider any theory to explain the origin of this incident, built on the accumulated evidence obtained by himself and Margaret Fry, he will not condone any conclusions arrived at by the presentation of inaccurate statements, for obvious reasons.

> *"There is no evidence to support a UFO crash. This was invented, sadly, by UFO enthusiasts, who tried to link noises from an earth tremor that same night with an impacting UFO. There was a seismic event that evening and a coincidental meteor shower. Debunkers have used these natural events to try and explain away what people saw. It is also the case that locals have been looked upon as rustic and ignorant and by definition, must be wrong about their observations.*
>
> *Whether or not there was a UFO about that night is, to me, not important. I am more concerned about the lengths certain persons have gone to, to cover up and debunk the event. Something must be frightening these people for such extreme measures to be enacted. I myself have persistently had Wikipedia entries (2009) countering the debunking versions removed.*
>
> *To this day, there are some who persist in claiming three witnesses saw a poacher's lamp rather than an alien craft, which is inaccurate, as the poachers had left the mountain range completely 45 minutes before that particular witness observation, and that they have testified to this on several occasions, that Police Officers did not conduct a foot search and thus their torches were mistakenly seen, and most important of all, it omits the fact that the UFO and the poachers/Police were actually on two totally different mountains, several miles apart.*
>
> *Another debunker deliberately omitted records of the distance travelled by Mrs. Evans and the distance concerned, which showed several miles difference. The idea being that a search had been carried out by the Emergency services on Cader Berwyn when, in fact, it was Cader Bronwen, some four miles away from where the UFO was seen, not forgetting the poachers were not even on the range after 9.30pm.*
>
> *When reports of activity on Cader Bronwen, above Llandrillo, began to come in, the authorities carried out a search of that location – the wrong location; without Mrs. Evans and her daughters' eye-witness accounts, there would be no Berwyn Mountain case at all.*
>
> *Contrary to much of the rubbish bandied about in books and reports, and on the Internet, Pat Evans regrets ever having reported this matter*

and was effectively hounded out of her home by disrespectful UFO enthusiasts. These days she spends much of her retirement abroad - small wonder that people who treat others like this are incapable themselves of analysing evidence and testimony and presenting it correctly.

She got hardly a moment's peace and in so harassing this woman, UFO enthusiasts themselves have probably done as much harm to this event's case as the debunkers. Fortunately, Mrs. Evans is well, but equally unhappy about being misrepresented by virtually everyone with whom she has spoken about the event, apart from North Wales based UFO researcher, Margaret Fry. Nor would she knowingly give any information to anyone directly or indirectly, which would be used to debunk her claim of what both she and her two daughters saw."

Scott is shown standing next to the telephone box, in the Village of Llandrillo, from where a number of calls were made in 1974 by the villagers, following the earth tremor at approx 8.35pm. Villagers using the box said they could see lights/beams etc., coming from over the horizon of the hill crest in the background. They were the lights of local hunters, lamping rabbits.

The coincidence of tremor sounds and the lights led residents, and then the Police, to conclude a plane had crashed on the slopes of Cader Bronwen Mountain, above and behind this ridge. Scott Felton continues:

> *"Some four miles away on a neighbouring mountain - Cader Berwyn - was a descending UFO, witnessed by residents of two separate properties. Property resident 1 saw the UFO at 8.40 pm, after leaving his abode following the tremor. Property residents 2 saw the object at 9.10pm, in the company of resident 1. All then observed the UFO slowly descend onto a lower slope of Cader Berwyn. In doing this, it left their field of vision at 9.25 pm, still descending. The resting UFO was later observed by Mrs. Pat Evans and her two daughters, who were yet a further mile away from Llandrillo, on the B4391 Bala to Llangynog road, at about 10.00pm.*
>
> *In later years, the tremor noises and lights, and Mrs Evans' sighting, were hijacked by misinformed UFO enthusiasts and poor researching, to create the myth that an impacting UFO had crashed near Llandrillo, and even caused the 'quake'. The UFO was nowhere near Llandrillo, and there is no first-hand evidence for a crash."*

The validity of the witnesses, especially Pat Evans, has never been in issue. Sadly, for having the courage to just report what she and her two daughters had seen, she was herself the target of inane comments made to her by sceptical locals. Unfortunately, the media has chosen to continue to portray this incident as a mystery of epic proportions, when common sense and rationality suggest otherwise.

The suggestion that an alien craft crash-landed at Berwyn will continue to attract the attention of those that wish to keep the myth alive, irrespective of no substantive evidence to corroborate this line of speculation. However, we learned that members of the army were in attendance, according to Margaret Fry. Evidence of this came from a woman witness living in Caernarvon, who told Margaret Fry that she was returning home from work, at 3.00am, on the Caernarfon to Bangor road, between the villages of Bethel and Pentir, a few weeks into 1974, when she was stopped by a military Policeman.

> *"He told me I had to stay there. About 20 minutes later, three army Lorries arrived and drove into the nearby electric power station. Two contained armed troops. In the centre of the third lorry could be seen stone oblong boxes, at which point I was motioned away by the soldiers. I was then escorted back to my home. About a month later, I received a visit from a member of the military, who asked me a number of questions, including my affiliation to the Communist party."*

We have to admit this sounds rather odd, and cannot understand why a member of the public would received a visit , by the army/intelligence services later unless it was a case of them being in the wrong place and the wrong time. We shall never know what was contained in the stone oblong boxes, it could have of course been anything!

Another important witness was Mike Saville, who contacted Margaret Fry, in 1996, and told her:

> *"In January 1974, I was living with my young family on a steep hill out-side Llandderfel, in one of three houses, Gart-Goch, Cae Pant and*

Tyn-y-fron, which were situated opposite the Cader Mountain range, some 5miles across to Cader Berwyn. On the 23rd January 1974, we felt the terrible earthquake, and ran out carrying the children down to Cae Pant Farm, where our neighbours - Arthur and Dyliss Prichard - were stood outside. We then all saw this enormous dark orange object, moving silently and slowly down the mountain, some three miles away from them. This then slowly settled down onto the mountainside, just below the plateau. It was so big we thought the world was coming to an end. After watching it for between 30-35 minutes, it suddenly went downwards and disappeared from view."

Margaret discovered that other people had seen a similar object, which corroborates what Mike told her. She is sure that this was the same object seen by Pat Evans, but at a greater distance away. She told us:

"Mike Saville and his neighbours did not see or hear any military vehicles because of the position of their houses on a steep concealed mountain slope, opposite the Berwyn Mountain range. Mike told me that it had a definite shape - it was a UFO. We were very angry when the Press passed it off as a meteor. There was no explosion or crash - it just blanked out. They covered the whole thing up. We stood outside for a while and then everyone came into my house and stayed for hours after."

In 2010, The National Archives released a number of de-classified MOD 'UFO' documents. They included a file referring to what has become known as the 'Berwyn Mountain incident'.

In a letter, dated 14th February 1974, it outlined five separate reports of *"unusual objects seen in the sky"*, in different areas over the UK, on the night of 23rd January 1974. According to the letter, these were all in the South of England and all described a bright light falling to earth. It suggests that these may have been a 'bolide' - a meteor disintegrating during its passage through the atmosphere.

Another document is an extract from the meteorological log book of the *SS Tokyo Bay,* travelling from Port Kelang (Malaysia) towards Southampton. This report describes *"five bodies, spectacularly incandescent... traversing the sky",* which the ship's captain - M. Lees - attributes the observation to a satellite, disintegrating, having re-entered the Earth's atmosphere, and an attached MOD memorandum suggests this was:

"...probably of the decay of the Soviet Communications relay satellite Molniya 2-8's rocket body, which decayed at about this time".

Another letter, sent from the MOD tells us:

"With regard to the events of the evening of January 23rd, in the Berwyn Mountains; we did receive a number of reports of an unusual object seen in the sky just before 10.00pm, on the evening in question...Later on, personnel of the Royal Air Force mountain rescue team participated in a search of the area where the object was thought to have come down, but as you probably know nothing was found."

Saturday, June 28, 2008 *Sun* 23

SPACE ODDITY

Riddle of molten lump off 'crashed spaceship'

Heavy metal . . . Russ with the UFO debris

Out of this world . . . melted blob found in Wales

By ALASTAIR TAYLOR

ALIEN hunter Russ Kellett yesterday revealed a lump of mystery metal which he says was recovered from a crashed UFO 34 years ago.

The shiny one-and-a-half inch melted blob was found near Llandrillo in Berwyn Mountains, Wales, after reports of a spaceship plunging to earth.

Russ says it is similar to melted aluminium, yet heavier.

Police logs described a "terrific explosion" shaking houses on January 23, 1974, and locals said hundreds of cops and military personnel ordered everyone off the mountain.

It has been claimed that alien spacemen were whisked off to a secret military installation — all hushed up by the Government.

Former building worker Russ said: "That and this piece of metal from the spaceship proves in my mind the existence of aliens.

"The metal was picked up by someone who was on the mountain at the time. They have since died and it was passed to me about a year ago.

"I passed it to a jeweller who showed it to an expert but they have no idea what it is."

Russ 45, of Filey, North Yorks, has amassed more than 30 years of data about flying saucers — but only unveiled the shiny metal after reading recent UFO reports in The Sun.

We told of three sightings in five days earlier this month — in Shropshire, near Cardiff and over the Brecon Beacons.

Russ, who started studying UFOs after being surrounded by inexplicable lights while on a motorbike in 1988, said: "None of these incidents surprise me.

"It is only a matter of time before we get conclusive proof."

a.taylor@the-sun.co.uk

Army spot UFOs over Shropshire

Sunspot . . page 1 story   LLand of Llegend — P34&35

On the 13th May 2011, the *Sun* newspaper published an article, entitled the 'Ros Welsh Incident' and showed an artist's illustration of a saucer-shaped object, hovering above the village of Llandrillo, accompanied by a story from Yorkshire based UFO researcher - Russ Kellett.

Russ claimed that following his acquisition of a document* released by the Marine and Coastguard Agency, code named 'photoflash', it was evidence of a military operation to light up the coast, in order to see submerged UFO craft in the sea, and that the MOD had been looking for crashed alien craft on that night. They tell, we understand, of an altercation that took place in the Irish Sea, when military vessels clashed with UFOs, and that, as a result of this action, one of the objects later crash-landed on Cader Berwyn. We have never seen those documents and leave the reader to form their own judgments about this matter, although it is quite likely such documents do exist, but whether they are genuine is, of course, another matter.

> "I believe there were three separate craft that were flushed out of the ocean that night. Military craft were involved and there was an engagement. I spoke to a fisherman, who saw one come out near Puffin Island. His colleagues at the time told him to say nothing about it because it was considered bad luck. He never spoke about it for years."

Russ said that he was in possession of correspondence with a group of men, who told him they were moved on by military personnel on the roadside at Llandrillo, where one of the craft had come down.

ABOVE: Scott Felton visits the 'Crash Site'
BELOW: A typically authentic picture from one of Britain's leading journalistic sources

> *"They saw the aliens getting out of the craft, helping two of their own, who were injured. They were then loaded onto a flat bed truck and taken away."*

He was asked if any of the eye witnesses are still alive,

> *"The eye- witnesses are all dead, but I am in possession of a strange piece of metal recovered by witnesses after the incident"*

Although we do not know the identity of these men, who were described as professional men, we traced J.W. who had approached Margaret Fry, in 2000 and discussed details of this incident with her. During an interview with him, he outlined a version of events that seemed to incredible to believe. We weren't prepared to accept that five men, all known to each other, had, by some miraculous circumstance, found themselves separately on the side of the Berwyns, the very same evening when the UFO incident had taken place!

We are also expected to believe that UFOs were constantly seen for three weeks before in the sea off Puffin Island, and under the continental shelf in the Irish Sea. This led to the arrival of Royal Navy ships, which fired torpedoes into the sea. (Allegedly to disrupt or destroy the objects) In addition to this rather bizarre story, to say the least, the informant claimed there was a NASA recovery vessel also present, and that its communications were rendered inoperative. (Presumably by the force fields of the UFO)

> *"One of the vessels fired upon the UFOs. The smaller of the 'craft' went up into the sky, leaving the larger one, which retaliated and 'zapped' one of the navy vessels with a beam, injuring some of the seaman; worse, it was said some were killed. It then flew off towards the direction of North Wales, pursued by RAF fighter planes from Anglesey, flew over Bangor, and continued on its flight towards Capel Curig, in the Snowdonia range of mountains, where a RAF Jet finally intercepted and shot at it.*
>
> *The object, now damaged, zigzagged across the sky before crashing in the Berwyn Mountain. Aliens, with big eyes and large heads, wearing grey jumpsuits, being led to vehicles which they entered by themselves, before being driven down a forest road - not forgetting they claimed the UFO had lifted itself onto a military transporter."*

Scott Felton said:

> *"The said documentation relates to an incident where an alleged military exercise was buzzed by two USOs (Unidentified Submerged Objects) It is claimed that both USOs emerged. One departed the scene, and the other ended up in a shoot out. In the course of this, the said UFO was hit by gunfire from a vessel and seemingly disabled to a point where it could not fly straight up into space, or re submerge. It had no choice but to run.*
>
> *What alerted me to the possible fake nature of the document were contradictory references to the location of the event. Puffin Island in the Irish Sea was mentioned and the continental shelf. Any 'O' level standard student of*

> *geography, geology, and ocean science, would have known that Puffin Island is a lump of limestone, about 500yds off the Island of Anglesey. The entrance to the straits from the east is a vast shallow area of sandbanks, most of which is exposed at low tide. In fact it is so shallow, there is an ancient route over the low tide sands from Abergwynegregyn to Anglesey still usable today. This means it is totally impossible for any warships to negotiate."*

Scott Felton, an authority on the events that took place in Berwyn, conducted a thorough investigation into this matter and believes, from the nature of his research, there is not the slightest scrap of evidence to prove that this military intervention took place, and believes it is likely this is yet another example of disinformation, deliberately put out to confuse the issue, which we wholeheartedly concur with.

Margaret Fry has said:

> *"At no time has either of us (Scott) ever said that a UFO crashed in the Berwyn Mountains. To the present date our research continues, but we have no evidence of a satellite or UFO having crashed on the night of the 23rd January 1974, on or near Cader Berwyn, or Cader Bronwen Mountain ranges.*
>
> *What did happen was that local witnesses saw a UFO hover in the air, quite a while, which then came down in a controlled way to sit on the mountain ridge of Cader Berwyn range; the witnesses were farming families from the Llandderfel Mountain, opposite.*
>
> *The UFO sat there for quite a while before going down on to Cefn Coch, opposite Cader Berwyn. It was there for some time, and seen by the Evans family. In all it was on the ground for one hour and 45mins before it flew up, where villagers in Llandernog saw it passing over."*

In January 2012, we spoke to retired Police Constable Neville Hughes living in the Denbigh area. We had spoken to him some years previously about a UFO he and a colleague had sighted while on duty during the 1970's. He remembered this incident very well and told us that many people had believed it was a piece of Russian satellite which had crashed to Earth, and that part of it had been picked up some years later and stored at a house belonging to a member of the North Wales NFU (National Farmers Union), from which it was later collected by the police. However, the truth was vastly different, and we shall be returning to this tantalizing case in the volume dealing with 1980.

While we intrigued about this revelation we knew there was no evidence available to back up the claim, and wondered if it was hearsay or local rumours which abounded in all variety of shape and form!

We discussed this with Scott, who had this to say:

> *"In the mid 70s in the Llandrillo area and of course across rural Britain, Policing was much different as you'll know. Police officers had a more personal relationship with people on their 'patches', so as in this case, this ex-PC Hughes knows Huw Lloyd and others.*

What was significant about the Berwyn case is that no Police Officers involved would directly talk to Margaret. I noticed that as soon as I got involved and indeed, that has proved to be the case with me. In fact I've received nothing but obstruction and interference when seeking Police Officers living locally at the time to come forward. Margaret was told by the guy running the Dr Who Exhibition in Blackpool, that the man running the same exhibition in Llangollen where I am now was involved in the Police operation that night.

Margaret one day called on this guy who was not at home, but his wife was very welcoming and invited Margaret into their home. When he turned up, he was very hostile to Margaret and demanded she leave immediately.

Anyone supplying info' which differs from the concept of a UFO event, i.e., Russian stuff should be treated with caution. Up to now, we have people coming forward saying as in this case, Russian equipment. I've had missile test flights going wrong, American satellites crashing to Earth etc. Only one or none can be correct.

I'm of the opinion that there was never a crash, but a controlled landing and departure. Crash stories came out of the tremor event that night and this has been manipulated by the Authorities to debunk. Pieces of metal in circulation have been seeded to support a crash scenario of both UFO and man-made devices to muddle up the story. The military mounted their operation against the UFO - to scare it off - on the 23 Jan 74 so as to use the meteor shower that night as a cover story. They expected the UFO because it had been landing regularly and I believe it continued to try and do so for several weeks thereafter. As a result, there was a long term stake out on the Berwyns by the military. I have no reason to disbelieve that further UFO sightings up to about 1980 wasn't in fact the same or related craft. The Berwyn Range was of some great interest to the occupants of this/ these craft".

At 10.00pm the same evening, Ken Haughton of Betws-y-Coed, and his wife, saw what they took to be sheet lightning, behind cloud, and then noticed what looked like *"a sphere, with a tail"* dropping down at a speed they estimated to be 1,000mph. Mr. Haughton believes the object fell into the sea north-east of Rhyl, or in the Dee Estuary. (**Source:** *The North Wales Weekly News,* **31.1.74**)

The following evening (24th January 1974) David Upton - then aged 14, from Gobowen - was in the back garden of his house, at 7.15pm, when he saw an object in the western sky. He ran into the house for a pair of binoculars. He looked through and saw:

"...a disc-shaped object, divided into four sections, each section a different colour - red, green, yellow and purple."

His sister, Elizabeth, and her mother, Mary Upton, came outside and confirmed the sighting. Elizabeth then contacted the Police. Unfortunately, a minute later, the object slid behind a cloud; when the cloud passed, so had the object. Elizabeth reported:

"When I first came out of the house, the light from the object was dazzling - like a street lamp. When we looked through the glasses, we saw its overall disc shape and the four sections." (**Source:** *Border Counties Advertiser,*

Oswestry, 30.1.74)

Horrifying Encounter at Brecon

Our friend, Margaret Webb, from Worcester - a past member of the locally based UFO group Sky Scan - was to be the source of various snippets of information over the years, relating to the group's activities and some of their investigations. Margaret believes (as we do) that there is much suppression of the UFO subject, and tells of occasions when she and other members of the organisation firmly believed they were being watched by the Security Services, and felt so strongly that their personal records were at risk that they were forced to hide them at various locations. This may sound like paranoia, but it probably wasn't!

During Easter 1974, Margaret and her daughter, Sandra (13) decided to visit an artist friend, who lived in a small cottage situated in Brecon, Wales, a few miles from LLangorse Lake, near LLangasty. Because the accommodation in the cottage was limited, their host suggested they rent a room at a B & B farmhouse - then run by a Mrs. Harris.

After arriving at the farmhouse at about 8.30pm, they booked in and had a cup of tea and slice of cake with Mrs. Harris, who made them most welcome. They were then shown to their room, which was very cosy, with hot water bottles already placed into the beds, as the weather was cold and miserable.

On the same floor were three other bedrooms and a bathroom at the end of the landing. In addition to Mrs. Harris and her two sons, aged 18 and 24, there was a group of young jockeys, who were taking part in a local point to point. Neither Sandra nor Margaret had the slightest inkling that the jocularity and good spirits of the assembled youngsters hid a dark sinister secret, which lay in waiting for them. Margaret picked the bed nearest the window, but Sandra asked if she could have that as she wanted to look out in the morning and see any horses that were about. Margaret gave in and the two girls then settled down and did some reading. About 10.30pm, feeling tired after the journey, they switched the light off and settled down to sleep.

Both Margaret and Sandra commented on how dark it was in the room, but thought this was because being from the City they hadn't appreciated how dark it was in the country.

Margaret was in that first lovely drowsy stage of dropping off, when she heard Sandra starting to breath heavily and quickly - almost panting. She asked her what was wrong and she replied that the bedcovers were too heavy. Margaret advised her to turn the eiderdown back, but she continued to be agitated, so in the end Margaret switched the light back on. As she did so, Sandra stumbled out of bed saying she felt sick, and was escorted to the bathroom where she recovered her former self.

They returned to the bedroom. Sandra stood at the edge of the bed and refused to get back into that bed. She was so adamant about this that, in the end, Margaret agreed to swop beds. She later told us:

> *"I snuggled down and felt a great stifling weight on my chest. I felt cold and started to shiver; a sensation of sickness swept over me. I hitched myself onto my elbow. This was ridiculous. How could I feel sick? I had been perfectly alright a few moments ago. I told myself to 'lie down and don't be silly. It must surely be psychological, brought on by worrying about Sandra'. By this time Sandra was asleep, breathing peacefully. I lay there, fighting this. My eyes were shut, but I could see great black clouds swirling and engulfing me - then the swirling blackness broke to reveal nightmarish faces and long claw like figures reaching for me. I tried keeping my eyes open, but that didn't help. It was like watching an awful horror film in black and purple. I sat up. I thought I was going crazy. I was not asleep, so how could I have been having a nightmare?*
>
> *I lay down again and it started up as before. Desperately, I concentrated my thoughts on the jewelled cross in the Parish Church and said the Lord's Prayer, and repeated over and over, the words, 'Deliver me from evil'. Eventually I drifted into sleep."*

The second night, Margaret was more prepared to face what she considered was going to be another 'repeat performance' and settled down into bed, concentrating on the mental picture of the bejewelled cross, while reading out the Lord's Prayer, time and time again. Despite the re-emergence of the previous discomfort, she finally dropped off to sleep.

On the third night, Margaret questioned Sandra about what it was that had made her change beds.

> *"It was all black and coming down on me and made me feel sick."*

Margaret pondered on what Sandra had said, knowing it had not been her imagination and that this was something real, but what? Her curiosity aroused, she decided to spend their third night far more prepared and brought a car torch into the room, and a good supply of cigarettes, as she had a feeling she was in for a long vigil.

> *"We went through the usual routine and Sandra was soon asleep. I lay down and it started – blackness, with weird forms floating past. I sat up and put the torch on - now I knew it was not me. I thought okay, I'll lie down and watch to see what all this was about. I settled down again, all the time mentally holding my only means of protection - the cross. The blackness descended again - then the forms appeared, whether my eyes were open or closed. Suddenly I heard a noise, like a huge iron door, slamming. It made me jump and I saw black metal bars of what looked like a portcullis - the type found in an old castle.*
>
> *I felt myself passing along tables, or benches, all laid out with old black metal equipment or tools, which I couldn't indentify. Behind them were chains, glinting, hanging from the wall, and the sounds of bolts being pushed hard into position.*
>
> *I sat up and reached for a cigarette and thought, had I just seen inside a medieval prison? Could they have been instruments of torture? Incongruously, against the backcloth of all of this, I could hear normal sounds of the house. There was a phone ringing. Someone was having a bath and the buzz of conversation was going on downstairs."*

Margaret stubbed out the cigarette and lay down. Immediately, there was a change in the events that swirled around her. A large old-fashioned cooking pot appeared. This was followed by a frog that grew larger, filling the space above her, its eyes bulging and its gills on the side of its head pulsing. She shrank away from it and cringed. A series of animals then passed in front of her eyes. She was unable to tell whether these were dead or alive, but saw a chicken and rabbit.

> *"...then horror of horrors - black candles, which gave no radiance, began to move around the bed. I watched, fascinated. I could see the shape of a flame on the top, but no light. On came the torch and out came the cigarettes.*
>
> *I sat there, taking stock. The room looked so normal. My companion was sleeping peacefully. Someone was still in the bath. I carefully went over the events again in my mind, seeking a rational answer. Could it be a drug, hidden in the pillows, that was causing this happen?*
>
> *I searched the bed and thoroughly examined the pillows and sheets, but there was nothing. I had an idea; perhaps I should take the covers off the bed and sleep on the floor, but then dogged determination dictated why should I adopt this course of action? I had, after all, paid for this bed!*
>
> *I heard the telephone ring and excited voices in Welsh I made out that there was a big race, the following day. Once again, I switched off the torch and lay down - this time on my stomach, my hands pressed together in the traditional attitude of prayer. I did wonder if I should go and tell*

Mrs. Harris - the Landlady - about the bed, but guessed what her reaction would be.

Once again, I methodically went through in my mind what had taken place - the frog, the candles, and what appeared to be a dungeon from the Middle Ages - I knew what to do, exorcise them, but I didn't have access to salt or

> I say aloud :-
> "In the Name of Jesus Christ leave this bed!"
> "In the Name of Jesus Christ leave this room!"
> "In the Name of Jesus Christ leave ME ALONE!"
> This final plea was said with the desparation of despair, not caring if the people hear me.
> Suddenly I was engulfed with the most terrible smell of burning. I immediately hitched myself up onto my elbows, alert, straining my ears for a shout from down stairs. My mind was racing, I would have to wake Sandra and get her downstairs, and how would I manage to gather up our things. (It was the old question of what to rescue in a fire). Because the weather was so cold, there was always great log fires downstairs, which spit and sent out sparks onto the hearth rug. Every nerve was tense ready for action, surley they must smell it. But everything went on the same. There was the general drone of voices. The chap was still on the phone. Someone was still in the bathroom. My cigarettes were safely out. What was that terrifying smell?

water. The only thing I could do was to say a prayer."

In the morning, Margaret told her daughter what she had experienced. She was horrified to learn of her mother's ordeal. Margaret pondered now, in the cold light of day, whether the manifestation was a fairly recent phenomenon, brought about by recent witchcraft activities, or was there a connection with what had taken place, hundreds of years ago? Did other people, who slept in the same bed, also experience the same horrifying presence? She spoke to Mrs. Harris, who was shocked to learn of what had taken place, and confirmed, to her knowledge, that none of the previous guests had ever brought anything like this to her attention.

Following her return home, Margaret was relieved to find that her sleeping pattern was fine and that the ordeal had come to an end. Consultation with someone from the local Churches fellowship of psychical

Margaret Brian CHRIS WIFE of FRED JAMIE TONY

Keith

Jane FRED Derek Stella WIFE of JAMIE

This final plea was said with the desparation of despair,
not caring if the people hear me.

Suddenly I was engulfed with the most terrible smell
of burning. I immediately hitched myself up onto my elbows,
alent, straining my ears for a shout from downstairs
My mind was racing, I would have to wake Sandra and get her downstairs,
and how would I manage to gather up our things. (It was the old question
of what to rescue in a fire). Because the weather was so cold, there
was always great log fires downstairs, which spit and sent out
sparks onto the hearth rug. Every nerve was tense ready
for action, surley they must smell it. But everything went on
the same. There was the general drone of voices. The chap
was still on the phone. Someone was still in the bathroom.
My cigarettes were safely out. What was that terrifying smell?

and spiritual studies, of which Margaret was then a member, revealed that she and her daughter had been in appalling danger. It was suggested an exorcism should be arranged. Unfortunately this idea had to be vetoed, as it was thought such an action would cause upset between Mrs. Harris and Margaret's friend, who knew each other.

We have nothing but admiration for Margaret, who is very much a down-to-earth lady and one of the nicest women we have ever met. She and her husband, Dennis, are good friends.

We carried out a search on the internet, in 2012 hoping to find other information that may have a bearing on what took place, but nothing of any consequence. Was it the bed which was haunted? Could it have been the ceiling immediately above the bed? What was below the bed, and where had the bed come from? One thing was assured she wouldn't have been the only one to have experienced this. At 1.20am on 22nd April 1974, Edward Harris - editor of *Cosmology Newslink*, who was keenly interested in researching the UFO subject (as he still is in 2012) - was driving home, when he noticed a strange 'ball of light' descending silently from the sky and grow in size, before falling onto the runway at Stansted Airport.

Was it ball lightning, or something else?

Is your neighbour a Martian?

Whilst there appears to be little interest in covering reports of UFOs at this current time (2012) by the National Newspapers, the local newspapers can often be relied on to assist with any appeals, or reports, of UFO activity that they would wish to bring to the attention of their readers. Unfortunately, there is a predisposition to occasionally attract the readers' attention with a banner grabbing headline, especially where UFOs are concerned.

In 1974, Roy Lake was contacted by a member of the *Dagenham Post*, who wished for any updates on reported UFO activity. Following an interview at the house, Roy mentioned the possibility of extraterrestrials being present on Earth. When the article was published, it was presented under the headline as above, which no doubt attracted disbelief and ridicule. This is, of course, why many witnesses regret later having contacted the Press with their stories, although it would be unfair to say that this is a general policy of the local newspapers - far from it, without their valuable assistance, *Haunted Skies* would be far worse off.

2012 - Roy celebrates nearly 50yrs of UFO research and investigation and is now head of London UFO Studies, which was launched in January 1990, in an attempt to fully investigate and evaluate the numerous UFO sightings that continuously occur throughout the UK. The chairman of London UFO Studies, for the past nine years, has been Roy Lake. Roy has spent a great deal of time, effort and money, in educating the public to the reality of the UFO situation. (**Source:** *Cosmology Newslink,* **Edward Harris**)

Strange 'stars' over Lincoln

At 8.10pm on 2nd March 1974, Thomas Albert Bradley from Ermine East, Lincoln - an amateur astronomer - was outside his home address, checking the night sky, when he noticed a 'double star' in the direction of the north-east. After watching it for ten minutes, he looked at it through binoculars and noticed:

> "...the right-hand 'star' pulsed once, then slowly moved downwards and
> away, towards the horizon, but abruptly and without slowing down, turned

right, heading now towards the east. My impression was that they were very high up on the edge of space. I had them under observation for ten minutes." **(Source: Richard Thompson)**

Between 6.30pm and 7.00pm on 13th March 1974, three children members of the Shepherd family, living in Reading, accompanied by two friends, together with a man walking his dog , sighted a disc-shaped object, hovering about 30ft above a nearby school playing field. The object was described as:

"...yellow orange in colour, with a light haze surrounding it, and flashing red and blue lights banded around the centre.

An orange beam of light could be seen coming from an indent in the underside of the object, illuminating the ground beneath. It hovered there in this position for about two minutes, emitting a steady humming noise. It then shot straight up to a considerable height, before halting momentarily and then moving away." **(Source: John Roylance, *BUFORA Journal*, Volume 5, Number 4, November/December 1976)**

At 10.35pm on 23rd March 1974, a Swansea resident, after hearing the sound of jets passing over the house, over the course of what appears to have been a number of evenings running, decided to capture them on photo.

"I decided to take a photo, when I heard it coming. The noise came. Standing on my bed, looking out of the window, I thought I had better take a photo quickly, as it would disappear, but it was not a jet I saw. This was round and all lit up orange, and was going very slow over the house. It reminded me of, if you hold a tangerine up in the air and look underneath, you see sections joining to the centre. It was exactly the same, with a darker light in the middle. I didn't have time to take a photo, as I rushed down to tell me parents to open the front door to see it. By the time they did, it was no longer visible from where I was standing. No further sightings, but it did start my interest off in UFOs." **(Source: UFOINFO Sighting Form Report)**

At 2.20am on 31st March 1974, Laboratory assistant - Mr. Ashlyn Brown from Bracebridge, Lincoln - was out fishing at a lake by the side of North Scarle, on a clear, cloudless, but cold night, when he saw what he first took to be a shooting star - blue and white in colour, with a glow around it, at an angle of 45° off the horizon - but felt this was unlikely, as it headed along a steady and level course through the sky, heading south, to the north, and out of sight 20-30secs later. **(Source: Richard Thompson)**

In the spring of the same year, teenagers - Angela Johnson and Lorraine Terry - were out playing near Ibbotson Way, Bournemouth, one evening, when the sky lit up with a brilliant flash, followed by the appearance of a *"dark orange egg-shaped object"* moving slowly through the sky, heading north-east. The girls ran home and alerted their parents, who rushed out of the house in time to see: *"...an oval-shaped object, showing a shadow effect across it in the design of a cross"*. **(Source: Leslie Harris, *Scan* Magazine, Bournemouth)**

UFO over Maidenhead

In April 1974, Yvonne Sanders was driving a Volkswagen Beetle about 40mph. through a place called Hawthorne Hill, between Maidenhead and Ascot, at 11.45pm, when she noticed a red and green light in the sky, some distance apart.

> *"...then my car was surrounded by light. Looking upwards, I saw an elliptical-shaped 'craft' hovering above my car, about 15ft above me. It was cream coloured and divided by a crucifix-shaped stainless steel cross, with a round, white, light in each small quarter - no other markings, no rivets. The body was very smooth - no wings, or appendages. In the time it took me to look away in shock, and return my gaze, it had gone. At the time I was persuaded into thinking that the object concerned was some sort of Ministry of Defence aircraft that was being tested, but that was over 30yrs ago, and I have yet to see anything resembling what I saw."*

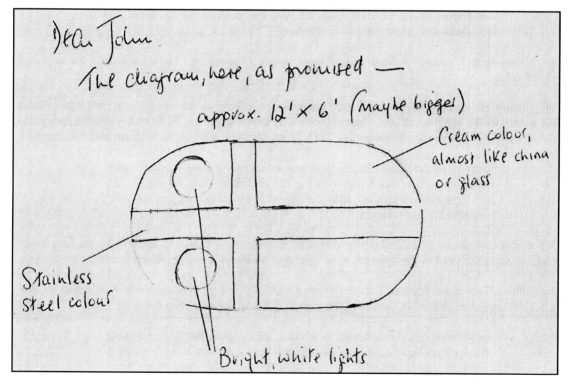

On the 9th April 1974, Margaret Fry from Bexleyheath, in Kent, who has been investigating and documenting UFO reports for nearly 50yrs, was celebrating her birthday with a visit to Penshurst Castle, Kent, accompanied by her husband, Ron, and friend, Myfanwy Parker.

"I stood there, taking a photograph of them against the backcloth of the Castle, just as a large, low flying, white cigar-shaped object, with a number of portholes set alongside its body, appeared low down in the sky, and moved slowly over the top of the turret, at what looked like a walking pace.

We jumped into the car and followed the object, but lost it near Hever Castle, so decided to stop and picnic there. Imagine our surprise when the object appeared a few hundred feet off ground level! People nearby watched with amazement, as it flew over at a leisurely pace. I followed it through the Italian gardens, down to the lake, and managed to take some photos, but was disappointed to find, when processed, that it was very small." **(Source: Margaret Fry, *Link to the Stars*)**

Ghostly figure seen, Farnborough

In May 1974, Mr. Wally Churn - a self-employed carpenter from Cove, Farnborough - was cycling to work, at 7.50am. As he crossed the road, intending to call into the paper shop adjacent to a shopping centre, known as the Queensway - part of his regular habit - a man spoke to him. Wally ignored him, as it was 8.10am and he was already late for work. The man spoke again, saying:

"I am Freka Alfreka, or something like that, and he held out his hand. I am from the saucer people, do you understand?"

Mr. Churn took his hand, walked two or three paces, stopped, and turned around - the man had vanished!

Mr. Churn went into the shop and collected his paper, remarking on the strange man, and later brought the matter to the attention of Mr. Omar Fowler - an Investigator for BUFORA/Surrey Investigation Group on Aerial Phenomena, in December 1975. In an interview with Omar, he described the man as:

"...having a round, smooth, face - almost without a chin, small hands - like a woman, cold to touch. His eyes - green in colour - had no pupils. He was wearing grey clothes, with a trilby, and was about six feet tall and looked in his early thirties."

Mr. Churn complained of suffering pins and needles in his right hand and forearm by the time he arrived at work, followed by the appearance of a red spot on his right thumb, which lasted for a fortnight.

Incredibly, this was not the only time we were to hear of a strange person seen in Farnborough. Mrs. Cheryl Chuter from Aldershot, told us of her own frightening experience in the same year.

"I was working for a company in North Camp, and on the way to deposit the day's takings into a bank at Farnborough. I noticed a man, wearing ordinary clothes and a hat, walking towards me. As he came closer, I felt an apprehension creep over me; my first thoughts were that he was going to steal the money. As he passed, I looked into his face and saw that his eyes were like no other eyes I had ever seen. They were like deep black pools, devoid of any colour, and he had no pupils - just deep black holes where his eyes should have been. By the time I pulled myself together and

turned around, all I saw was him fading away. The following week, I read in the local paper, the Star, *that a man had reported seeing a UFO land in a school field, while out exercising the family dog. I am fairly sure it was the same day, although I cannot be sure of the exact date."*

UFO over Portsmouth

Stanley Pitt of Old Wymering Lane, Cosham, Portsmouth, was visiting shops in Pebmarsh Road, with his younger brother, at 5.35pm, during 1974, when they heard an unusual buzzing sound. On looking up they saw:

"...a silver-grey, apparent large object, shaped like a flattened pith helmet, or bee-keeper's hat, with a dark area on the top, stationary in the sky, at an elevation of about 50°, and was slowly revolving. After about five minutes, the buzzing began to increase in volume and the object tilted and began to move away, towards the direction of north-east, before disappearing over Portsdown Hill." **(Source: WATSUP/Nick Maloret)**

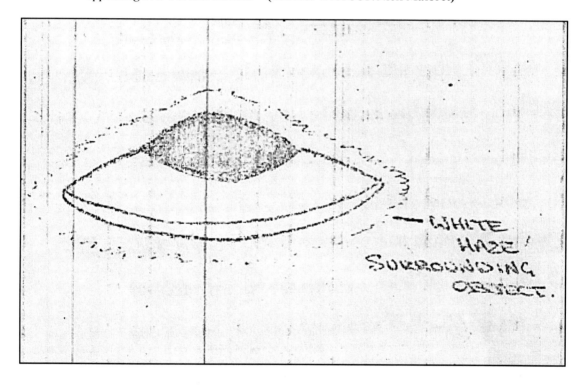

Close Encounter, at Barn Hill

A close encounter of chilling proportions took place at 8.45pm on 11th May 1974, involving Dagenham based BUFORA Investigator - Barry King - and Chingford Investigator, Ian Vinten, who were driving back from Leighton Buzzard, in Bedfordshire. When nearing Chingford, they decided to make a detour and visit Barn Hill, off Sewardstone Road, as there had been previous reports of UFOs seen in the area.

The two men pulled off at the side of the road and left the engine running of Ian's Ford Anglia, while they stood at the wire fence, casting their eyes over the ridge opposite, some 400yds away, with a copse of trees to their left, noticing two grey vans parked along the road, but thought nothing of it at the time. Barry King wrote:

> *"Ian shouted out something. I couldn't hear what he was saying because of the noise of the car engine. I asked him to repeat it. He shouted out, 'there's someone over there' and pointed over towards the ridge."*

Barry saw nothing, to begin with, but after further scrutiny, saw someone standing near the trees, not moving. They fetched their binoculars, and trained them on the figure. Barry continues:

> *"A feeling of unease spread over me when I saw a tall figure, dressed in a full length gown, with long blonde white hair. What scared me was its completely featureless face. It stood there, not moving, facing us. I lowered my binoculars and reached for a cigarette. My hands were shaking. Ian shouted, 'It's gone', and looked around for any sign of the figure - then we saw it a little further along the ridge. Suddenly, out of the corner of my eyes, I saw these strange white, featureless blobs, darting about at terrific speeds, close to a hedgerow, approximately 200yds away. In an instant they had gone."*

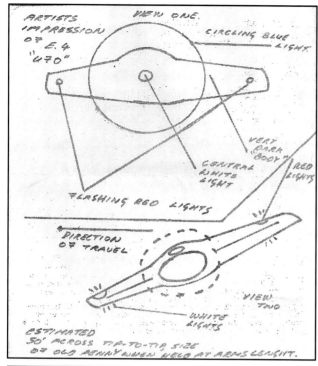

ARTISTS IMPRESSION OF E.4 "UFO"

VIEW ONE.

CIRCLING BLUE LIGHT

VERY DARK "BODY"

CENTRAL WHITE LIGHT

RED LIGHTS

FLASHING RED LIGHTS

DIRECTION OF TRAVEL

VIEW TWO

WHITE LIGHTS

ESTIMATED 50' ACROSS. TIP-TO-TIP. SIZE OF OLD PENNY WHEN HELD AT ARMS LENGHT.

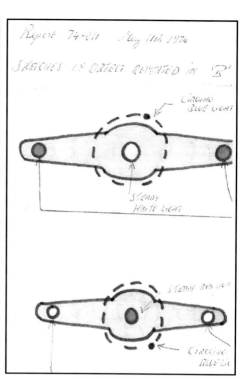

Report 74-011   Aug 11th 1974

SKETCHES OF OBJECT REPORTED IN 'B'

CIRCLING BLUE LIGHT

STEADY WHITE LIGHT

STEADY RED LIGHT

CIRCLING BLUE LIGHT

X UFO

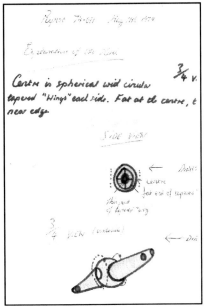

The two men tried to fathom out what on earth the two white blobs had been, and what their presence meant to the weird figure they had seen previously. Above the tree tops appeared a small red light, which rose slightly upwards and became two red lights, with a white light in the centre, *part of something* that began to head towards two men, whose attention was on this object - the strange figure being momentarily forgotten. Barry says:

> *"A distinct outline could now be seen. It was spherical in the centre, with cone- shaped sides (like a tennis ball with an ice cream on either side). It displayed large, round lights; the red ones flashing in unison, the white one stayed on, with a small blue light circling the centre, clockwise. There was a strange pinging noise, two-tone, like a ship's sonar. It continued its flight towards us. A combination of fear and amazement swept over me.*

Ian ran to his car and picked up his camera, and managed to take several shots of the UFO as it passed overhead."

Incongruously the traffic continued to flow past, as if ignoring the passage of the object through the air. The two men looked around for any potential witnesses and noticed two young girls, talking nearby. When asked if they could see the UFO, they took one look at it and ran off. Barry continued:

> *"We noticed a guy standing at the front gate of his house, intently watching the object. All of a sudden I had this really weird sensation, as If I was actually inside the object - then I was back on the road looking up at it. All then went quiet - no sounds, no traffic. The next thing I was aware of was seeing the object heading west, over Enfield, before being lost from view."*

Now very subdued, the two men returned home. Barry reported, not surprisingly, that he had slept badly that night, and believes there may well have been some *missing time* as *Match of the Day* was just starting when he arrived home.

Following consultation with Ken Philips - National Investigations Co-coordinator - enquiries were made at the scene with the male witness, who denied even being there, clearly concerned about getting involved.

Examination of the locality revealed extensive treetop damage, with burnt branches lying on the ground. Following this discovery, a comprehensive report was submitted to the MOD and to Professor J. Allen Hynek - (CUFOS, in the States)

The film was sent to Omar Fowler - then head of SIGAP (Surrey Investigation Group of Anomalous Phenomena). Unfortunately, while being removed from the camera, the film jammed and was rendered useless. Worse, Ian went to the Press against the wishes of Barry, as a result of which the whole matter was sensationalised out of all context. The story does not end here - another frightening incident was to occur on the 10th August 1974. Barry continues:

> *"I was contacted by many newspapers, asking for an interview, but declined. Ken suggested I contact Ian and see how he was reacting to all the public interest. When I telephoned his house, a stranger answered and told me nobody of that name lived there. I was astounded and went around to the house and spoke personally to the occupier. He invited me in. I was shocked to see the décor and wallpaper were different. I telephoned Ken and explained what had happened. He promised to make some enquiries. A few days later, he advised me that Ian had abruptly left and gone to live in the West Country. I have never heard from him since."*

We spoke to Barry about this case in 2012, after learning that Ian was alive and well. Unfortunately he did become the focus of attention a few years ago when he blamed his problems on researching the UFO subject, the less said on that the better. **(Source: Barry King/Credit Dave Sankey, BUFORA & Mark Rodeghier, CUFOS)**

Close Encounter, Hartlepool

In 1974, Hartlepool teenager - Dianne Sudron - was babysitting her brother and younger sisters at her home in Elphin Walk, Hartlepool, when she sighted a strange object above the houses between her street and Brierton Community School.

> *"It was like a big headlamp, but not as big as a football, and hovering above the rooftop. It then moved away, towards Owton Manor primary school. I wasn't scared and decided to follow it, accompanied by two friends".*

On another occasion, she was babysitting again when, to her amazement, six entities with creamy-coloured bald heads, pointy chins and eyes like almonds, entered the house through the French windows.

> *"I remember it vividly. We had ornaments on a shelf next to the window and part of the wall became a control panel. An alien, that seemed female, pressed buttons on the wall. There were flashing lights and it just seemed to be part of the UFO. I asked them, 'How long are you going to be? I don't want you here when my mam and dad come in'. We used to speak in telepathy and they would immobilise me. I used to just sit there. My mind is blank. I don't know whether they took me somewhere, or whether they did something to my body.*
>
> *They used to come in through the French window at the back of the room and float out through the front window. I wondered if our house was in the way, in the middle of the alien highway, or something."*

On another occasion, Dianne alleges that she telepathically became aware of an 'alien 'pulling up in an expensive Honda car, one early morning, and then parking up outside the house. The next thing she knew was that 'they' were at the bottom of her bed.

"They looked like doctors. One had a clipboard. I had been suffering from cystitis at the time, but I know they gave me an operation on my forehead. They cut through a piece. I was aware of it and sort of conscious. It seemed to hurt, but as soon as they had gone it went. I don't know whether they were trying to make me more psychic. If you have an operation on your third eye, you become more psychic."

In our conversations with Dianne Sudron, we judged her to be a genuine and truthful woman, who had endured a series of what, some might have found, frightening close encounters with a non-human agency. She believes that she has been taught much by them and was courageous enough to contact to the local paper and tell them her story. Dianne said she was always going to write her own book, entitled *Alien Dreamland,* about what had transpired, and we wish her well. (**Source:** *Hartlepool Mail,* **7.3.2008 - 'Alien doctors treated my cystitis'/personal interviews)**

UFO over Worcester
At 11.00pm on 28th May 1974, Mrs. Margaret Webb - a member of a Worcestershire based UFO Group, Skyscan - was in the back garden of her home in Cromer Road, Worcester.

"I was looking up into the clear night sky, noting the various constellations, when I noticed what looked like a mass of stars, grouped in a triangular shape, with a bright centre, hazy at the edges, crossing the night sky - unlike anything I've ever seen in the night sky."

UFO over Combe Martin
John Keen, an ex-resident of Combe Martin - a seaside village of much character and charm - spoke about what he and his brother saw, when young boys playing on the football pitch, during summer 1974.

"It was broad daylight, when we saw this shining silver, cigar-shaped object, hovering silently 30ft above the ground. It had five circular shapes or portholes around it, with a dome or fin on its blunt end, with a wire or rope hanging from it, trailing sparks. It then moved away, and we watched it following the contours of the countryside. When we told our parents they laughed at us, but I know what w saw and will never forget it, despite it being over 40yrs ago."

An auxiliary nurse, from Worcester, was at her kitchen window, just after 2.00am on the 3rd June 1974, when she sighted an unidentified flying object, estimated to be about six times the size of normal stars in the sky, emanating long rays of light, travelling in a southwards direction. Imagine her surprise when, a few minutes later, a second object appeared behind the first and was seen to hover briefly before continuing its course.

She had the impression that they were distant but moving very fast, and was followed by a shadow of indefinable shape. There were several other witnesses to this case, including a train driver and his mate, who observed the object hovering. When the train stopped, the object stopped with them. **(Source: Skyscan)**

At 12.00pm, a '*pulsating white light*' was seen hovering over Grantham Common, on the 6th June 1974. During the evening of 7th June 1974, two brilliant lights, a few minutes apart, were seen heading across the sky over Worcester, by a number of people, including a local councillor **(Source: *Evening News*, Worcester, 7.6.74)**

Early radio talk and UFO meeting

On the 8th June 1974, Rex Dutta held a lecture on the UFO subject, in Manchester, which was hailed as a great success. Representatives from various UFO groups attended. During the same evening, there was a meeting of the North-East London Astronomical Society (NELAS) at Wanstead House, London. The guest speakers were the committee of the Essex UFO Study Group. David Prockter wrote about this event in his magazine, the *UFO News,* Number 6, 1974.

> *"As a committee member of the Essex Group I was, for the most part, over-shadowed by other members of the committee, and therefore said very little. The meeting was one of the best attended NELAS had ever experienced, in many years. Roy Lake was the first member of the Essex group to speak. He gave details of the group and chatted on this level, for a few minutes. Ron Markwick began by asking the audience how many of them had seen what they considered to be a UFO. Only one or two rose their hands, but they almost unanimously put their hands up when the question of belief of life on other planets was brought to their attention."*

David then goes on to mention that, after the meeting, the conversation was extended over half pints of beer in the presence of Ian Vinten - a member of BUFORA - and Barry Crawford and his wife. Two days later, on the 10th June 1974, an object resembling *"a yellow torpedo"* was seen over Derby, by a number of people. **(Source: *Derby Evening Telegraph* - 'Yellow torpedo seen as UFO season opens', 10.6.74)**

This was followed on the 13th June, with a sighting of an *"orange, glowing, oval object, a mere 100ft off the ground"*, over Hornchurch, by two men, who called the Police. By the time they arrived, it had gone. The MOD were contacted, but declined to give any statement. **(Source: *Herts. Advertiser and St. Albans Times*, 13.6.74)**

On the 14th June 1974*, "a rusty-red revolving ball of light"* was sighted rushing through the sky over Halifax, Yorkshire, for a few minutes, travelling at a speed of about 100mph and at an estimated height of 200ft. **(Source: *Evening Courier*, Halifax)**

UFO display over Birmingham

In mid June 1974, a number of residents living in Wentworth Drive, Harborne, contacted the Police, after sighting a number of mysterious glowing objects darting about in the sky over the nearby Harborne golf course.   We spoke to retired Police Officers - Margaret and Geoffrey Westwood who were responsible for the running of a Birmingham UFO group, UFOSIS, and living in Wentworth Drive at the time. Margaret told us:

> *"I can confirm a report was submitted to the MOD about the incidents,*

which were brought to our attention by some of the residents, one of whom described a frightening experience when one of the objects swooped down over her head, while near the golf course. I saw some of these objects for myself, flashing across the sky. They looked like globes of light constantly changing colour, leaving red trails behind them.

When I looked through binoculars, I could see a number of bars of horizontal light moving downwards over the face of the UFO - like the sort of effect you get when frames of interference roll down over the face of a TV screen.

It reminded me of the film taken in 1978, of the UFOs over New Zealand that attracted such huge publicity at the time.''

One evening Margaret, on her return home, was told by the baby sitter that she had seen a vivid lime green coloured light shoot over the house. The following morning, she discovered the top of a young eucalyptus (transplanted 12 months previously) was blackened, as if burnt.

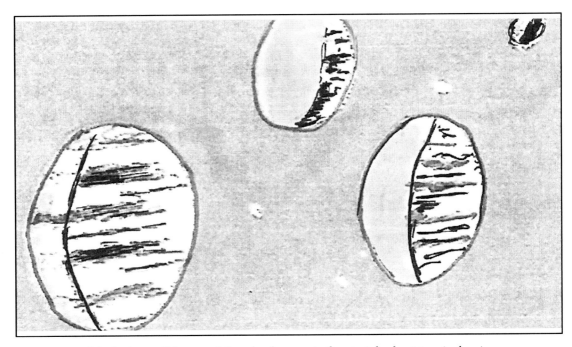

*"At the base of the tree, I found a fragment of material, about two inches in size, that I hadn't seen there before. When later analyzed, it was found to be rich in **aluminum,** with large traces of **silicon** and smaller amounts of **iron** I don't know whether it was connected, but the leaves on the tree grew very elongated. The tree itself grew to a height of 16ft over 12 months - an abnormal*

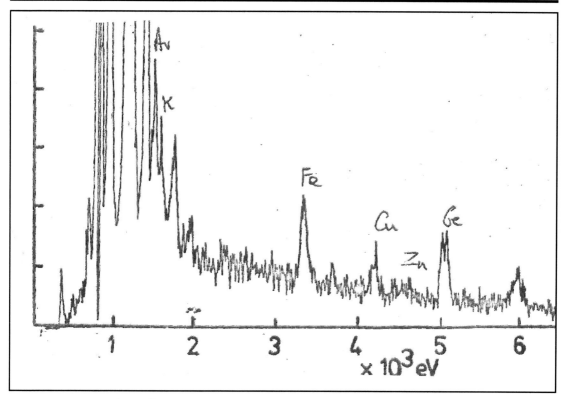

growth rate."

We discovered that MOD Officials had written to several people, living in the Bourneville Park estate, confirming that their reports were, *"being examined, to see if there are any Defence implications".* Margaret told the *Birmingham Evening Mail,* at the time:

> *"One of the sightings was very frightening. It seemed to hover right overhead and then drop suddenly. More than a dozen people living near their home in Wentworth Way had seen the unidentified objects. Among them were a Doctor and electrical engineer. Initially, the lights travelled in a south to north direction but, following a spell of inactivity during cloudy weather, had changed to an east-west direction."*

We sent a copy of the incomplete Graph supplied by Margaret to Nick Reiter a scientist in the States, who has worked on numerous cases involving the alleged recovery of UFO debris, in 2012, he told us

> *"I did some comparative study of the old Harborne plot versus known sample plots of my own. Attached is the annotated version. It looks like that metal was magnesium primarily, with aluminium and sodium being the other two main missing peaks. I would call it a magnesium alloy, with Al, Fe, Cu, and Ge added.*
>
> *It makes for a strange blend, I'll give you that."*

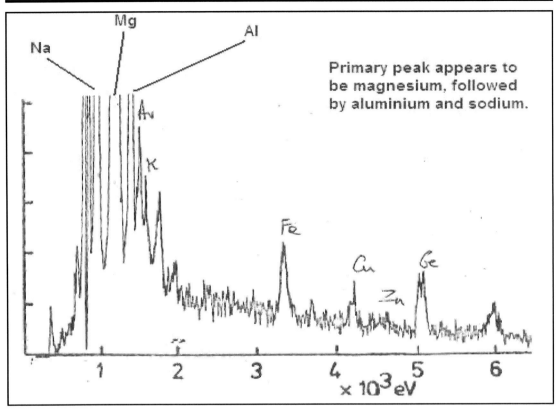

Many years later, we were to come across what appeared similar sighting of Unidenified flying objects filmed over New Zealand in 1978 and Scotland during 1996.

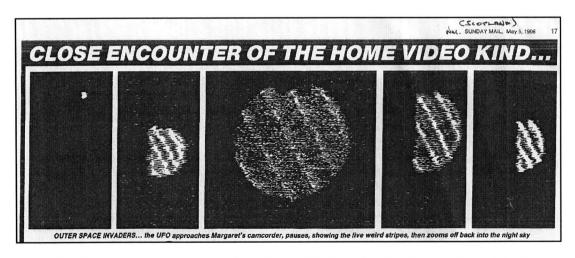

The stills, shown above, were extracted from the Scottish film taken by Margaret Ross of Stenhouse-muir, and show five clear stripes on the surface. These were later examined by Archie Roy, Glasgow University's emeritus Professor of Physics and Astronomy.

"I've never seen anything like this before. Around 92 per cent of sightings can be easily explained, but this is one of the 8 per cent of phenomenon which science cannot recognise. I have seen things like this before, but not changing shape the way this does."

Northern UFO News (NUFON)

This was a monthly periodical published by a group of Northern UFO Societies, chronicling reports of UFO activity between 1974 and 2002, and edited by Jenny Randles. In 1980, she had this to say about the role:

"Due to a lack of regionalisation and consequent isolation of the North from the [British UFO] scene, the idea emerged for an alliance between the various UFO factions existent within that region. Hence, the Northern UFO Network (NUFON) came into being in the spring of 1974. NUFON was never intended to rival the national organisations but to work with them, helping to integrate the North more fully into the UFO system in Britain. Chiefly for this reason it maintained an air of informality, which proved a useful feature in its development.

The main function of NUFON is as a liaison medium. It is open to groups and independent researchers, and counts amongst its associates virtually all of those who are active within the region's Ufology. The differing commitments between various types of ufologist is recognised and catered for by there being two levels of involvement. This consists of association, for the more active participants, and affiliation for those only peripher-ally involved. Meetings are frequent and decisions made because they are seen to be to the common good. They are adhered to by trust. There are no rules or regulations, no membership to the network and the independ-ence of all the contributors is a key factor in the concept.

Investigation standards vary, but it is policy not to dictate technique but to allow the possibility of improvement by working with others more ex-perienced. This does appear to be working, and the NUFON files (available to all participants for reference) have built up into an impor-tant repository of data on investigation work within the region, and are housed in a building owned by the Nottingham area group, NUFOIS, associated with the network.

NUFON co-ordinates the activity of researchers within the North, and works with the national and ultimately international organisations so that a sense of integration is maintained. A monthly newsletter, **Northern UFO News***, is published to give up-to-the-minute information on sighting reports and investigation activity."* **(Source: Taken from Randles, J. and Warrington, P. (1980)** *UFOs: a British Viewpoint,* **London, UK; Robert Hale)**

Scientist Nick Reiter and his work

We were intrigued with the composition of the metals found at the scene, and conducted a search of the internet in 2009. We came across the work of Nick Reiter - a scientist at a solar research facility in

Toledo, Ohio – who has also spent over 20yrs researching UFOs and anti-gravity concepts.

Nick has had the opportunity to work with many well-known investigators and authors, including Bud Hopkins, David M .Jacobs, PhD, and Linda Moulton Howe and was one of the 'behind- the scenes', formerly anonymous analyzers, asked by Linda Moulton Howe, to examine the alleged Roswell UFO metal fragment that appeared on the Coast to Coast 'Arts Parts' show, in the mid 1990s.

Nick's many original, technical developments and instruments are currently being tested in the field for their effectiveness in providing solid quantum physics based solutions to anomalous experiences. You will find Nick's innovative techniques mentioned in the *Fortean Times, New Energy News, Journal of Borderland Research, UFO Forum, The Bulletin of Anomalous Experiences,* and *Nexus* magazines. He has also been featured in *Glimpses of Other Realties* (Volume II) by Linda Moulton Howe, and *Electric UFOs: Fireballs, Electromagnetics and Abnormal States,* by Albert Budden.

Examination of metallic debris found in Ohio USA

In March of 2003, Nick Reiter received a phone call from his father, Bruce Reiter, concerning an interesting piece of news from his old rural neighborhood, north of Tiffin, Ohio. His father related to Nick that his nearest neighbour - 'Ed' - had found a mysterious piece of metal in his side yard, while raking up the last fall's leaves and twigs. The object had been obscured over the winter by two heavy snowfalls and

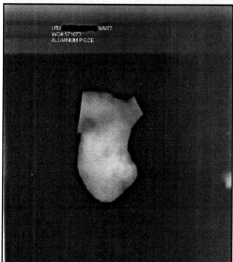

numerous lesser ones. 'Ed' had no explanation for the irregular metal blob, which was roughly six inches by two and a half inches, with a maximum thickness of one half inch, or so.

The blob had very apparently been molten at some point, and had solidified against a fairly flat or solid surface. While the piece had been found in the yard on the earth, the bottom side of the blob when found was generally smooth, with some white oxides present. By reviewing the weather, over the course of the winter that year, He concluded that the 'blob' of metal – if it had not been placed by artifice at a later post-snow date – had apparently fallen onto a hard packed ice crusted snow drift that had remained their since January of the year, up until the thaw in March. The blob may have then melted into the snow and ice a ways, but then apparent, that same month, Nick interviewed 'Ed' carefully, and borrowed his blob of mystery metal after being granted permission to cut it open as desired.

Nick ended up sawing a roughly 2 inch portion from the main blob. The interior of the metal appeared homogeneous. A small shaving was taken from both the interior and the surface and analyzed by Nick with a Jeol 840 scanning electron microscope, fitted with EDS.

The sample was originally analyzed using EDS (Energy Dispersive Spectroscopy) by Nick Reiter, which determined the metal was primarily **aluminum**, with traces of **carbon** and **silicon**. A crude Archimedian test of density indicated that the aluminum was within a couple percent of appropriate mass weight, thus meaning it was likely not an unusual isotope. It was not noticeably radioactive when surveyed with our Baird Atomic rate meter (Geiger counter).

Metallic debris found after UFO sighting

In late 2006, an uncannily similar account came to Nick's attention, by way of the Ohio UFO investigative community. The witness to this event was a Vietnam veteran, named Bennie Foggin, living in rural central Ohio, southeast of Newark. He told of sighting:

> *"... a large dark box like UFO - the length of a commercial airliner - glide silently over my home, at an estimated altitude of 100 to 200 ft. I say silent, but I did hear a rhythmic sound near one end that reminded me of the drum of a washing machine, scraping on bad bushings. As this noisy end of the craft passed over, I heard a dull 'thud' from somewhere nearby, but was transfixed by the dramatic object above."*

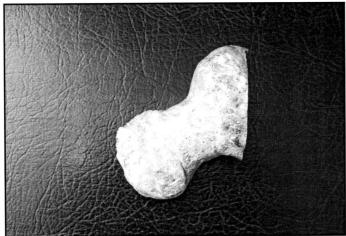

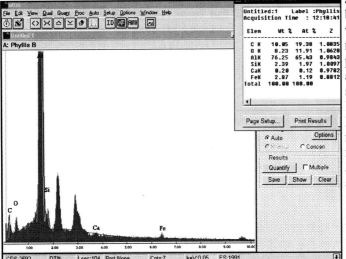

It was only after the 'craft' had vanished to the west, over the tree-line, that Bennie (opposite, then and now) thought to look for the source of the thud sound he had heard, a few minutes before, and discovered what appeared to be a blob of solidified and still hot aluminum lying in his gravel and dirt driveway. The material was recovered and placed into in a box, intending to show it to some of the Ohio UFO research community.

However, domestic and personal issues at the time prompted him to delay, and within a few months, the box had been misplaced and Bennie and his wife had, by that time, moved to a new home in the area. In 2006 the piece was re-discovered by the owner, and in late 2006 and early 2007, the sample was analyzed by EDS and IR spectroscopy. In early 2006, Bennie found the box containing the mysterious metal and took it to Ohio researcher, Joe Stets, in Columbus. Joe apparently had an un-named party at his own work establishment take an informal analytical look at the material. However, another piece of the aluminum blob was also sawed off and sent to Phyllis Budinger, of Frontier Analytical Services, Cleveland, who has done high quality analysis on 'unusual event' residues and artifacts, for some years.

Phyllis performed Infrared Spectroscopy on the sample and EDS was performed, in turn, by a colleague of Phyllis' - Dr. Sampath Ayengar. Dr. Ayengar is also well-known as analytical expert on matters of unusual or anomalous artifacts and materials. With permission granted from Frontier Analytical, a copy of the EDS spectrum plot is included herewith. (**Source: personal interview/***Birmingham Evening Mail,* **8.7.74 - 'Flying Saucer Probe in City'/Avalon Foundation)**

UFO display, Bournemouth

In 2010 Paul Usher contacted David Sankey, seeking any further information or knowledge of a UFO, sighted by him at 11.00pm on 20th June 1974 (approx. date) over the Bournemouth area.

> *"I saw what appeared to be an orange coloured torpedo-shaped object, with a central flashing light pulsing on and off, twice a second, following a random course across the sky. I got the impression the light was also*

12/26/2011

rotating around the whole object, which was spinning like a drill. The central light could change colour from white, or red/orange, then very bright. The object was moving in a zigzag manner or, 'castle' formation. Sometimes it would travel along for about 10 to 20secs in this odd fashion, then suddenly disappear, then reappeared instantly in another part of the sky, and so on. Direction could change and was impossible to predict. Its altitude must have been very high, some 80 to 180 miles (as a rough guess) and, as such, its speed must have been quite fast. However, it sometimes came to a full stop!"

Paul still seeks an answer for what he regards as being one of the most baffling things he has ever seen. He cannot understand how anything would behave in such a manner, nor instantly appear in other parts of the sky - sometimes a considerable distance away and then reappear in any part of the sky zigzagging around, doing 90° turns for probably half an hour. Incredibly, Paul saw the same 'display' for four nights in a row.

On the 21st June 1974, amateur astronomer Philip Wheeler, and three friends, sighted UFOs over the town. **(Source: *Bournemouth Times*, Poole, 21.6.74)**

Also, on this date, Mr. Brendan Taylor was in Brumby Lane, Scunthorpe, at 11.00pm, when he and his female companion sighted, *'a yellowish-white metallic object'* crossing the sky, heading eastwards. **(Source: personal interview Richard Thompson/*Scunthorpe Evening Telegraph*, 28.6.74)**

The following day, *"red pink green and blue lights"* were seen on two separate occasions, by people living in Exeter, in Devon. Through binoculars, a solid shape could be made out. **(Source: *Express & Echo*, Exeter)**

A meeting that never was to be

David Prockter - editor of *UFO News* decided to visit Starr Hill, Warminster, on Saturday, 22nd June 1974, and interview Arthur Shuttlewood, and wrote to Arthur. Arthur wrote back, confirming, and told him to meet up at Starr Hill, at 9.00pm. David set off, accompanied by John Hopping. After visiting Salisbury on the Friday night, they met up with their friend, Renato Bernandin, and visited Stonehenge.

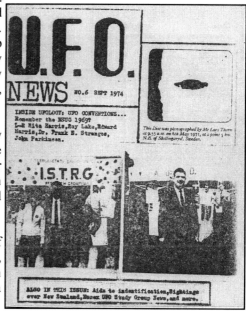

As this was National Sky Watch week, David was eagerly looking forward to being part of the crowd that would be assembled on the Warminster slopes and presumed, after having spoken to Arthur, that there would be no problem finding their way to Starr Hill, which Arthur had told them was on an O.S map.

Frustratingly, they were unable to locate the position of Starr Hill and, although they made enquires in Warminster, nobody seemed to know where it was located. They then made their way to 17, Portway, and were told by a woman that Arthur had gone to Cradle Hill with a party of French students. At 8.25pm they gave up and went home!

June and July 1974 were very busy months, with literally hundreds of sightings of UFOs reported in the local newspapers, but very rarely in the Nationals. Why? The reader is invited to conduct their own research into these incidents, through personal contact with the local library, or newspaper archives, as time and space prevents us from obtaining this information. (These dates may not be exact. If they are not found on the date given, try the day before or day after.)

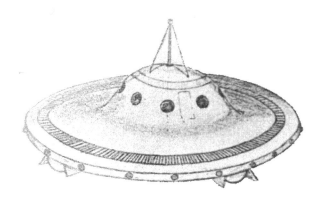

CHAPTER 6
JULY - DECEMBER 1974

Rex Dutta and 'D' Notices

On the 5th July 1974, veteran UFO researcher - Rex Dutta - gave a talk on Radio Piccadilly, Manchester, hosted by Roger Finnegan. He then gave a second talk during a 45mins broadcast with Steve Beard, on the same day. The live 'on air' interviews attracted a surge of letters from the public, which went on for eight weeks, emphasising the public's interest in the UFO subject, now over 35yrs ago. According to the magazine *Viewpoint Aquarius,* many of the letters expressed puzzlement at what they considered to be the attitude of an authority who tried to repress and play down sightings, and to minimise the importance of the staggering fact that UFOs were here. The magazine claimed the editor of an unidentified world-wide Magazine, with a circulation of ten million, had privately said, in conversation with Rex Dutta, who had been commissioned to prepare an article on *'Flying Saucers',* that: *"The British Government does not like saucers and has 'D' notices (plural) on them."* He then apologised for having to sub-edit the article 'to present both sides' and altered the headline to *'Flying Saucers are Real'.* We don't know who the editor was; sadly, little has changed over the attitude of authority in general as to the existence of UFOs. On 6th July 1974, a brilliant pulsating light, judged to be one third of the Moon in size, was seen motionless in the sky over London, in broad daylight, before commencing to fly in a series of triangular movements. (**Source: *Aquarius Viewpoint*, London, Number 29, 1974**)

On the 12th July 1974, an object, resembling a white golf ball, was sighted in the sky over Walthamstow, accompanied by reports of UFOs sighted over Staffordshire and Gloucestershire. The *Evening Echo* newspaper, at Basildon, also carried a double column about UFOs being sighted, along with three shots of the UFO. It was said that the negatives had been sent to the MOD, who made no comment. (**Source: *Evening Echo*, Basildon/*Stafford Newsletter*, 12.7.74***)

Also on the same day was the sighting of an object over Warrington, described as: *"...pearl coloured, brilliant, and absolutely controlled - unlike anything seen before."* (**Source: *Warrington Guardian*, 12.7.74**) *The Forest Guardian* - '**Mysterious object in Banbury reservoir'** (approx. 12th July 1974) told a curious story that, after the reservoir had been emptied at Banbury, on the 12th July, divers carrying out essential work had discovered a 'metallic object' on the bottom. Despite it being drained of its million of gallons of water, nothing was found. We were unable to obtain any further information about this intriguing matter. The following day (13.7.74) a resident of Gloucester sighted two bright red objects, described:

> *"...as huge as a block of flats; five minutes later, 'the two lights' merged and took off at fantastic speed."* (**Source:** *Gloucester Citizen,* **13.7.74**)

Five days later, on the 18th July 1974, high-pitched electronic noises were heard, after a vaguely circular light was seen shining through the clouds, causing strange beeping noises on the domestic television sets at Cheltenham, Gloucestershire, along with bright red 'stars' seen over Stroud. (**Source:** *Gloucestershire Echo -* **'They're back, after months of comparative silence')**

Mr. H. Page of Albert Road, Peel Common, Fareham, Hampshire, was weeding the front garden in July 1973 (it may have been 1974 - he can't be sure) at 4.30pm, when he saw:

> *"...what looked like three large 'dinner plates in size', bright orange objects, motionless and low down in the sky. After five minutes they moved away towards the direction of Gosport. I contacted the* Portsmouth Evening News *and told them about it. After they published the sighting lots of people contacted them, reporting having also seen it go over."* (**Source: Nicholas Maloret, WATSUP**)

A triangular object, with what looked like the sun's rays emanating from it, was seen in the sky over Halifax, Yorkshire, by an amateur astronomer. (**Source:** *Evening Courier,* **Halifax, 18.7.74**)

Also on the same day, was a report contained in the *Romford Express* (18.7.74) of a bright ball of light, seen by a local resident, *"...that seemed to glide along before dropping out of sight, behind houses."* The Police attended and examined the locality, but found nothing untoward. Further reports of UFO activity for this period included: *"...a rugby ball-shaped object, topped with brilliant white, with grey dots",* seen over Middleborough sparking-off numerous calls to the Police, on the 22nd July 1974. (**Source: Teesside Evening Gazette**)

On the 23rd July 1974, the *Herald Express,* at Torquay, told its readers about:

> *"...six UFOs, forming a crescent shape, sighted over the town, which broke into a perfect half-moon formation, before joining up again".*

A silver cone-shaped UFO was seen over Kidsgrove, Staffordshire, on 26th July 1974, by a number of people, who contacted the Police. (**Source:** *Evening Sentinel,* **Stoke-on-Trent, 26.8.74**)

Vanished into Thin Air..

At the time of researching Volume 5 of *Haunted Skies,* we were intrigued to come across details of a highly unusual incident widely disseminated on the WWW (2012) alleged to have taken place on the 28th July 1974, according to Colin Parsons, who wrote about it in his book *Encounters with the Unknown* (Robert Hale, 1990). It involved a Somerset resident Peter Williamson, and his wife, Mary, who were having a barbecue in their backyard garden, when the proceedings were interrupted by a heavy electrical storm.

As Peter went to rescue his dog, which was cowering under a nearby tree, there was a bright flash and Peter vanished into thin air! The Police were called and a thorough investigation and search were conducted, without success. At 8.00am three days later, Peter was found in some nearby bushes, with one foot in a pond - as if he had just appeared there, out of nowhere. Peter began to experience increasingly lucid dreams. He saw himself standing in an unfamiliar garden, soaking wet, and wandering along roads, dazed and confused. In his dream, he was found and eventually taken to a hospital. Here he spent some time undergoing tests. He was able to recall the names of a doctor, a sister, various nurses, and the ward where he was cared for. He also remembered how the hospital would 'shimmer' around him in a sort of haze, and furniture would appear in places where none had previously stood ... then the ward would return to normal.

As Peter's condition improved in this dream hospital, he was allowed out for a walk around the grounds, going down a lane outside. Pete began to get a sense of familiarity and the next thing he knew was on waking up by the pond.

The hospital Peter described was traced; it was a cottage infirmary nearby. It had a ward, a doctor and a sister, with the names Peter had reported. The doctor did not recognise Peter, and the hospital records showed that he had never stayed there. It was suggested that he must have invented his dream from fragments of information lurking in his subconscious (perhaps a conversation once heard about the hospital).

This was a case that once again fired the imagination, but we had to rein in our excitement and endeavour to focus our attention on discovering the facts of what lay behind these startling revelations. While we had no reason to disbelieve that events of similar high strangeness have, and will, continue to take place, we were surprised not to find any corroborating evidence from the media during this period, or from established UFO researchers from the Bristol/Somerset area, who had no knowledge of this matter at all.

We contacted the Somerset Libraries but were told that, without an exact location, any research work would cost us £30 per hour, with of course, no guarantee to find anything. The fact that we were unable to substantiate, in our own minds, that this incident actually took place, does not imply any fabrication on behalf of Mr. Parson (whom we understand has passed away). It is just that we were unable to obtain any answers to questions; such as, were there any other witnesses to the event, apart from Peter and his wife, Mary? Was the incident taken from his own testimony? What was the involvement of the Police, and Ambulance services? Would they have conducted investigation(s) into an alleged 'missing person' incident so early? One cannot believe that the Police would have treated this as a missing person initially, bearing in mind that if someone had mentioned the circumstances of how this man had disappeared, to me (John) as young 'copper', on duty back in the 1970s, I may have wondered if a bomb had gone off, and would have despatched an immediate Police response. Something else to consider would be if it was suitable weather for a barbecue on that day? One would think that any sudden freak changes in weather would surely have been noted by any enthusiastic weatherman in the area.

It might also be prudent to look into any medically related problems that the alleged witness might have suffered from – such as blackouts, fits, epilepsy etc. – or perhaps he was just inebriated from drinking at the barbecue, wandered off and collapsed somewhere. This matter was discussed at length with Bristol based UFO researcher Terry Hooper who is convinced (as indeed we are) after conducting an investigation into the matter, that there is no evidence whatsoever to support this claim.

On 31st July 1974, a tiny point of light appeared over Watford, which was soon joined by a second and then a third light, which was seen to circle a tree. Another three lights appeared in the sky - this time they flared into brilliant light. Soon a fourth appeared, but did not according to the witness 'flare up' like its predecessors.

"Suddenly they all disappeared from sight, followed by the arrival of small

Jet aircraft, making its way to where the objects had been. After the aircraft had gone, two lights returned. Shortly afterwards, they were gone for good."

This was not the only sighting for this date. According to the *Southern Echo* (31st July 1974) four people, including a coastguard, sighted an object in the sky, *"like looking through a slot in a furnace"*, and visible for fifteen minutes, at 2.00am. **(Source: *Aquarius Viewpoint*, Number 29, September 1974 - Peter Merriot)**

In August 1974, the *East London Advertiser* carried the start of a number of articles, including the sighting by people from Catford and Downham, during the early part of the month, of:

> *"...curious pink balls of light, seen carefully avoiding buildings as they slowly floated through the air, sometimes just above the road."*

At 9.40pm on 8th August, a bright saucer-shaped object was seen moving slowly across the sky, by East Sussex resident - Peggy Mason - author of *Tales of Two Worlds,* who had this to say, at the time:

"The sky was not yet dark, still remains of sunset. I saw this enormous light, and went into the garden to watch it, <u>hoping</u> it could tune in to me. After about ten minutes it expanded and dimmed out, leaving a point of light that slowly travelled northwards from the direction of Ashdown Forest. I had the strong sensation that it wanted me to see it." **(Source: *Aquarius Viewpoint*, Number 29, September 1974)**

Close encounter, Dagenham

Barry King, still curious as to what he and his colleague had seen previously, in May 1974, was sat at his bedroom window on the late evening of 10th August 1974 - a warm and stuffy night - watching out for any sign of the Perseids meteor shower, visible from mid July each year, with the bulk of its activity falling between the 8th and 14th August. His attention was drawn to a small red light, seen moving from right to left. As it drew level with his position it bounced up and down, a few times in the air, then carried on to Barry's left, before stopping in mid-air and reversing its direction, where it once again began to retrace its original journey, occasionally bouncing up and down.

> *"I flashed a large heavy duty torch at it. To my surprise, it responded with a bounce in the air. I flashed twice - it bounced twice. I flashed three times - it did it three times. This went on for a few minutes and then it disappeared, so I recommenced my observation for any sign of the meteor shower. Suddenly, I heard a noise from the garden below and shone the torch, thinking it was a cat. The beam caught a figure standing near the shed. I*

froze with fear, realising this was the same figure we had seen at Barn Hill, back in May. Oh My God! I thought it's moving towards me. I dived away from the window and crouched down next to the wall, at the bottom of my bed, terrified.

After some time had elapsed, I gingerly went over to the window and plucked up the courage to look out - there was nothing to be seen. Relief flooded through me and I got back into bed."

The next morning, Barry went out into the garden and examined the ground. There was nothing to be seen. Within a few weeks of the event, he became afflicted with a strange rash on his hands and face - a medical condition the Doctor was unable to diagnose. Fortunately, with the application of ointment and bandages, the condition cleared up.

On the 12th August, a red sphere was seen over the Leicestershire area, at 1.30am, described as:

> "...moving low down in the sky, clearing the tops of houses, before changing to a yellow colour, lighting up the whole street with its illumination - then changing course and heading out of sight."

UFO over Cheltenham

Brian Savory from Cheltenham, Gloucestershire, was observing Jupiter through binoculars, at 1.55am on the 14th August 1974 - a clear night, with a little haze in the distance, accompanied by his father.

> "I was turning to look at Sirius, when I noticed bright red and green lights over Leckhampton Hill, moving towards us. As the lights came closer overhead, I could see a distinctive crescent shape, with a domed top and a riot of multi- coloured lights swirling around the object. It then began to swing to and fro, like the pendulum of clock, rose slightly, and then descended". **(Source: personal interview)**

UFOs over Stone-on-Trent

At about 9.30pm on the 16th August 1974, a Stoke-on-Trent housewife living at Milton, told of sighting a bright shining light heading across the sky, from South, South-west to North, North-east, before disappearing behind a clump of large trees. Seconds later it reappeared, and headed towards the horizon and vanished from view over it.

> "Another two objects appeared then, followed the same course, and then faded over the horizon. Another three objects appeared, two of these following the same path as the other objects, the third one travelling from west to north. All of these sightings lasted for about 2 minutes, and except for the latter object, all disappeared over the horizon; the latter sighting faded out above the horizon.
>
> At about 11 o'clock, a star like object appeared, and travelled eastwards at a steady rate, and then accelerated upwards at an angle of approximately120° - then it faded out of sight. At 11.20pm a similar object appeared, still travelling in the same direction, but this time it speeded up and disappeared at an angle of about 130°."

UFOs over Surrey

At 9.45pm on 20th August 1974, Mrs. Mills - a housewife from Camberley, Surrey, and former member of the Royal Observer Corps - sighted a UFO moving through the air over a local youth club, at an estimated height of 100ft off the ground. The following evening, she was stood in her back garden, taking in the air at 9.45pm, when she saw:

> "...a bright beam of light approaching the house, so close I thought a light aircraft was about to crash-land, so I ducked behind the side of the house. After nothing happened, I peered into the garden and saw the amazing sight of a 'ball of light', about ten feet in diameter, accompanied by a number of smaller red lights darting about, just above the ground where I

had been standing.

I decided to pluck up my courage and confront the object, now making a humming noise. Suddenly it moved a few feet upwards and crossed over into my next door neighbour's garden, where it was joined by four or five similar objects, all of them bobbing up down, before moving away out of sight." **(Source: Peter Paget, *Fountain Journal*, No. 8, 1977)**

UFO over Hertfordshire

Mrs. S. Eaton of London, was driving her open topped sports car to meet some friends for a drink in Hatfield, Herfordshire, one warm evening, in August 1974, and was travelling along the A1000 road, through Brookmans Park, when she noticed an object in the sky, towards the north-east.

"I slowed down to about 5mph, so as to get a better look, and saw a long craft 2-300yds in length, travelling at a height of about 3-4,000ft in the sky. I pulled the car over onto the side of the road to obtain a closer look, bearing in mind that dusk was falling.

This was no aircraft - it had no wings and was tremendous in size. There were no visible protrusions on the upper and lower surface of the object, but along its length were a number of lights in a line, not bright but bright enough to be seen.

The body of the vessel was darker in colour but not black - possibly a matt or satin finish, which didn't reflect the light; it was making this deep humming noise, accompanied by a whirring sound. It was stationary in the sky at this point, positioned very close to Brookmans Park Aerial - a TV and aircraft flight beacon. After about five minutes it moved away, its course taking it almost directly overhead. I continued on my journey. My emotions were mixed feelings - both thrilled and terrified." **(Source: Dan Goring, *Earth-link*, Winter 1979/80)**

Close Encounter, Bournemouth

Ron and Jackie McClure would never have guessed that they were to be the victims of another bizarre experience, twelve months later, after their 'encounter' with the weird figure on the slopes of Cradle Hill, Warminster.

Ron was getting ready for bed, when he noticed a narrow beam of light shining onto the roof of a nearby house, which he brought to Jackie's attention before getting into bed. Within a short time Jackie fell asleep, leaving Ron restless. The next thing that he became aware of was a dog, barking, outside.

"I decided to ignore it. About fifteen minute, later, the dog stopped barking. Right away, the noise of the animal was replaced by a strange whining noise - its tone low and high-pitched. Now wide awake, sensing something was going to happen, I looked out off the bedroom window, from my prone position on the bed, and saw a brilliant half-moon shaped yellow object shining through the clouds, before it dropped downwards, sharply etched against the background of the sky, followed

by the unnerving sight of a black, transparent silhouette, about five feet tall - not dissimilar in shape and size to what we had seen on Cradle Hill, Warminster - then the whining stopped.

I felt a strange calmness descending over me. At this point Jackie sat up in bed and told me her eyes were sore after watching bright lights, and promptly fell back to sleep.

I heard the bedroom door swing open, a few inches.

I looked - there was nothing there. When I looked back at the window, the silhouette was gone.

I found myself unable to sleep most of the night, puzzling about what had happened, falling asleep at 4.00am. The next morning, during conversation with Jackie, I asked her if she remembered anything unusual taking place in the night.

She told me about having seen some brilliant lights, which seemed rather odd, because from her position in the bedroom, she wouldn't have been able to see through the window." (**Source: Leslie Harris, *Scan*, Bournemouth**)

UFO over Hampshire

Ian Glasby from Cosham, Portsmouth, was with two other youths watching the night sky, in late autumn 1974, with a pair of binoculars, at 8.00pm. They noticed a bright, stationary light in the sky, towards the south-east, flashing green and red lights, which they first thought was a helicopter. On looking at the 'lights' through binoculars, they were staggered to see a gigantic object, *"the size of a battleship"*. Ian said later:

"It had a rectangular body, surmounted by a raised dome, with a number of protrusions along it length. Midway along the base of the structure was a single row of oval portholes, out of which spilled green red and white lights into the sky.

At both ends of the UFO were what looked look antennae. The surface was covered with what looked like grey coloured squares and rectangles - almost metallic in appearance. There was a beam of white light projecting downwards, towards the horizon.

We ran around to the local newspaper office, but found they were shut.

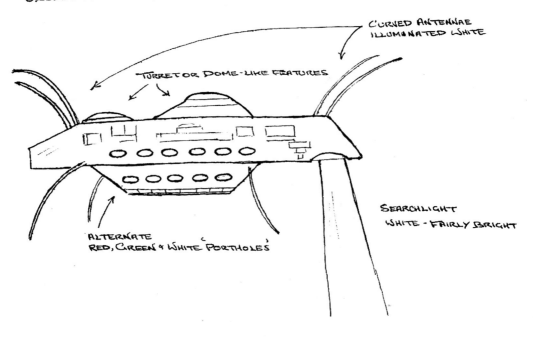

OBJECT AS OBSERVED THROUGH BINOCULARS.

CURVED ANTENNAE
ILLUMINATED WHITE

TURRET OR DOME-LIKE FEATURES

SEARCHLIGHT
WHITE - FAIRLY BRIGHT

ALTERNATE
RED, GREEN & WHITE 'PORTHOLES'

When we looked back into the sky it had gone, although we actually saw it again in the same place two nights running." (**Source: Nicholas Maloret, WATSUP**)

UFO Display over Bedfordshire

At 7.00pm on 15th September 1974, Leslie Moulster - then aged 47 from Billington, Bedfordshire, well experienced in aircraft recognition, and employed as an instrument fitter - was driving between Stanbridge and Billington. He noticed an unusually wide vapour trail running in a north-south direction across the sky, before being lost in cloud, towards the horizon. Leslie thought it might have been a Boeing 747 on Trans polar over flight, and continued on his journey, turning right onto the A4146 at Billington Junction, heading towards Leighton Buzzard, with the vapour trail still above him. He then became aware of:

"...a silvery object, flying parallel with the trail, heading northwards, offset slightly to the west of it. I thought it must be another aircraft, travelling along the same route but was surprised not to see any vapour trail.

I had just passed through Billington when I saw a clear disc-shaped object, similar to the other one but coloured a distinct reddish-brown. I slowed down my car, as I formed an impression they were on a collision course.

Within seconds, they collided with a brilliant flash of light that temporarily blinded me, obscuring everything in the near vicinity. I was horrified and expected to see pieces of wreckage falling from the sky.

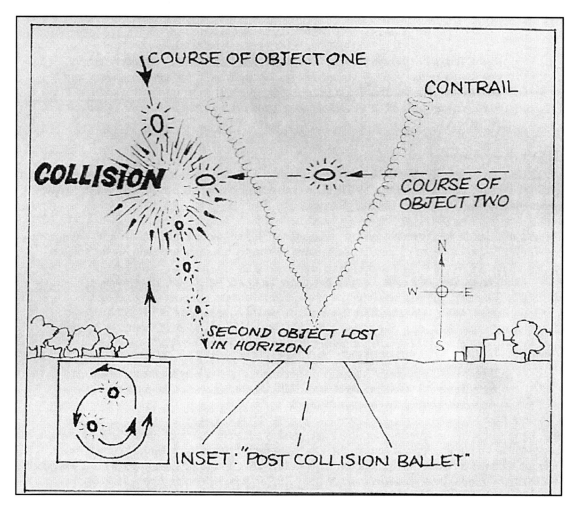

A few seconds later my eyes adjusted sufficiently for me to see an amazing aerial ballet, involving the two objects, which were circling each other in the sky - far too tight a turn to be aircraft. At this stage an irate driver in a Rover 2000, behind me, sounded his horn. After allowing him to overtake, I looked upwards again and saw the reddish-brown object had gone - the silver one was still there and now back on its original course." **(Source: personal interview, 2012/***FSR***, Volume 24, No. 6, Ken Philips - 'Bedfordshire mid-air collision')**

On the 21st September 1974, Kevin Knight was with members of the family on a boating holiday, cruising down the River Thames, at 8.30pm. They decided to moor up for the night at Marlow, in Buckinghamshire, close to several large fields, with a few scattered trees.

"My father asked us to come up on deck, as he could see something strange across the fields. At first I thought it was a bright fire burning in the trees, 5-600yds away, but then I realised the 'fire' was about 15-20ft above the trees; its colour was changing constantly from red to orange and then to yellow, and back again. After about five minutes, it rose slightly higher in the air.

By this time there were eight of us watching it. The light was now moving relatively slowly across our field of vision. My uncle looked at it through binoculars and shouted out that it was a bright orange disc, spinning on its own axis. Suddenly, it hurtled away from us, at incredible speed, and disappeared from view." (**Source: BUFORA**)

UFO over Dorset

At 12.10am on 24th September 1974, ex-RAF Michael John Byatt from Bridport, Dorset - an experienced gliding instructor, then employed as a TV Engineer - was returning from Maiden Newton, with a companion, and heading towards home in his Bedford motor van.

As he turned left at the crossroads on top of Eggardon Hill, an ancient hill fort, with its commanding views over Eggardon Downs, reputed to be haunted by ghostly baying hounds and Roman soldiers.

"We both became cold. I turned the heater up to full but it made no difference. The engine began to lose power, and the electrics dimmed, but did not go completely. Had we not been travelling downhill, we would have stopped. An object appeared to our right, at a fairly high altitude, approximately 300-600ft above us, at the same time as the vehicle lost power, before disappearing vertically from view.

Whether it disappeared before we left I cannot say, as I was frightened and beat a hasty retreat. On looking back at the hill, we could see it at the top rather like a parachute flare, only not quite as bright".

Mr. Byatt still seeks an answer, over 30yrs later, and is adamant that what he saw was no aircraft, as suggested to him, following publicity in the local newspapers. After the event he told us that it looked like a circular neon tube, moving backwards and forwards, in the sky. (**Source: Frank Marshall, BUFORA/personal interview/***Bridport News, **27.9.74/***Dorset Evening Echo, **25.9.74**)

UFO over Portsmouth

At 12.30am on 29th September 1974, Mr. and Mrs. Oliver were driving westwards along Romsey Road, in an Austin A60 Cambridge, near Hursley, and had just reached the crest of a hill. They noticed a flashing light in front of them, which they took to be an aircraft, but on reaching the base of the hill, realised the light was stationary and they were almost underneath it. Mr. Oliver later told Nick Maloret:

"It was clearly visible and made up of a circular arrangement of 'V'-shaped white lights, flashing on and off rapidly, as it hovered over open field, about a hundred feet away from the road. I slowed down to about 5mph and watched it through the side window.

My wife kept her eye on it by looking through the windscreen. A car in front had stopped. The occupants were already outside watching the object, which

Page 3

BRITISH U.F.O. RESEARCH ASSOCIATION - SIGHTING REPORT FORM

14) Did you observe the object through any of the following? (Please circle if yes):

Spectacles ;   Sunglasses ;   Window Glass ;
Car Windscreen ;   Binoculars ;   Telescope ;
Theodolite ;   Other ; *FIRST SEEN THROUGH CAR WINDSCREEN, THEN THROUGH OPEN WINDOW.*

15) Describe the following properties of the object :-
Sound ; .... NONE
Colour ; .... WHITE
Shape ; .... CIRCULAR ARRANGEMENT OF X-SHAPED LIGHTS

16) Draw a picture of the object :-

NO SOLID STRUCTURE WAS VISIBLE BEHIND THE ARRANGEMENT OF LIGHTS.

17) The edges of the object were :- (Please circle one)
Blurred of "fuzzy" ;   (Sharply outlined)   Other ; ....

18) If there was more than one object, how many were there? ....

19) Draw a diagram to indicate the course of the object(s), indicating any changes of direction. Put "A" at the start of the course and "B" at its termination :

was under cloud level. We eventually lost sight of it, as our view was obscured by trees bordering the side of the road." (**Source: Nick Maloret, WATSUP**)

Steven Furk - a TV Engineer by occupation - was out fishing off Portland Bill, with his friend - Mr. Hartley - just after midnight on the 4th October 1974, when their attention was drawn to a luminous 'white ring', slightly blurred at the edges, stationary in the sky, out of which projected a beam of light arcing over towards the horizon. Twenty-five minutes later, it disappeared from sight. (**Source: Frank Marshall, BUFORA**)

At 1.00am on 14th October 1974, Mr. and Mrs. Haughton from Mossley Common, Greater Manchester, were awoken by brilliant white light flooding into their bedroom. The couple rushed to the window, and wondered if there had been an accident. They were astonished to see:

"...a huge object, about 80yds away, hovering low down over trees; it had a domed top and rectangular underside, showing a row of seven framed windows, out of which poured white light. The object then silently rose up just above tree level, and halted in the sky before moving away - still at tree top height." (**Source: *UFOs: a British Viewpoint*, Jenny Randles & Peter Warrington, Page 76**)

Amateur astronomer - Dave Stringer - from Clapham Village, Worthing, Sussex, was out walking with his wife, at 6.00pm on 17th October 1974, when they saw an enormous bright light hovering in the western sky above their position, before veering off at incredible speed. Apparently they were not the only ones to see it; two other Worthing residents also reported having sighted:

> *"...objects, like pink clouds moving in formation, two abreast, from south to north-east, at 6.00pm."*

Another witness told of seeing what looked like:

> *"...oval, pinkish objects, like candy floss in the sky."*

Mr. Stringer stated that research into these and other events indicated a connection with Devil's Dyke, at Brighton, as many of these objects were seen hovering over this local landmark.

UFO photographed over Bournemouth

The *Scan* newsletter was produced by Bournemouth based Leslie Harris, whom we had spoken to on numerous occasions, over the years, with regard to a number of interesting 'Close encounter' sightings, involving Alien beings, and humanoid shapes seen bordering more on the paranormal, rather than UFO, personally investigated by him during the 1970s, many of which were included in his *Scan* Magazine, often accompanied by artwork provided by John Ledner.

On this occasion, we discussed a photograph taken by Bournemouth man - Greg Marchant - of a UFO seen during the evening of the 23rd October 1974, which was to be the subject of considerable media attention. It was featured on the BBC News, TV and Radio, and was reported in the *Bournemouth Evening Echo* (23.10.1974). We contacted Greg, who told us:

> *"I was in the bedroom and looking out of the window when, suddenly, I noticed a bright blue-green light moving across the sky. I grabbed my Polaroid camera, which had a few exposures left, and ran downstairs and into the garden. The object was moving across the sky, quite fast, in a straight line from West to North-east. The stars were bright and there was a moon quite low down.*
>
> *The object did not hover. By the time I got there, it was moving fast. I leaned right back, quickly followed it in the view finder, and took the photograph when it was almost overhead - brighter than the Moon. When I took the photo I didn't realise it, but there was a flash in the camera. When I took the camera away from my eyes, the object had gone from view. There was absolutely no sound from the object. This I couldn't understand. I had seen aircraft - in fact lots of them, as we are on the flight path to Hurn Airport."*

Greg then went into the front room where his parents were, and 'peeled the film', waving the photograph in front of the fire for exactly 30secs, then peeled the two parts of the film away.

He then watched, with baited breath, as it appeared. Excited, he showed his father, who thought he *"was mucking about"*. The next morning Greg's father tackled him again about the photograph, but Greg assured him it was genuine. This was followed by the threat of *"a thick ear"* by Greg's father, after his son had told him that he was going over to the Airport to show them the photo.

Instead, his father took the photo himself and was told the radar had been switched off that night. What the relevance of that is, bearing in mind there were no flights, isn't known, although Greg appears to have suspected, albeit erroneously, that there was something suspicious about this.

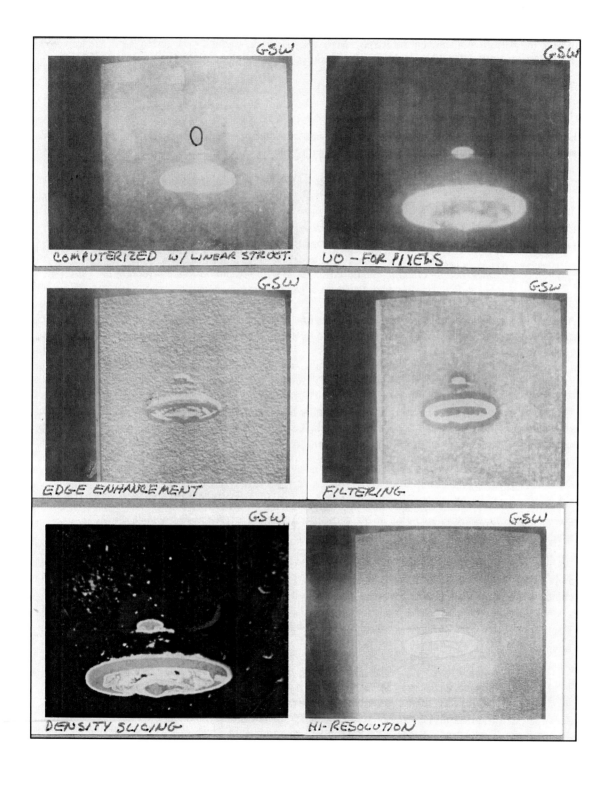

GSW

COMPUTERIZED w/ LINEAR STRUCT.

GSW

UO - FOR PIXELS

GSW

EDGE ENHANCEMENT

GSW

FILTERING

GSW

DENSITY SLICING

GSW

HI-RESOLUTION

The matter was brought to the notice of *Scan* members -Ron McClure and Malcolm Terry - who went over to the Airport and showed the Airport Manager - Harry Longhurst - the photograph. He looked at it with amazement and confirmed there were no aircraft flying at the time In fact, one man said:

> *"That is one of the best photographs I have ever seen of a UFO and I, for one, believe in them."*

Leslie tape-recorded an interview with Greg, which was later released to Radio Solent, and concluded, in his opinion, that the photo was apparently authentic, the UFO being described as:

> *"It had green top, dark sides, bright white rim at the bottom, and orange underneath."*

On the 24th October 1974, the *Bournemouth Evening Echo* covered the story, '**UFO - was it an aircraft?**' and made reference to an unnamed spokesman from the Airport, who suggested:

> *"Under certain climatic conditions, a plane with navigation lights revolving and headlights on can look rather spectacular from certain angles."*

Another suggestion was *'a helicopter, with lights on, could also look strange'* - not forgetting the fact that there were no flights made in the locality that evening. The photo was judged important enough to be sent to the well respected Ground Saucer Watch - a now defunct organisation, founded in 1957, with a membership of scientists, engineers, professionals, and educated laymen interested in taking scientific action to resolve the controversial elements in UFO reports.

Their aim was to provide an accessible outlet for anybody who wished to report any aerial phenomena without fear of ridicule or undue publicity; to 'edify a confused media' with factual press releases, lectures, conferences, and interviews; to research and evaluate all UFO cases to which scientific criteria can be applied and analysed, with the use of specialised talents and instrumentation. GSW concluded damningly,

> *"...that Greg's photograph represents a crude attempt to stimulate a UFO experience, and that there is no photographic evidence to support an extraordinary flying object."*

We wrote to Greg in 2000, enquiring about the matter. He was insistent that this was a genuine photo and that the suggestion it was hoaxed had attracted a lot of nasty letters accusing him of hoaxing, to the extent he withdrew from getting involved in the activities of *Scan*.

> *"The film type was an 87 film - just aim and shoot. I don't use it any more. It's part of history anyway. I was 21 then - now I am 47! I still look around at night. You never know now armed with a digital, 80 times zoom. When I got home that evening, on the 22nd October 1974, I found the picture and story in the paper, via a new man, who was at Bournemouth Airport, and took it upon himself to put it on radio. I was stunned with all of the rush - then the* News of the World *contacted me. Some months later I appeared on the* Mary Parkinson *programme, at Thames TV. It's still the best photo around."*

According to Leslie Harris, the initial experience had a marked effect on Greg, who took time off work, found it difficult to write and could not sleep facing the window.

> *"Greg's interest in UFOs became intense. He spent many evenings (when conditions were favourable) out on his motorcycle, and was to witness a number of further sightings of UFOs.*
>
> *One night, while riding his motorcycle through the Fordingbridge area, he saw four diamond-shaped objects, described as 'brilliant white, with a dark area or black hole in the centre', moving across the sky, making a humming sound.*
>
> *On another occasion he filmed an object, resembling a saucepan-shaped object, from the excavation site at Rockwell, but unfortunately, incinerated the film, while trying to photograph the projected picture. Not that this appeared to have put him off - far from it. He was to also claim having photographed other UFOs as time went on."*

Leslie, told us the most spectacular, mysterious, and unusual incident (number nine sighting) occurred at a road junction known locally as 'Three Legged Cross', at 8.00pm. (Date unknown) when, after having parked his bike, Greg noticed a light moving silently through the air, at tree top height.

> *"I noticed, as it went across the tree tops, it was very unusual. It had a light bulb top - like a strip light, without the glass. There was a figure inside, wearing a blood red helmet. You could see a discerning white chin underneath it, as though the thing inside was made of metal.*
>
> *The only part of the 'being' directly visible was the lower face. The rest of the 'body' was covered in a one-piece suit, right down to the boots - more like wedges than normal boots. The garment was luminous green, like the luminosity found on clocks or watch faces. The 'being' appeared to be contained within some sort of energy field - like power beams of light all going around. There were bullet-shaped things travelling in the beams of light, being propelled around 'him' in these transparent red lines, and they never seemed to cross each other."*

At this stage, after several unsuccessful attempts to start his motorcycle, Greg rode away - the 'object' now travelling away from him, keeping just above the bushes which flanked the road, on the right-hand side. Greg followed, increasing his speed up to 70mph, driving on the wrong side of the *"dead straight road"* to keep pace, flashing his light and sounding the horn, and managed to get within 10ft of the 'thing' still about 20ft off the ground.

He then became aware of a car approaching from the opposite direction, and slowed down. Inexplicably, the vehicle suddenly vanished in front of his eyes. Greg pulled up and was astonished to see the rear lights of the car moving away from him. How had this happened, he pondered, when he had no memory of seeing the car pass? By this time the object was ascending upwards into the night sky, before being lost from view.

Greg was to claim that, following this incident, his right hand was to glow with greenish luminosity.

People would scoff and laugh, but Leslie Harris says he saw his hand glowing himself and has no idea what caused it, other than the explanation given by Greg. Medical examination failed to diagnose the cause of the malady. Greg has also developed the ability to guess or have precognition of future events, albeit trivial ones. Leslie told us:

> *"Greg has photographs to back his claims, which would be very difficult to fake, and you cannot ignore the evidence of his hand. He is a very clever liar, illusionist and photo faker, or he is a genuine man, who has had genuine experiences. If so he is also a brave man."* **(Source: personal interview/*FSR*, Volume 20, No. 3, Page 31/*Scan*, as above/*Scan*, number 10, July 1975)**

Close Encounter, Aveley

Over the years we were to hear of numerous occasions involving reports of strange globes of light seen by motorists, while driving along lonely country roads. Many of the reports concern an initial sighting of a globe of yellow or white light, approximately the size of a rugby ball/football, which would often fly alongside the vehicle, sometimes for many miles, before inexplicably shooting up into the sky.

A well documented case at the time, involving a close encounter between a UFO and motorist, followed by a number of mysterious incidents, bordering on the paranormal, took place at 9.50pm on 27th October 1974. However, this was not, in fact, brought to the attention of Andrew Collins until August 1977. He conducted a very professional investigation into the matter, assisted by fellow researcher Barry King, and later wrote an extensive article in *Flying Saucer Review*, which was published in 1978, although he referred to them, at the time, as the Avis family. On the 27th October 1974, John (32) and Elaine Day (28) accompanied by their three children, Karen (11) Kevin (10) and Stuart (7) went to Elaine's parents house in Harold Hill, Essex.

John and Elaine's father went to the school to collect Elaine's sister – Anne - from school, following a trip to Belgium. Unfortunately, she was four hours late getting to the school and didn't arrive there until 9.00pm.
After Anne had been taken home, the family set out from Harold Hill at about 9.50pm, anticipating that they would be home within 20mins.

John drove along Hacton Lane, a mile away from Hornchurch, in his white Vauxhall Victor car, on what was a beautiful clear night - mild and dry, with little traffic about.

Karen and Stuart were asleep in the back of the car.

Kevin was awake in the back, looking out of the window. Suddenly, Kevin brought his father's attention to a light he could see above a line of terraced houses, to their left. John and Elaine glanced around and saw:

> *"...an oval-shaped light, bluish iridescent, resembling a large star, about 30° off the horizon, approximately 500yds away; it seemed to be traveling in a similar direction to our car, in a series of stopping and starting movements. We thought it was a helicopter's light and continued to watch as it moved behind a small wood."*

Within seconds of seeing the 'light', they passed the end of houses on their left-hand side and lost sight of it, due to their vision being momentarily obstructed by a small wood. When they looked again it was still there, travelling in the same direction, but slower than before. They noted the time was 10.10pm. Throughout, Karen and Stuart remained asleep. John again remarked on the absence of traffic on the road. At this point they were now driving through the darkness of the open countryside. This enabled them to obtain a good view of the 'light', which was still about the same distance away some 500yds. They continued along the road and turned 90° left and drove along Park Farm Road, with the *White Hart* public house on their right-hand side. John drove steadfastly on heading east, towards Aveley, commenting once again, at the lack of traffic to his wife. About half-a-mile east along Park Farm Road, the 'light' appeared to have changed course to south-easterly, and was now observed heading towards the road at an angle of 50°. John explained:

> *"It picked up speed and passed in front of us, at a high angle. I slowed down the car, and craned my neck upwards to see it, before it was obscured by bushes on the right-hand side of the road. As the car went down a dip, we thought this was the end of it and our initial excitement began to fade."*

After the 'dip', the road bends to the right and continues along Averley Road. They drove on for about a mile, passing gravel pits on his left, and the road to Upminster. As they began to negotiate a right-hand turn, with a block of four terraced houses to their right, they had a terrible feeling that something was wrong, as the sound of the engine and tyres on the road receded into the background - just the radio still playing.

> *"In front of us, some 30yds away, covering the whole road, was this green mist or fog gas bank, about 9ft high, bordered on the left by bushes, its right-hand part curved to the ground behind a thin line of trees along the verge of the road. Its top was flat; the bottom was touching the ground.*
>
> *The car radio began to crackle and smoke. I pulled the wires out of the back of it and disconnected the appliance - then the lights on the car failed. Everything went black as darkness settled – the 'fog' unlike any fog I had ever seen engulfed us. The windows were up; Kevin was standing on the floor behind, the other two children who were still asleep. It was 'light' inside the fog and very cold, dead silent, I could feel a tingling sensation - things seemed hazy - then there was a jolt, like the car going over a hump-back bridge* and seconds later the mist or fog was gone. The oddest thing was that I felt I was alone in the car. My next recollection was being aware of driving along the side of White Post Wood, exactly half-a-mile away!"*

---

* The bridge marks the boundary between London and the Essex boundary of Greys Thurrock – this was the location of another remarkable close encounter

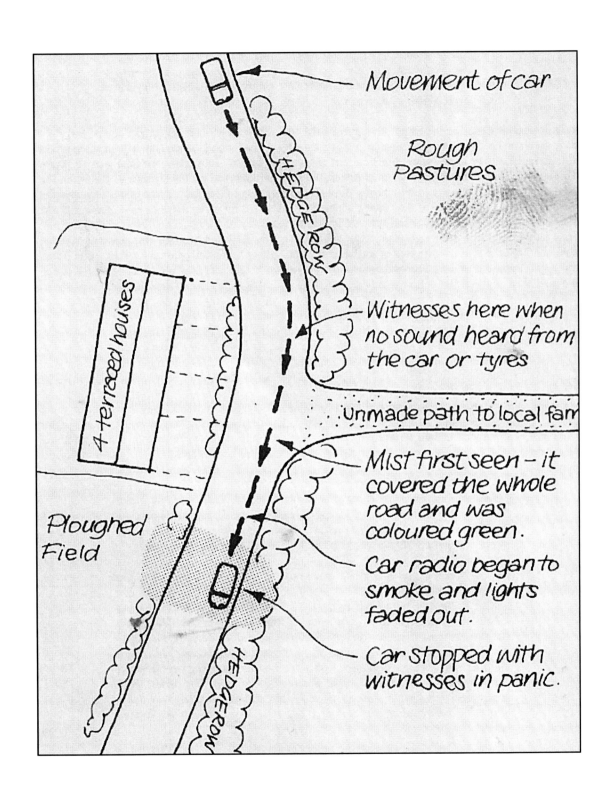

Movement of car

Rough Pastures

Witnesses here when no sound heard from the car or tyres

Unmade path to local far

Mist first seen – it covered the whole road and was coloured green.

Car radio began to smoke and lights faded out.

Car stopped with witnesses in panic.

4 terraced houses

HEDGE ROW

Ploughed Field

HEDGEROW

ABOVE: Couple stand by the four little terraced houses.
BELOW: Looking south along Aveley Road

Elaine's recollection began about half-a-mile further up, near to Running Water Woods, at which stage the car was now behaving normally - the coldness had gone.

On reaching home John rewired the radio and carried the two children, Karen and Stuart, still asleep, up to bed, but was surprised to discover the time was now 1.00am, which seemed impossible, as they expected to have arrived home at 10.20pm, which meant there were three hours of time they were unable to account for. The next day, Elaine telephoned her mother and told her about the incident, but didn't mention about the 'missing time'. Both John and Elaine felt tired, but all three children went to school as normal. In conversation about the matter, the couple decided they should try and forget about it.

The car started breaking down after the incident and suffered a broken crankshaft, which required a replacement engine and clutch renewal. In early 1975 they scrapped the car.

Shortly after the incident John, a talented carpenter and joiner, suffered an inexplicable nervous breakdown, sometime before Christmas 1974, forcing him to give up employment until September 1975, when he found a job working with mentally handicapped people - something he had wanted to do for years, (feeling much more confident of himself), before going on to University, where he obtained a Degree in Art. We were not surprised to hear that, after the event, John was to develop a new found interest in art, craft, and writing poetry. Such changes in behaviour appear common, following UFO close encounters like that described by John and Elaine. In addition, the couple were to complain of physical interruptions to power supply and electrical devices within the family household, together with sightings of strange noises and shapes seen.

Similarly, Elaine, now much more self confident, decided to take up a college course in September 1975 - something she had intended to do for years. Kevin, who had been awake during the UFO encounter, the first one to sight the mysterious light, suddenly began to improve his reading ability, and was soon way ahead of his reading age, whereas previously, he had been backward in his reading at school.

Additionally, John, Elaine, Kevin and Karen, gave up eating meat and couldn't even stand the smell of it. They sampled fish, but the taste made them ill and began eating health foods to some extent, avoiding foods with preservatives and additives, becoming teetotal, and giving up cigarettes.

Shortly after the encounter, John and Elaine became aware they were being followed, on a number of occasions (individually) by three cars - a small red 'sports' car, a blue jaguar, and a large white car (Ford Executive?). The number plates were the British new style yellow at the front, with white at the rear. All of them had darkened windows.

John told us:

> *"I was being stopped at least five times a week by the Police, while driving the car, and given a ticket to produce my driving documents. When I did produce at the Police Station, the officer there was very curious as to why, on occasion, the Officer's details had not been included on the HORT/1 slip. This took place in December 1974. This harassment lasted well into the summer of 1975."*

One is bound to ask why and who sanctioned this action against Mr. Day, and for what purpose? Unfortunately, this was not the first or the last time we were to come across witness intimidation, following a report of a UFO to the authorities.

Based on drawing made by John of the "green mist"

In addition the couple began to have strange recurring dreams, involving 'being operated on' by small, ugly beings, resembling gnomes.

John and Elaine also took part in three hypnotic regressions, which took place on 25th September 1977, the 2nd October and 16th October 1977. During those sessions, conducted by Dr. Leonard Wilder - a qualified hypnotherapist and dentist by profession - John described meeting.....

> *"...tall hooded beings, with pink eyes, wearing one-piece suits, and tables made out of a peculiar substance - not wood or metal - an a thick metal honeycombed bar, 30 ins long, by 10 ins wide, which was moved over my body, causing a vibrating sensation.*
>
> *There was also a small being present, clothed in 'fur' - but not fur.*
>
> *He touched my left shoulder and I passed out. When I regained consciousness, I*

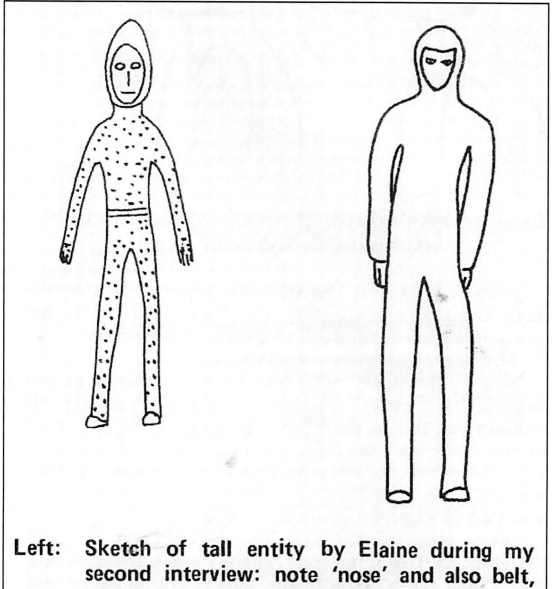

Left: Sketch of tall entity by Elaine during my second interview: note 'nose' and also belt, which was worn by 'leader' only.

Right: John's sketch of tall entity. Nose and belt are omitted, although he says he believes that at least one entity was wearing one.

found myself lying on a table, two and-a-half feet wide, a few feet off the ground. The surface of the table was soft and covered with small grey bubbles. Eighteen inches above my head was a 'scan' type of apparatus, rectangular-shaped, 30-36ins in length, about 3 ins. in width, approximately one inch thick, with an underside of honeycombed design, supported by two circular rods, one on each side of me. The device took about one minute to pass over my body, creating a warm, tingling, sensation on the area being apparently scanned I was aware of three tall entities to my right, and two small ugly looking ones to the left, referred to as 'examiners'. They were four feet tall - no apparent neck - with large, slanted triangular eyes, light brown nose or beak, a slither for the mouth, pointed, slanted back ears, large hairy hands - four digits on each, with claws or long nails. This 'being' walked awkwardly, making an occasional guttural chirp."

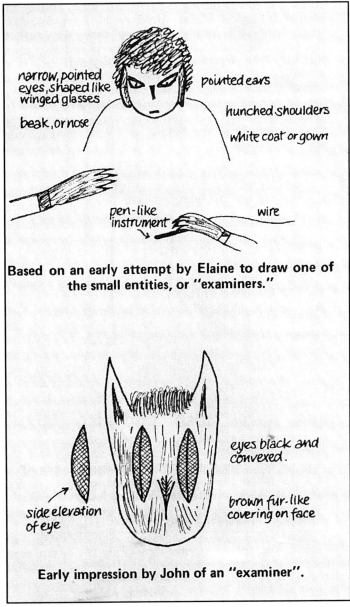

narrow, pointed eyes, shaped like winged glasses

pointed ears

beak, or nose

hunched shoulders

white coat or gown

pen-like instrument

wire

Based on an early attempt by Elaine to draw one of the small entities, or "examiners."

eyes black and convexed.

side elevation of eye

brown fur-like covering on face

Early impression by John of an "examiner".

John asked the tall entities if he could get up. *"Sit there for a while"*, he was told, startled, realising that the words were not spoken, but received telepathically.

Shortly afterwards, he was allowed to get up. The 'examiners' then left the room, at which point he became aware that he was dressed in a one-piece garment, similar to what the tall entities were wearing.

"The room was oval-shaped, perhaps 20 ft in length, by 12ft in width, and about 7-8ft high - very smooth, like being inside a bubble, the only furniture being the table and two overhead lights."

John described the taller entities to be 6ft. 6ins tall, except the 'leader', who appeared to be 2ins taller.

They all appeared to be wearing a one-piece suit, made of material resembling lurex or synthetic felt, that even covered their hands and feet.

"They had two eyes, slightly larger than ours, with pink irises and creamy eyeballs.

No nose or mouth was seen, and I speculated whether they were wearing masks. I saw what appeared to be only three fingers on each hand, and their skin looked very pale almost transparent. They reminded me of a 'bendy toy' or 'blow up doll' when they moved, as they seemed devoid of joints in their arms or legs, yet walked gracefully but with no long strides."

During his entire onboard encounter, the tallest entity was the only 'being' that John had direct contact with. John asked these beings what they did when they went outside their ship, and was told that they used a visor, which was shown to him.

We felt this was one of the most detailed accounts we had ever come across, involving considerable conversation between the parties known as the 'Watchers', who told John they had formerly inhabited the Planet long ago. All manner of topics were discussed, including, the 'aliens' form of communication. They were also given a 'guided tour' of the layout of the 'craft' and shown maps, charts and instrumentation.

Sadly, the couple split up many years later, as they both entered separate lives. Sue became a pagan witch and midwife, who served with the Allies in Iraq, during the first Gulf War. John now lives in a rural part of Scotland. Andrew Collins (left) was to tell of *"strange happenings inside the house"*, which he himself witnessed:

"I find it intriguing that in European occultism, eggregori (Greek for Watchers) was the name given to the balls of etheric light that watched over the affairs of mankind. Perhaps John might have been closer to the truth than he could ever have imagined. The family are very credible, and what is important is that they have always attempted to analyze what happened from grounded perspective, suggesting even that the whole thing had been an astral experience, after they all entered the green mist. In my opinion, the whole incident happened instantaneously for the family and car, but outside usual space-time for the rest of the world, leaving them with a three hour time loss. I am sure I could eventually work out that something like this is possible on a quantum level, using Einstein's Special Theory of Relativity.

It seemed the more we talked together on the subject, the more information would be released. As Elaine put it, 'Its like if you hit the right note, the flood gates will open'.Myself and Barry King would camp round at the Day's home every Friday night, to see whether any paranormal phenomena might occur, and sometimes it did. Another night John, Barry and I, sat up chatting until the early hours.

Sunday Mirror

KIDNAPPERS FROM OUTER SPACE

SCIENTISTS BAFFLED BY COUPLE'S STORY

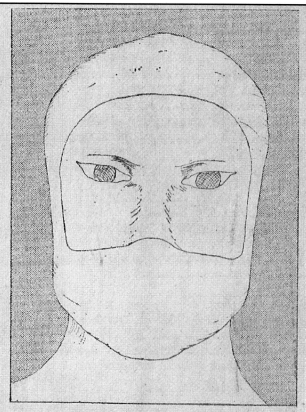

THE ALIEN: John's sketch

We found ourselves in a giant room. I was standing next to two or three beings. They were about seven feet tall, and all dressed in a one-piece costume.

It was like a silver-grey stocking, with a balaclava-type hood which came halfway up their faces.

The most startling thing about them was their eyes. They were bright pink, and they had no eyelids.

I found I knew what they wanted me to do. I think they communicated with me by telepathy. I knew they wanted me to walk across the room, so I did.

There was a doorway leading to another room. We all went through it.

This was obviously an examining room, and they asked me to lie on what looked like an operating table. I did so and a metal arm swung over me.

MAGNETS

I got the impression it was scanning me. Then some smaller beings appeared. They were very squat and ugly, almost dwarflike.

Only one seemed concerned with me. He kept prodding me with a pen-shaped object.

After a while, he seemed to have finished and I asked if I could see around the ship. They agreed.

On a table, which was moulded into the wall, like the rest of the furniture, I saw a game.

It was a pile of cubes, which had magnets on every side. The idea of the game was to build the small cubes into a big one.

Towards the end of the tour the aliens left me alone in a room and suddenly an incredibly beauti-

liquid. Then they it off.

prodded me all h a pen-like object, idn't spare my Then I screamed. of the tall beings ver and put his h my forehead. I t likt a light.

VANISH

r they took me ur around the ship. howed me a screen d, 'That is Earth.' pointed out Eng- it. Then we seemed m in, and they me where I lived. ld the beings I vant to go back I. I could stay on the nd they agreed. w John climb into

the car, and it started to vanish. As it disappeared, I said I had changed my mind, and wanted to go back. Then I found myself sitting in the car."

Hypnotist Mr Wilder, said: " I have no doubt that Mr Day is telling the truth.

" I say this because when I first hypnotised him I conditioned him to tell only the truth.

Mr Barry King, member of the UFO Investigators Network, said: " We've made exhaustive inquiries and are convinced this couple had a close encounter.

" Certain aspects of it are similar to other abductions, like the design and furnishing of the rooms. We can find no reason to doubt its authenticity."

So as not to disturb his wife, Sue, who was asleep, John remained with Barry, and I. As we settled down for the night, John and Barry were in sleeping bags on the floor, and I was on the sofa. I slept, and was then awoken around seven o'clock that morning by the sound of the door handle moving behind my head, at which I craned my neck to see in the dawn light - the door opening just feet away.

I thought that John or Barry had got to the toilet upstairs, and were returning to the room. A tall, silhouetted, figure stood momentarily in the doorway, before moving quickly out of sight, as if walking away. It was at that moment that I glanced on to the floor and saw that both John and Barry were clearly present and both fast asleep.

I became slightly anxious, but assumed that the person had to be Sue, the only other adult in the house. This was despite that no sound of anyone going up the stairs followed the figure's disappearance, and these were right by the door. It could not have gone anywhere else, as it had stood in the house's tiny reception area, which leads only onto the stairs.

It was then that, very suddenly and unexpectedly, I was engulfed by an extremely pungent smell, like rotten eggs, which stifled me, and then instantly I fell back to sleep and woke up around 10 o'clock. The whole thing eventually came back to me, and I recounted what had happened. Sue assured me she had not come down at all, which made sense as the figure was, in my opinion, male.

Moreover, Sue was quite sure there was definitely no-one in the house and an intruder can be ruled out, as the doors to the outside were locked. The strangest aspect was the pungent smell, which we know is associated very strongly with UFO entity cases. The person/entity was unquestionably physical and not etheric.

There has been a great deal written about the case, over the years - much of it without any communication with myself and family, and much of it incorrect. The 'Watchers', as they have become known, have a great sense of humour.

They are like children. When it comes to new experiences, they need to feel. They have always been here and always will be. They have progressed from the physical being and, in doing so, have lost so much. The desire for perfection only leads to despair and it is that which drives them. They fear humans, for they know that they are so insignificant in the scheme of things and yet so very rare and very fragile."

We wish John, Sue, and his family, all the best with their new lives. (**Source: Andrew Collins, UFOIN/The Aveley Abduction,** *FSR,* **Volume 23, No. 6, April 1978/Volume 24, No. 1,** *FSR,* **June 1978, THE AVELEY ABDUCTION/personal interviews, John Day)**

UFO over Hornchurch, Essex

Whilst the next sighting lays outside the period of time covered in this Volume, we judged it important enough to be included, bearing in mind the previous case........

During 1988, Geoffrey - who had experienced flight in a RAF Chipmunk, Tiger Moth, Jet Provost, Douglas DC3 and a Robinson R22 Helicopter - was driving home from London to South Ockenden, in Essex, at midnight, with his (now) ex wife, who was asleep at the time. They had just passed Aveley, when he noticed:

> *"...two red lights in the sky above South Ockenden Railway Station, travelling through the air towards my direction. After crossing the M25 along the B1335, I turned left into Stifford Road, and then left into Foyle Drive*.*

The red lights by this time were heading straight towards me, flying above and along the same road.

About two thirds of the way down Foyle Drive, I turned left into Humber Avenue (to get to my house in Hamble Lane). The lights, at this point, were now on course directly above me. I stopped the car and turned off the engine. It was drizzling, so I knew it was unlikely to be an aircraft. I then got out and looked upwards and noted that whatever it was to be moving silently and very slowly, approximately 5-10mph and was tubular-shaped, with the absence of any wings. I estimated it was 200ft off the ground.

As the tail end passed over me, I heard what I can only describe as a silent roar, along with a faint red glow. I assumed this was coming from the engine, or power source.

I had been standing in the road on my own, and apart from the almost silent noise, you could have heard a pin drop; anyone sleeping in the houses around me would not have heard a thing.

As it moved away from me I wanted to follow the object, but at the end of the road was a small forest called Brickklin Wood, and running right down the middle of this forest was the M25. This made it impossible for me to follow. From that point I have no recollection.

My mind from that moment until the next morning was, and still is, a complete blank; I don't recall getting back into my car and driving the last 100yds to my house, or anything else, until the next day. (**Source: WWW. British Earth Aerial Mysteries Society**)

*A long road about a mile in length and dead straight

UFOs over Rossendale Valley, Lancashire

At 4.10pm on the 24th November 1974, Mr. Daniels and his wife were crossing the street, towards their home in Haslingden - a small town, situated between Burnley and Bury - when they sighted three golden-bronze coloured objects, sweeping across the sky in a long arc, heading from SSE to NNW, accompanied by a feint buzzing sound.

According to the couple, who were later interviewed by members of the Rossendale Astronomical Society, they estimated there was about half-a-mile separation between the first two and a little further between them and the third, and that the overall length was 50-80ft. Another witness was Mrs. Tate. She told of having sighted two small objects:

> *"...like bullets, showing flat and rounded ends. They were moving against the prevailing wind. Moments later they joined together, the junction being marked by a fuzzy region. It was a glowing golden colour and moving in and out of the cloud."*

Mrs. Tate rushed into the house and telephoned Mr. Timothy Evans, of the Rossendale Astronomical Society. By the time he arrived, the object was in the far distance and he was unable to see anything. **(Source: Jenny Randles, *Lancashire Round-up/FSR*, Volume 21, Number 6)**

On the early morning of 1st December 1974, a bright object was seen in the sky over Beckington. Through binoculars, a triangular-shaped object was seen to head north-west, for a few seconds, and descend at a 90 °angle, before vanishing inexplicably. It then reappeared three times in the sky and finally disappeared. **(Source: Lawrence W. Dale, BUFORA)**

'Sky Watch' at Somerset

During a sky watch by members of a UFO organisation, held on the early morning of the 1st December 1974, at Beckington, Frome, Somerset, which included Peter Walsh from St. Pauls Cray, Orpington, Kent, a bright object appeared in the sky.

With the aid of binoculars, *a triangular object was seen within the light.* It was then plotted as heading north-west for four seconds, before dropping downwards for six seconds, followed by a 90°turn south-east, for four seconds, these movements being repeated three times - until it disappeared from view. From calculations carried out, it was established the object was seen:

> *"...at an angle of 100° elevation, height 1.4104 miles, distance 8.1235 miles, downward speed 846.24mph, diameter of object 384ft, lengths of sides adjacent to acute angle of a triangle 190-190ft."*

Whatever it was, it certainly was unlikely to be any conventional aircraft. **(Source: BUFORA/ Lawrence Dale)**

UFO sighting, Ben Nevis

Police Constable David Dawson, of the Strathclyde Police, and his companion - both veteran climbers - were descending Ben Nevis, after a gruelling climb lasting 16 hours, in winter 1974. The two men decided to stop and take a break at the Red Burn, halfway down the Mountain.

David told us:

> *"I was lying down, exhausted. Kerr shouted out in an alarming tone, 'look at that, Dave!' I forced myself up and looked outwards, seeing an object - the size of a full moon - approaching, increasing in size as it grew closer. It was about the size of a double-decker bus, and silver all over, making a noise like an electricity transformer, moving at about 30mph - barely a hundred yards - just above the ground. I studied it, trying to determine a regular shape, or windows to it - there were none. We watched, as it headed towards Polldubh, where we lost sight of it."* **(Source: personal interview)**

UFO over Colchester

During December 1974, a UFO was sighted over Colchester, by a local resident, who had this to say, at the time:

> *"I saw it approach initially from the south-west direction, stop, and reverse away from me without running around. It went behind some trees and then rose to the west and just 'messed about' in the sky, before disappearing. A few minutes later, the light reappeared - this time showing a cluster of red lights around it.*
>
> *These faded away -   then it proceeded to go through a series of aerobatics, accelerating and slowing down, silently and gracefully. Finally, it shot off towards the west."* **(Source: *Colchester Evening Gazette, 6.12.74*)**

UFO over Kent

Mr. Norman and his wife and son, Adrian, were driving along the A2, towards London, near the Dartford Heath turn-off, at 8.00am on the 16th December 1974, when his wife brought her husband's attention to a strange light in the sky, which he thought might have been a factory light.

> *"It then moved across to our left. The sun had not yet risen, so the light could not have reflected the light. The object was moving very quickly; the sky was clear. suddenly, the light disappeared but further along the A2, by the* Black Prince *Pub, I could see the* object. *It looked grey. I then noticed a jet overhead, at high altitude. My husband told me it was a RAF Jet.*
>
> *We turned off the A2 at the Danson Interchange, and had only intermittent glances of the object as we were driving in a near circle. While going along High Street, Welling, towards the British Rail Station, we glimpsed it again. Object and Jet were now visible, heading towards London. When the light of object went out, I thought I could see smoke - not very dense - coming out of the left-hand side."*

BUFORA, Investigator Mr. Castle who was told about this incident made enquires with the Kent UFO Society, and discovered that they had received other reports of a similar object seen in the sky around the Dartford and Welling area.

14) Did you observe the object through any of the following? (Please circle if yes):

        Spectacles ;   Sunglasses ;   Window Glass ;
        (Car Windscreen) ; Binoculars ;   Telescope ;
        Theodolite ;   Other ;... *THROUGH OPEN WINDOW*

15) Describe the following properties of the object :-
Sound ;..*N/A*
Colour ;..*GREY WHEN DARK* ... *WHITE/YELLOW WHEN BRIGHT*
Shape ;....*OBLONG*

16) Draw a picture of the object :-
    BRIGHT   *DARK*

17) The edges of the object were :- (Please circle one)
Blurred of "fuzzy" ; (Sharply outlined) ; Other ;..........

18) If there was more than one object, how many were there?...*N/A*....

19) Draw a diagram to indicate the course of the object(s), indicating any changes of direction. Put "A" at the start of the course and "B" at its termination :

On 9th January, Mr. Castle paid a visit to the scene and was fortunate enough to see a strange light in the sky, 5-6 miles away. Unfortunately, by the time he arrived at the exact location of the previous sighting, made by Mr. Coles, it had gone. (**Source: James Castle, BUFORA**)

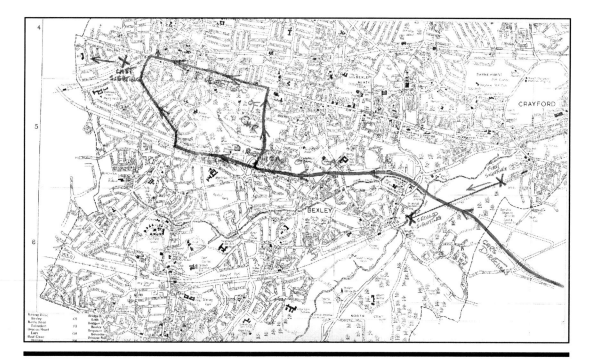

flying object seen descending in the area recently.

Many villagers spotted a "red ball" floating to the ground and they determined to find a solution to the mystery—but in vain.

Now one of the searchers will be sending a report on the incident to an international organisation dealing with UFOs.

though the fireball might be traced to fireworks set off some miles north of the village.

But a report of the fireball being sighted travelling over the area from the SOUTH seems to have exploded this theory.

WOODS SEARCHED

Two of them, Mr. Cyril Hughes, of Oakhurst, Pill Road, Hook, and Mr. Robert Annesley, of 53 New Road, Hook, have since made a search of the wood and shoreline in the area in a bid to find some trace of the fireball.

retired veterinary surgeon, lives at Roch.

So far, their search has failed to come up with a clue to the strange phenomenon.

FIREWORKS

At about the same time as the Boxing Night sightings, several fireworks were set off about two miles north of the village, at Fern Hill, near Haverfordwest.

Mr. Jim Teesdale, of Fern Hill, explained that a few young lads had set off the fireworks near the property. "One of the fireworks was a special one, which lighted up the sky," he said.

He timed the incident at between 9 and 10 p.m.

New twist to 'fireball' mystery

The report of the fireball being sighted travelling south from the direction of Pembroke Dock came from the Downes family, who live in Newtown Road, Hook.

The two young Downes brothers sighted the object from the lounge of their home.

At the weekend, they took part in another search of the area, without success. A further search is planned shortly.

On the 26th December 1974, a curious 'ball of red light' was seen descending through the sky, at about 9.55pm, over Hook, Dyfed, by a number of villagers, who rejected the suggestion, later made, that they had seen a flare. A search of the locality by Mr. Randall Jones Pugh of Roch, near Haverfordwest, on Boxing Day, accompanied by a number of villagers, failed to locate anything of value. **(Source:** *Western Mail, 30.12.74/Western Mail, 6.1.750/Western Telegraph, 9.1.75)*

ADDENDUM FOR 1974

If a person was asked to supply details of English UFO sightings from the early 1970s, it is unlikely that he or she would be able to offer few, if any, examples at all, taking into consideration the difficulties which would be experienced in tracking down these reports, now 40yrs ago. Fortunately, as a result of liaison over the years with many individual UFO enthusiasts, who bothered to catalogue an astonishing number of UFO sightings covering this period, we can now see for ourselves the extent of many hitherto unpublished UFO reports, the majority of which will not be found in declassified Top Secret files made available by the MOD.

JULY 1974: Spate of sightings reported over the UK
JULY 2nd 1974: *Northern Echo Darlington,* Report of a yellow orange object with black markings, flat and dome shaped on top, disc-shaped underneath seen moving across the sky
JULY 2nd **1974 -** *Huddersfield Daily Examiner,* 'brilliant tadpole-shaped light'
JULY 6th 1974: *Solihull News,* 'A bright white light seen over the borough, and reported to Birmingham Airport'
JULY 12th **1974** *The Citizen Newspaper Gloucestershire,* Local people contacted the Police after sighting UFOS.
JULY 12th **1974** *Stafford Newsletter,* A disc shaped object was observed through binoculars for ten minutes before it moved away at speed.
JULY 12th **1974** *Evening Echo Basildon* Three Photos taken of UFO and published, negatives sent to the MOD who apparently declined to comment
JULY 12th **1974** *Warrington Guardian,* A pearly white object was seen flying through the sky apparently under control and moving unlike anything the witness had ever seen before.
JULY 14th **1974**
At 11.00pm, Mrs. D. Marks was driving along Goresbrook Road, Dagenham, Essex, when she noticed a bright light in the sky. As it was so big, she decided to stop the car to obtain a closer look.

> *"It appeared to be above the River Thames, or in that vicinity, travelling fast from the direction of London, towards Southend. I saw it pass quite close to an aircraft, travelling in the opposite direction, before stopping still in the sky for about a minute, during which time it dimmed and grew brighter at regular intervals. The light then proceeded to return in the direction taken and passed out of my view behind two blocks of flats. I waited for it to reappear but it didn't, to begin with. After about three minutes it reappeared in the sky, heading towards the estuary. When it reached the position I had first seen it, the light vanished from view."* **(Source: Letter to Gordon Creighton of** *Flying Saucer Review***)**

JULY 18th 1974, *Evening Courier Halifax,* a triangular object with what looked like the suns rays emanating from it was seen in the sky over Halifax by a number of people including an amateur astronomer. The Police were notified but were unable to offer any explanation for the phenomena.

JULY 18th 1974 *Havering Romford Express,* Reports of a ball of light seen gliding through the sky before dropping out of sight behind houses. Police made as search of the area but found nothing

JULY 22nd 1974 *Teeside Evening Gazette* Middlesborough- many people contacted the Police after sighting an object described as resembling a brilliant white rugby ball showing gray dots on its outer surface *'topped by a bubble'* seen flying across the sky.

JULY 22nd 1974, The *Mail West Hartlepool,* UFO seen over Stockton-Police informed.

JULY 23rd Herald *Express Newspaper,* Six UFOs, forming a crescent-shaped arc in the sky, was seen over Torquay, by a number of people, who gave identical descriptions. The objects were seen heading across the sky, at great speed, before suddenly breaking away from the perfect half-moon formation and then rejoining themselves into the original formation. *Authors* -This process of behaviour is common to the movement of these objects and, while they often appear to move in a fixed formation, they have been seen to fly off in different directions, for an undetermined purpose, before joining up again.

AUGUST 1st 1974 *South East London Mercury,* confirmation from witnesses regarding the previous weeks sightings over the South East London, Catford, Downham areas.

AUGUST 2nd 1974: *East London Advertiser,* 'sighting of curious pink balls of light seen, avoiding buildings as they floated through the air'

AUGUST 5th 1974: *South Wales Evening Post,* 'bright white objects moving at speed'

AUGUST 5th 1974: 'V' or 'W'-shaped formation of UFOs at 10.50pm. Castle Vale, Birmingham, with larger light at base, seen for five seconds (UFOSIS)

AUGUST 7th 1974: *Havering Romford Express,* 'More witnesses come forward'

AUGUST 8th 1974: *Letchworth and Baldock Citizen,* 'metallic object seen'

AUGUST 8th 1974: *Stroud News,* 'metallic object seen'

AUGUST 19th, 1974: *Enfield Weekly Herald,* 'Two humanoid figures seen floating above ground'

Same date, E*ast London Advertiser,* 'pink balls of light seen' over Queen Mary College, London

AUGUST 10th 1974 *Isle of Wight County Press,* orange light seen.

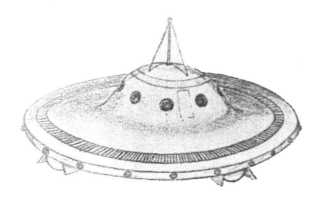

INDEX

BUFORA
JOURNAL
Volume 3 No. 8 Autumn 1972

Published by The British U. F. O. Research Association

Mark, C. - 179
Marks Tey - 179
Marks, D. - 287
Mason, Peggy - 254
Mason, Robert - 54
Mathews-Granville, Diana - 39
Mayfield Golf Course – 191
McClure, Ronald - 66, 257
McDermott, Mary - 132
McDermott, Patricia - 132
McManus, Sharon - 132
Mera, Steven-102
Mera, Alex-102
Mills, Mrs. - 256
Monks Wood - 149
Moorend Park Hotel, Cheltenham - 120
Moreton - 101
Morris, Leslie - 35
Morris, Marlene - 35
Mossley Common - 263
Moulster, Leslie - 260
Mulberry Bush, Birmingham - 189
Munday, Barbara - 81
Munday, Damon - 80
Munday, Wayne - 80
Murray, Mike - 24

N

Naylor, Margaret - 193
Naylor, Michael - 193
Nettleship, Lillian - 55
New Forest, Farmington - 55
Newchapel Observatory - 45, 122
Norman, Mr. - 284
Norridge Common, near Cley Hill, Warminster - 39
Norris, M. - 99
North Scarle - 230
Northamptonshire UFO Forum - 139
Northern UFO Network - 243
Nunn, Paul – 78,79

O

Oldham - 74
Oliver, Mr. and Mrs. - 262
Orpington, Kent - 157, 283
Overchurch Middle School - 39

P

Page, H. - 252
Parsons, Colin - 252
Parsons, Ken - 167
Patching, Joan - 98
Pensarn, Abergele - 156
Penshurst Castle, Kent - 231
Perrin, Mike - 123
Philips, Robert - 71
Photoflash - 218
Pike, Neil - 59, 216, 153
Pike, Sally - 62, 69
Pitt, Stanley - 140, 233
Police
Police Constable Brian Nicholls - 54
Police Constable David Dawson - 283
Police Constable David Harris - 48
Police Constable Keith George - 54
Police Constable Maurice Barsley - 191
Police Constable Neville Hughes - 221
Police Constable Walter Buswell - 191
Police Constable William Hunt - 96
Police Sergeant Clive Williams - 71
Police, Hounslow - 62
Police, Hoylake - 102
Police, New Scotland Yard - 62
Porter, Hilary - 167
Porter, Mr. - 41
Porton Down, Wiltshire - 58, 195, 197
Prisbrey, Dennis - 147
Prockter, David - 239, 249
Punch Bowl Hotel - 121
Purbecks - 26, 111

Q

Quebec UFO sightings- 183-185

R

S

T

U

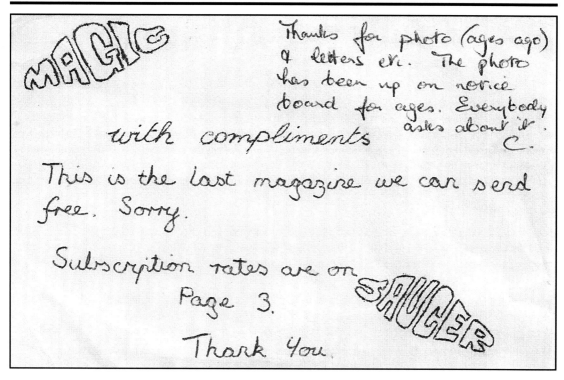

ABOUT THE AUTHORS

John was born in Didcot, Berkshire in November 1945. His grandmother was Spanish and his grandfather was English. During the war his mother was in the Land Army and his father was in the RAF and upon returning to civilian life his father became an RSCPA (Royal Society for the Prevention of Cruelty to Animals) officer. John's childhood was happy and during the course of his father's employment the family moved homes every seven years. When they were living in Halifax, John went to work as a chef in Cheltenham before joining Birmingham City Police in 1966. He settled in Birmingham for over 27 years.

John worked in the CID in the West Midlands Police for 14 years and after 27 and-a-half years in the police force, he retired in 1995. He has three children, one of whom is now a Police Inspector and one is a civilian radio operator at Bourneville Lane Police Station in Birmingham.

It was in January 1995 that John's curiosity in UFOs began, after a colleague telephoned him to tell him about a massive saucer-shaped object he and his officer partner had seen in the Stirchley area of Birmingham, and for the next two to three years John began to gather information of other sightings

that had been witnessed on that same evening. It was also in 1995 that John first met Dawn.

Dawn Holloway was born in Selly Oak, not far from Birmingham to an Italian mother and Welsh father. She undertook a course in office procedures in the 1970s at Turves Green Secondary Girls' School, Northfield, which involved gaining RSAs in shorthand and typing. After leaving school Dawn worked for a company in Kings Norton for around six months before gaining more experience in another company. She left in 1977 to have children – a daughter and a son – and took a few years off work to look after them. In June 1995, Dawn visited a college where John was giving a lecture and he propositioned her into helping him write a book about UFOs, which she thought was only going to last 12 months, but which has - in fact - taken 15 years!

Dawn has met some very interesting people in assisting researching this book including pilots, police officers, and general members of the public who have been most helpful and have had a lot of fascinating accounts to recall. With John, Dawn has visited the length and breadth of the country collecting various UFO reports and has chronologically written these up in various volumes of *Haunted Skies*. It has been a very challenging task, but one which has helped to satisfy the curiosity of the general public. It has been a hobby which Dawn has found immensely enjoyable. Their research has seen them investigating crop circles, WWII foo fighters, strange lights in the sky as well as on the ground, together with flying objects in the skies from Scotland to Cornwall, and they have built up a comprehensive and detailed log which spreads over several volumes.

They are both animal lovers and used to look after Maud (sadly now passed away) the dog who was a regular companion on their trips when Chris her owner was at work. Dawn had a cat called Breeze - so named after the way he 'breezed' into their life some years ago, after being apparently abandoned locally.

Sadly fate was to decree that he only lasted a few years due to his age, but they were happy years and he was pampered, and now lies at rest in his favourite place in the garden.

PICTURE CREDITS

Page 1 - Front cover David Sankey © 2006

Page 3 - Photo of HM Queen ©Bob Tibbitts, 1963

Page 4 - Photo of Margaret and Ron Fry © M. Fry, 2012

Page 5 - Photo of Margaret Westwood © J. Hanson, 2008

Page 5/6 - Photos of Wendelle Stevens © Cece Stevens, 2012

Page 7 - Photo of Matt Lyons © John Hanson, 2011

Page 8 Photo of Maude and Breeze © J Hanson

Page 11 - Photo of Peter Hough © Peter Hough, 2012

Page 18 - Fanzine of UFO books

Page 23 –UFO Illustration,© Steven Franklin

Page 27 - Photos of William Dowman © Richard Thompson, 1972

Page 28/29 - Illustration © Francis Chard, 1998

Page 36 - Sketch of Warminster creature © Peter Mantell/Ken Rogers, 1972

Page 37 –UFO Illustration, ©Wayne Mason, 2012

Page 42 - Karen Hills/original drawn sketch of UFO © K. Hills, 2012
/Staffordshire UFO Club/Graham Allen/Irene Bott

Page 43 – UFO Illustration, Wayne Mason © 2012

Page 43 - Photo of Karen © K. Hills, 2012

Page 45 - Photo © J. Hanson, 2012

Page 46 – UFO Illustration, Wayne Mason, from original © 2012

Page 50 - Bob Tibbitts © 1972

Page 52 – UFO Illustration, Wayne Mason © 2012

Page 56 - Nettleship UFO original © L. Nettleship, 1972

Page 56 – UFO Illustration © Wayne Mason, 2011

Page 63 - Photo of Neil Pike © N. Pike, 1970s

Page 65 - Cetin Bal Illustration, copyright not identified

Page 68 - Photo of Paul Tricker © Paul Tricker, 1970s

Page 75 - Illustration by John Byrne

Page 76 - Illustration © Richard Thompson, 1972

Page 78- © Paul Nunn TAPIT

Page 81/82 - © Stephen Shipp

Page 83 - Original illustration © D. France

Page 83- Photo of D. France © P France

Page 84 –UFO Illustration by Wayne Mason © 2012

Page 85-Quest International report form © Tony Dodd

Page 92 - Photo of Howard Johnson © H. Johnson, 2009

Page 92 -Black Pear Poetry © J Hickman

Page 93 –UFO Illustration Wayne Mason © 2012

Page 94 /95 Images permission ©Lee Elders / Cece/Wendelle Stevens, 2012

Page 98 - Image © Brian @Olive Langford, 1994

Page 100 –UFO Images © Jonathon Hill, 1972

Page 102- photo of Mair Jeffery © J. Hanson

Page 102- UFO Photo © Alex Mera 2005 check page number

Page 108-Photo of John Spencer © Mrs E. Spencer 2012

Page 110 - Illustration © Carl Whiteley

Page 112 - Photos of Carl Whiteley © *Bournemouth Daily Echo*

Page 113- Photo of Mr. & Mrs. Wilson © J. Hanson, 1998

Page 115 – UFO Illustration © Steven Franklin, 2012

Page 116/17/18/Illustrations © Nicholas Maloret, WATSUP

Page 119 - Photo © Nick Maloret

Page 120 - BUFORA ID card © Nick Maloret

Page 122 –UFO Illustration © David Bryant, 2012

Page 123 - Illustration © Barry King, 2012

Page 124 - Photo of Barry King © B. King, 2012

Page 130,131, 132 - © Bob Boyd/*Probe,* Ian Mryzglod, 2012

Page 134 – UFO Illustration © Wayne Mason, 2012

Page 135 - Photo of Mrs. Good © T. Good, 2011

Page 137 - Photo © Ron Halliday, 2012

Page 139 - Photo of Diane Shepherd © M. Fry, 2011

Page 141/42 - Nicholas Maloret/© Harold Tamplin

Page 144 - Photo of Alconbury © J. Hanson, 2010

Page 144 - Illustration of 'Creature' © Wayne Mason, 2012

Page 145 - Photo of RAF Alconbury © J. Hanson, 2012

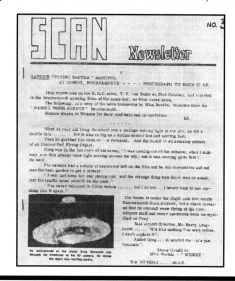

Warminster UFO Newsletter

Presented as an Information Service for Persons Interested In Keeping
In Contact with Unusual Happenings in the Warminster District.

No. 5

PRICE 10p

THE SKYWATCHERS ARE HERE -

AND SO ARE THE LATEST UFO REPORTS. (PAGE 2)

HOW TO START A PUBLISHING EMPIRE

Unlike most mainstream publishers, we have a non-commercial remit, and our mission statement claims that "we publish books because they deserve to be published, not because we think that we can make money out of them". Our motto is the Latin Tag *Pro bona causa facimus* (we do it for good reason), a slogan taken from a children's book *The Case of the Silver Egg* by the late Desmond Skirrow.

WIKIPEDIA: "The first book published was in 1988. *Take this Brother may it Serve you Well* was a guide to *Beatles* bootlegs by Jonathan Downes. It sold quite well, but was hampered by very poor production values, being photocopied, and held together by a plastic clip binder. In 1988 A5 clip binders were hard to get hold of, so the publishers took A4 binders and cut them in half with a hacksaw. It now reaches surprisingly high prices second hand.

The production quality improved slightly over the years, and after 1999 all the books produced were ringbound with laminated colour covers. In 2004, however, they signed an agreement with Lightning Source, and all books are now produced perfect bound, with full colour covers."

Until 2010 all our books, the majority of which are/were on the subject of mystery animals and allied disciplines, were published by `CFZ Press`, the publishing arm of the Centre for Fortean Zoology (CFZ), and we urged our readers and followers to draw a discreet veil over the books that we published that were completely off topic to the CFZ.

However, in 2010 we decided that enough was enough and launched a second imprint, `Fortean Words` which aims to cover a wide range of non animal-related esoteric subjects. Other imprints will be launched as and when we feel like it, however the basic ethos of the company remains the same: Our job is to publish books and magazines that we feel are worth publishing, whether or not they are going to sell. Money is, after all - as my dear old Mama once told me - a rather vulgar subject, and she would be rolling in her grave if she thought that her eldest son was somehow in `trade`.

Luckily, so far our tastes have turned out not to be that rarified after all, and we have sold far more books than anyone ever thought that we would, so there is a moral in there somewhere…

Jon Downes,
Woolsery, North Devon
July 2010

CFZ PRESS

Other Books in Print

CFZ Yearbook 2012 edited by Jon and Corinna Downes
ORANG PENDEK: Sumatra's Forgotten Ape by Richard Freeman
THE MYSTERY ANIMALS OF THE BRITISH ISLES: London by Neil Arnold
CFZ EXPEDITION REPORT: India 2010 by Richard Freeman *et al*
The Cryptid Creatures of Florida by Scott Marlow
Dead of Night by Lee Walker
The Mystery Animals of the British Isles: The Northern Isles by Glen Vaudrey
THE MYSTERY ANIMALS OF THE BRTISH ISLES: Gloucestershire and Worcestershire
by Paul Williams
When Bigfoot Attacks by Michael Newton
Weird Waters – The Mystery Animals of Scandinavia: Lake and Sea Monsters by Lars Thomas
The Inhumanoids by Barton Nunnelly
Monstrum! A Wizard's Tale by Tony "Doc" Shiels
CFZ Yearbook 2011 edited by Jonathan Downes
Karl Shuker's Alien Zoo by Shuker, Dr Karl P.N
Tetrapod Zoology Book One by Naish, Dr Darren
The Mystery Animals of Ireland by Gary Cunningham and Ronan Coghlan
Monsters of Texas by Gerhard, Ken
The Great Yokai Encyclopaedia by Freeman, Richard
NEW HORIZONS: Animals & Men issues 16-20 Collected Editions Vol. 4 by Downes, Jonathan
A Daintree Diary -
Tales from Travels to the Daintree Rainforest in tropical north Queensland, Australia by Portman, Carl
Strangely Strange but Oddly Normal by Roberts, Andy
Centre for Fortean Zoology Yearbook 2010 by Downes, Jonathan
Predator Deathmatch by Molloy, Nick
Star Steeds and other Dreams by Shuker, Karl
CHINA: A Yellow Peril? by Muirhead, Richard
Mystery Animals of the British Isles: The Western Isles by Vaudrey, Glen
Giant Snakes - Unravelling the coils of mystery by Newton, Michael
Mystery Animals of the British Isles: Kent by Arnold, Neil
Centre for Fortean Zoology Yearbook 2009 by Downes, Jonathan
CFZ EXPEDITION REPORT: Russia 2008 by Richard Freeman *et al*, Shuker, Karl (fwd)

Dinosaurs and other Prehistoric Animals on Stamps - A Worldwide catalogue by Shuker, Karl P. N

Dr Shuker's Casebook by Shuker, Karl P.N

The Island of Paradise - chupacabra UFO crash retrievals, and accelerated evolution on the island of Puerto Rico by Downes, Jonathan

The Mystery Animals of the British Isles: Northumberland and Tyneside by Hallowell, Michael J

Centre for Fortean Zoology Yearbook 1997 by Downes, Jonathan (Ed)

Centre for Fortean Zoology Yearbook 2002 by Downes, Jonathan (Ed)

Centre for Fortean Zoology Yearbook 2000/1 by Downes, Jonathan (Ed)

Centre for Fortean Zoology Yearbook 1998 by Downes, Jonathan (Ed)

Centre for Fortean Zoology Yearbook 2003 by Downes, Jonathan (Ed)

In the wake of Bernard Heuvelmans by Woodley, Michael A

CFZ EXPEDITION REPORT: Guyana 2007 by Richard Freeman *et al*, Shuker, Karl (fwd)

Centre for Fortean Zoology Yearbook 1999 by Downes, Jonathan (Ed)

Big Cats in Britain Yearbook 2008 by Fraser, Mark (Ed)

Centre for Fortean Zoology Yearbook 1996 by Downes, Jonathan (Ed)

THE CALL OF THE WILD - Animals & Men issues 11-15

Collected Editions Vol. 3 by Downes, Jonathan (ed)

Ethna's Journal by Downes, C N

Centre for Fortean Zoology Yearbook 2008 by Downes, J (Ed)

DARK DORSET -Calendar Custome by Newland, Robert J

Extraordinary Animals Revisited by Shuker, Karl

MAN-MONKEY - In Search of the British Bigfoot by Redfern, Nick

Dark Dorset Tales of Mystery, Wonder and Terror by Newland, Robert J and Mark North

Big Cats Loose in Britain by Matthews, Marcus

MONSTER! - The A-Z of Zooform Phenomena by Arnold, Neil

The Centre for Fortean Zoology 2004 Yearbook by Downes, Jonathan (Ed)

The Centre for Fortean Zoology 2007 Yearbook by Downes, Jonathan (Ed)

CAT FLAPS! Northern Mystery Cats by Roberts, Andy

Big Cats in Britain Yearbook 2007 by Fraser, Mark (Ed)

BIG BIRD! - Modern sightings of Flying Monsters by Gerhard, Ken

THE NUMBER OF THE BEAST - Animals & Men issues 6-10

Collected Editions Vol. 1 by Downes, Jonathan (Ed)

IN THE BEGINNING - Animals & Men issues 1-5 Collected Editions Vol. 1 by Downes, Jonathan

STRENGTH THROUGH KOI - They saved Hitler's Koi and other stories by Downes, Jonathan

The Smaller Mystery Carnivores of the Westcountry by Downes, Jonathan

CFZ EXPEDITION REPORT: Gambia 2006 by Richard Freeman *et al*, Shuker, Karl (fwd)

The Owlman and Others by Jonathan Downes

The Blackdown Mystery by Downes, Jonathan

Big Cats in Britain Yearbook 2006 by Fraser, Mark (Ed)

Fragrant Harbours - Distant Rivers by Downes, John T

Only Fools and Goatsuckers by Downes, Jonathan

Monster of the Mere by Jonathan Downes

Dragons:More than a Myth by Freeman, Richard Alan

Granfer's Bible Stories by Downes, John Tweddell

Monster Hunter by Downes, Jonathan

Fortean Words

The Centre for Fortean Zoology has for several years led the field in Fortean publishing. CFZ Press is the only publishing company specialising in books on monsters and mystery animals. CFZ Press has published more books on this subject than any other company in history and has attracted such well known authors as Andy Roberts, Nick Redfern, Michael Newton, Dr Karl Shuker, Neil Arnold, Dr Darren Naish, Jon Downes, Ken Gerhard and Richard Freeman.

Now CFZ Press are launching a new imprint. Fortean Words is a new line of books dealing with Fortean subjects other than cryptozoology, which is - after all - the subject the CFZ are best known for. Fortean Words is being launched with a spectacular multi-volume series called *Haunted Skies* which covers British UFO sightings between 1940 and 2010. Former policeman John Hanson and his long-suffering partner Dawn Holloway have compiled a peerless library of sighting reports, many that have not been made public before.

Other forthcoming books include a look at the Berwyn Mountains UFO case by renowned Fortean Andy Roberts and a series of books by transatlantic researcher Nick Redfern.

CFZ Press are dedicated to maintaining the fine quality of their works with Fortean Words. New authors tackling new subjects will always be encouraged, and we hope that our books will continue to be as ground breaking and popular as ever.

Haunted Skies Volume One 1940-1959 by John Hanson and Dawn Holloway
Haunted Skies Volume Two 1960-1965 by John Hanson and Dawn Holloway
Haunted Skies Volume Three 1965-1967 by John Hanson and Dawn Holloway
Haunted Skies Volume Four 1968-1971 by John Hanson and Dawn Holloway
Grave Concerns by Kai Roberts

Police and the Paranormal by Andy Owens
Dead of Night by Lee Walker
Space Girl Dead on Spaghetti Junction - an anthology by Nick Redfern
I Fort the Lore - an anthology by Paul Screeton
UFO Down - the Berwyn Mountains UFO Crash by Andy Roberts

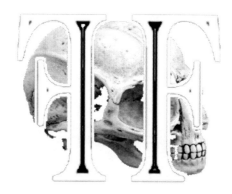

Fortean Fiction

Just before Christmas 2011, we launched our third imprint, this time dedicated to - let's see if you guessed it from the title - fictional books with a Fortean or cryptozoological theme. We have published a few fictional books in the past, but now think that because of our rising reputation as publishers of quality Forteana, that a dedicated fiction imprint was the order of the day.

We launched with four titles:

Green Unpleasant Land by Richard Freeman
Left Behind by Harriet Wadham
Dark Ness by Tabitca Cope
Snap! By Steven Bredice

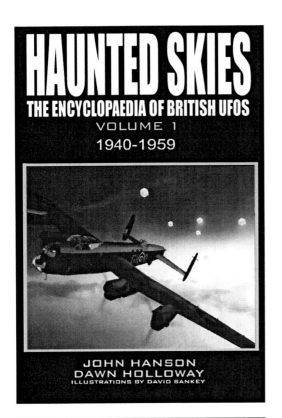

HAUNTED SKIES
THE ENCYCLOPAEDIA OF BRITISH UFOS
VOLUME 1
1940-1959

JOHN HANSON
DAWN HOLLOWAY
ILLUSTRATIONS BY DAVID SANKEY

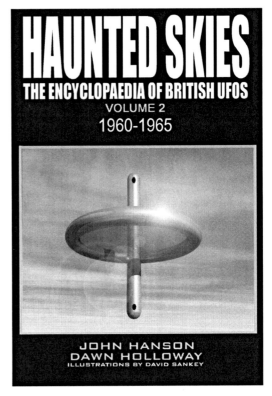

HAUNTED SKIES
THE ENCYCLOPAEDIA OF BRITISH UFOS
VOLUME 2
1960-1965

JOHN HANSON
DAWN HOLLOWAY
ILLUSTRATIONS BY DAVID SANKEY

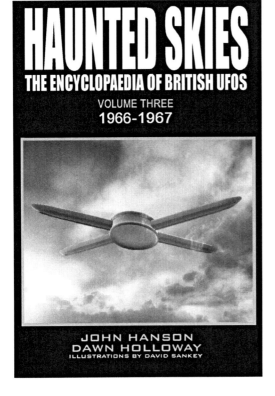

HAUNTED SKIES
THE ENCYCLOPAEDIA OF BRITISH UFOS
VOLUME THREE
1966-1967

JOHN HANSON
DAWN HOLLOWAY
ILLUSTRATIONS BY DAVID SANKEY

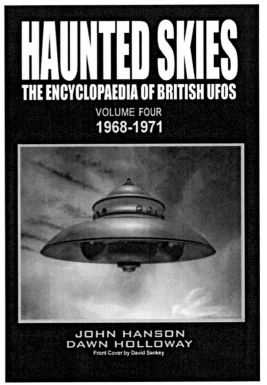

HAUNTED SKIES
THE ENCYCLOPAEDIA OF BRITISH UFOS
VOLUME FOUR
1968-1971

JOHN HANSON
DAWN HOLLOWAY
Front Cover by David Sankey

Lightning Source UK Ltd.
Milton Keynes UK
UKOW01f1537070114

224095UK00001B/4/P